FROM NAKED APE
TO SUPERSPECIES

FROM NAKED APE
TO SUPERSPECIES

A personal perspective on
        humanity and the global eco-crisis

DAVID SUZUKI AND HOLLY DRESSEL

Published in 1999 by Stoddart Publishing Co. Limited
34 Lesmill Road, Toronto, Canada M3B 2T6
180 Varick Street, 9th Floor, New York, New York 10014

Distributed in Canada by:
General Distribution Services Ltd.
325 Humber College Blvd., Toronto, Canada M9W 7C3
Tel. (416) 213-1919   Fax (416) 213-1917
Email customer.service@ccmailgw.genpub.com

Distributed in the United States by:
General Distribution Services Inc.
85 River Rock Drive, Suite 202, Buffalo, New York 14207
Toll-free Tel. 1-800-805-1083   Toll-free Fax 1-800-481-6207
Email gdsinc@genpub.com

03 02 01 00   2 3 4 5

Canadian Cataloguing in Publication Data

Suzuki, David, 1936–
From naked ape to superspecies: a personal perspective on humanity
and the global eco-crisis

Includes bibliographical references and index.
ISBN 0-7737-3194-6

1. Nature — Effect of human beings on. 2. Human ecology. 3. Social ecology.
4. Renewable natural resources. I. Dressel, Holly Jewell. II. Title.

GF75.S99 1999   304.2   C99-931469-6

Every reasonable effort has been made to contact the holders of copyright for materials
quoted in this book. The authors and publisher will gladly receive information that will
enable them to rectify any inadvertent errors or omissions in subsequent editions.

Jacket Design: Bill Douglas @ The Bang
Text Design: Andrew Smith Graphics Inc.

Printed in Canada on recycled paper

*We acknowledge for their financial support of our publishing program the Canada
Council, the Ontario Arts Council, and the Government of Canada
through the Book Publishing Industry Development Program (BPIDP).*

We remember, with admiration and gratitude, the love of nature that motivated Rachel Carson to write *Silent Spring*. She was a role model for generations of writers, activists and concerned citizens.

H.D. also dedicates this book, with love, to her husband, colleague and friend, the late Gary Toole.

CONTENTS

ACKNOWLEDGEMENTS

This book, like the radio series that spawned it, is the culmination of three and a half years of research, travel and thought, of delightful and distressing conversations with hundreds of wonderful and a few frightening people. It wouldn't exist without the cool lucidity of Jane Lewis, the Montreal producer of our series, or the watchfulness and experienced judgement of our executive producer, Bernie Lucht. We would also like to express our deep appreciation to Jennifer Glossop, Marnie Kramarich, and all the other people at Stoddart who worked so hard to make the book what it is.

Lisa Hayden, my secretary, cannot be thanked enough, not only for her unfailing cheerfulness, but also for her deep interest and constant involvement in every stage of the series and the book. Joel Silverstein, who is also a Montreal photographer, ended up with the exhausting and very demanding task of transcribing nearly all the tapes we had collected. He did this not only with enthusiasm, but also with a probing interest that went far beyond the call of duty and turned him into a true research collaborator.

Many other people also went beyond the call of duty in sending information quickly and without complaint, no matter how often we asked. They include Andy Kimbrell of the International Center for Technology Assessment, everyone at the Sierra Club of Canada, Christine von Weizsaecker of Ecoropa, Beth Burrows of the Edmonds Institute, Danny Kennedy of Project Underground, and particularly Brewster Kneen, publisher of the *Ram's Horn*. We are also especially grateful to the Third World Network.

On a personal level, my collaborator, Holly Dressel, would like to thank the following friends, who kept up with all the issues so brilliantly and tirelessly allowed her to bounce ideas off them, often far into the night: John Hughes and Martha Hughes; Jack Kofman; Gwynne Dyer and Tina Viljoen; and, for his invaluable post-mortems, Jim Latteier. And no such list would be complete without mention of her daughter, Thea; her son, Jack; and all the other friends and family who had to bear the highs and lows of such all-consuming work.

Finally, I want to acknowledge Jim Murray for his years of friendship and patience. He kept me in broadcasting when I wanted to quit and return to the lab, and he deepened my understanding of the human place in the natural world. The generous and uncomplaining support and enthusiasm of Tara Cullis, despite many weeks of absence, can never be fully acknowledged, but I make a meagre gesture of gratitude with a promise to put a lid on any new projects. I thank also Severn and Sarika, for being so supportive even though I was often away when they wanted me to be with them and too often responded, "Not now. I've got to finish this book."

INTRODUCTION

Humankind is on the brink of a momentous transition from the twentieth century to the twenty-first, from the second millennium to the third. Even though these dates are arbitrary social constructs in geological and cosmological processes, they give structure and significance to human events. And because of the power history holds over humans, few of us can resist believing that something significant is about to happen. In many ways, the furore over the computer glitch dubbed the Y2K crisis is indicative of our anxieties and our expectation of some kind of monumental change. So it seemed to me that this was an opportune moment to assess the past century, and even the past millennium — to look at where we, as a species, are right now, and how we have set about aiming towards the future. It's time to ask whether we are going in the right direction, and if we aren't, to decide what we can do about altering course.

Human beings entered the second millennium more or less as we began our sojourn on Earth — as intelligent, inventive creatures with numerous cultures to our credit, but tied to the Earth in every way imaginable. Back in the year 1000, most human beings were still nomadic hunter-gatherers or traditional agriculturalists, completely dependent on the vagaries of weather, climate and the generosity of the web of living things. A tiny minority of people lived in towns and cities, where they had laws, markets, stores and the trappings of civilization, but little control over natural forces like climate and disease. Industrialization occurred only in the past two or three centuries, and then total human populations began to climb steeply as Europeans rapidly colonized most other places and peoples of the world.

When the twentieth century began, many countries were well along in industrialization, and there were more than a billion people overall. While most of nature remained untouched, we were beginning to have an impact on the forests, waterways and soils on a large scale. The second half of this century witnessed the emergence of most modern societies from economic collapse and world war into a period of spectacular economic growth and social change. The accelerating growth in population, technological prowess, consumer demand, transnational corporations and the global economy has created a new force on the planet. We have been transformed from naked apes into what I call a superspecies. We are now transforming the biosphere — depleting the oceans, poisoning the air, levelling mountains and altering the composition of the atmosphere — and we are doing it all in a mere instant of geological time. In the nearly four billion years that life has existed on Earth, no species has possessed this capability for changing the biophysical makeup of the planet and thus affecting every other species on Earth.

For most of human existence, the natural world seemed to be the unlimited source for our physical, social and spiritual needs. Natural systems readily absorbed the impact of our activities, and even when we exceeded the finite limits in one area we were able to move to new spaces unoccupied by our kind. But those seemingly limitless vistas have disappeared far faster than our culture has proved able to comprehend and adapt. There are no new lands to be exploited, and the diversity and abundance of every natural system on Earth are being rapidly degraded by human activity. This crisis has to be faced collectively, yet the driving forces of our current culture are still aimed in the wrong direction, still pursuing endless growth in a world that is perceived as an infinite source of wealth and opportunity.

I've been working on environmental issues for almost four decades. I was first moved by Rachel Carson's 1962 book *Silent Spring,* which warned of unpredictable negative consequences of new technology. As a scientist, I still had a profound faith in the benefits of science and technology, but her book made me re-examine many of my assumptions. I didn't begin my career in broadcasting and journalism thinking that all natural systems were in peril. But I was concerned about the profound implications of advances in genetics, which is my area of expertise, and I felt a responsibility as a scientist. It was only after many years of observation, reflection and discussion with many people that I began to realize the magnitude and gravity of what was happening on the planet. For the past twenty-five years, I've been making films about people who are fighting to save the last woods or endangered species or habitat; I have noticed the quality of air, water and soil rapidly diminishing and the productive capacities of forest and marine ecosystems being stretched beyond their limits. And I've watched our governments and businesses respond reluctantly and too little to these escalating crises.

Like most other people, I'd rather spend time with my family, go to the lab and do research in my field of genetics, or pursue my hobbies. But I have children and grandchildren. I have a profound stake in the future. I'm only one person, and I have no illusions or conceits about saving the world. But I hope my grandchildren will never look at me and tell me, "Grandpa, you could have done more for us." If we adults fail to put the environment on the front burner, our children and their children will not have any hope of experiencing the abundance and diversity of life's creatures that existed when we were still young. I have read the statistics on contaminated water, asthma and cancer rates, allergies and immune problems, climate change and the loss of topsoil; I realize that the very things that give our children health, and even life, are in jeopardy.

These were the concerns that led me in 1988 to do a radio series called "It's a Matter of Survival" on the CBC with producer Anita Gordon. The programs documented the horrific level of human impact around the world and warned of the dangers we face. The public response was incredible; an unprecedented 16,000 letters were received at the CBC. Now, just a little more than a decade later, all of the dangers we warned of have increased, and others we didn't know about, like hormone mimics in plastics and pesticides, have come to our attention. Yet we've become increasingly distracted by such matters as globalization, the deficit, the economy and the information revolution.

In 1996, I approached the writer and researcher Holly Dressel with the idea for another radio series. I had worked with her in the past and knew that, apart from being one of the top people in her field, she had a deep understanding of and concern for the global eco-crisis. Together we proposed to the CBC an eight-part series that would move beyond a simple description of the degradation of the environment. What we wanted to investigate was why, when there is so much consensus among scientists that the biosphere is being altered catastrophically by human activity with results that will be disastrous for our own species, are governments and businesses failing to respond appropriately to reduce our ecological impact? After we interviewed scores of scientists, activists, politicians and businesspeople, it became clear that it is the deep-seated beliefs and values of modern culture that are both creating these problems and blinding us to their consequences.

We repeat like a religious mantra the unquestioned benefits and power of science, information and economics, without inspecting the structures and methodology on which they are built. Many of these beliefs are insupportable and dangerous. For example, the notion that human beings are so clever that we can use science and technology to escape the restrictions of the natural world is a fantasy that cannot be fulfilled. Yet it underlies much of government's and industry's rhetoric and programs.

Another dangerous assumption is that science can penetrate all of life's mysteries and extract the information we need to manage everything around us, thereby giving us total control over our own destiny. Science has generated many of the wonderful technologies that we enjoy today, but its methodology, which separates nature into narrow specialties, has prevented us from seeing the big picture. In real life, environmental issues cannot be separated from the economic, informational or cultural aspects of our lives. They are intertwined.

For all these reasons, the radio series looked at many aspects of culture, not just those considered to be "environmental" issues. If we can see where we are now and where we are heading, then we might be able to assess whether we really want to continue on the same path. Some areas we investigated for the series, like the rapid and unregulated progress of biotechnology, have frightening implications, while others, like the way people in the Third World are recognizing and fighting the recolonization of their countries by the global economy, are inspiring.

Overall, we interviewed nearly 200 people and spent more than two years gathering tape and editing the results. Our ambitious eight-hour series attempted to provide a picture of the steady loss of our natural systems in the context of the global culture that is currently shaping all our lives. We tried not only to analyze what is happening to our physical support systems but also to suggest some areas of our culture that are ripe for change. Public response to the radio series was very gratifying. It attracted a large listening audience, and the audio package has sold more copies than any other such package in the history of the CBC. To us, this means that people are indeed very concerned about environmental issues, and that they will go out of their way to get information about them.

The reality of radio, however, is that once each show was cut and assembled, we were able to include only a small fraction of all the interviews we'd done. The number of topics and ideas we could cover in each hour of radio was also restricted. But we had so much wonderful raw material that we wanted to get more information out. This book is built around the radio interviews, both those that were included and those that for a variety of mostly technical reasons didn't make the final cut. Our intention was to look at all the things that affect the environment in our culture. We wanted to show that one reason we're in so much trouble is that our modern culture is paradoxically behind the times, still assessing the world the way it did in the nineteenth or even eighteenth centuries: as a place of inexhaustible resources, where man is at the pinnacle of creation, separate from and more important than anything around him.

This book is in many ways a departure for me, a discussion of modern media, economics, culture and history that might seem some distance from my real expertise, science and nature. But culture controls how we treat the Earth, so those of us who want to assess the correctness of our approach have no choice but to look at the big picture. The reason we're looking, however, is to assess the state of the natural world, the state of our life support systems. For that reason, in the first two chapters of this book, I felt we had to do an inventory of what we've done to nature, how much we use and how much we have left. That inventory is always at the core of our discussion of the belief systems — modern culture, economics, politics and media — that have led us to consume our natural resources so excessively, and so quickly.

We began our first chapter, "Bugs Я Us," with a kind of history of the cultural assumptions on which we have based our present use of the natural world. One major assumption we make is based on size. We continue to be impressed with megaflora and -fauna, the big things, when in fact it is the insect and microbial world that keeps this planet habitable. We are only just starting to realize that worms, ants and microorganisms are more important than humans or their technology when it comes to the continuance of life on Earth. We are also just starting to realize that ancient human cultures held belief systems that dovetail with the most recent discoveries of science.

The second chapter, "Bigfoot," takes an inventory of natural resources on Earth. How much was there before humanity's great expansion? How much is left? And how much would each of us have if resources were shared out equally? These basic questions must be addressed if we are to learn to live in balance with the natural world.

The third chapter, "Sez Who?" establishes just what is being conveyed through the media and how destructive values such as the glamour of consumption are perpetuated. This chapter also suggests ways that concerned citizens can wade through the morass of information and use the media to present issues that shape the planet's future. The fourth chapter, "Unnatural Selection," explores how the desire to conquer and control nature has led to biotechnology and the deliberate redesigning of life through the manipulation of DNA. The chapter explains why this manipulation is not only dangerous but is also doomed to fail in the long term because of its reductionist base. The fifth chapter, "Your Money or Your Life Forms," shows how this search for gold inside our own bodies is tied to an increasing lack of capital in the world. Most of the world's true wealth has already been exploited. We investigate the implications and justice issues surrounding the commodification of life itself.

Chapter 6, "Follow the Money," examines the economy — an entity that late-twentieth-century culture has not only reified but also deified. What is the economy really, and, as Lewis Carroll asked, "Which is to be master?" Chapter 7, "Globalization Blues," explores what it means to extend the paradigm of the ever-growing, ever-insatiable economy to the entire planet. How does globalization both help and harm the environment and local communities? Who reaps the benefits? Are there alternatives?

Chapter 8, "The Other World," includes many voices that were left out of the radio series. Ironically, people in the Third World, who are perceived as poor and in need of aid from industrialized nations, are themselves the focus of treasure hunters trying to cash in on biological and human diversity. In fact, it is the rich nations that are sometimes poor in varied approaches to resource conservation, and the lesser-developed societies that have much to teach us about sustainability.

The final chapter, "Complex Pleasures," tackles the logistics of sharing, taking action and working for change. In our research, we discovered that these strategies not only benefit the environment, but also satisfy basic human needs far more than the infantile ones currently being served by a society focused on consuming everything in sight.

Designating the multiplicity of cultures and societies in the world simply as "nations" already glosses over the wonderful diversity of humanity. We compound this oversimplification by identifying countries as industrialized and non-industrialized, rich and poor, developed and developing. A more current distinction is made between countries of the northern and southern hemispheres, and we have used those classes in this book. The terminology in the extensive literature dealing with global development has now recognized that there are "poor" and disadvantaged conditions in northern countries like Russia, as well as many "rich," advantaged classes in southern countries like Australia or Argentina. So we have capitalized the terms North and South when they are used in this context, to distinguish them as references to states of development, not as directions. However, most of our interviewees continue to use the phrase "the Third World," which has come to be seen by many in the so-called developing countries as a desirable term. It expresses a third way, a different approach to living on the planet that is neither capitalist, as in the old terminology, nor communist. In deference to this usage, and to such organizations as the Third World Network, we have primarily used that term.

Throughout this book, we have written from the point of view of the senior author. But that person is really an amalgam of both David Suzuki and Holly Dressel. It has been a joint effort all the way, a dual offering for the next millennium.

David Suzuki
Vancouver
August 1999

CHAPTER 1
BUGS Я US

We don't know nearly enough to manage the ecosystems on our own. If we think that we can eliminate those natural ecosystems and substitute prosthetic devices, like creating clean air or water with fusion energy or sustaining the stability of cropland — in fact, [if we think we can] keep the planet in that delicately balanced, highly peculiar state on which humanity depends for its continued existence — then we are kidding ourselves.

— E.O. WILSON, ECOLOGIST

Back in the fall of 1991, there was a great deal of hoopla surrounding a $200 million scientific experiment getting under way in Arizona. Eight people were sealed in a giant bubble called Biosphere II in the middle of the desert. It was meant to be a miniature version of Earth's natural systems. The project was undertaken not only in anticipation of long flights in space but also to demonstrate how well we understand the world around us.

Like Biosphere I — the Earth — Biosphere II contained a variety of ecosystems and a sampling of plants and animals that were supposed to provide the same "ecosystem services" that nature does; it would purify and produce water, recycle wastes, provide oxygen and absorb carbon dioxide, use photosynthesis to capture sunlight, and produce plants and food. The bubble covered several acres and housed a variety of ecosystems, including a desert, a miniature ocean, a grassland and a tropical forest. Nearly 4,000 different plant and animal species were deliberately assembled to populate this airtight system. It was a kind of ark of technology that was supposed to provide a self-sustaining environment that would support the "bionauts" for two years. Biosphere II was intended to provide proof that we humans have learned enough about the world to recreate it at will, wherever we choose, and there was enormous media excitement the day the crew was sealed in.

I'm a scientist, and I've spent a great deal of my career studying ecosystems. I remember, as a boy, watching a sealed flask containing water, a plant and a fish. The fish and plant lived for weeks, giving the illusion that each was providing what the other needed and that they therefore had created a harmonious balance. Eventually, of course, microorganisms took over and the fish and the plant died. But the illusion is striking. I remember thinking at the time of Biosphere II that this was just a bigger version of the sealed flask, and that it was doomed to fail. We simply haven't yet reached the stage where we understand the workings of things like the water cycle and air purification enough to duplicate them. Yet the media and many experts were treating the event as if it were already an accomplished triumph, a portent of things to come as we rocket off to the stars.

Once the bionauts got inside, however, things started to go wrong pretty quickly. Oxygen levels plummeted, primarily because the mix of soil organisms was not correct and did not produce the proper proportion of gases. Oxygen concentration dropped to a level found above 17,000 feet of elevation. As a result, the bionauts suffered some of the alarming problems associated with low oxygen intake. Then nitrogen levels skyrocketed, creating a risk of brain damage. Most of the insects that had been carefully selected to pollinate the plants died off, dooming most of the bionauts' intended sources of food and air and water purification. And many other species careered out of control — cockroaches, katydids and a species aptly named crazy ants swarmed over everything. Some plants and vines also proliferated wildly. The bionauts spent increasing amounts of their time killing insects and hacking back vines. Eventually, the defeated pioneers, malnourished and sick, gave up and came out. Had they stayed much longer, they might have died. There was very little hoopla surrounding this failure; in fact, most people still don't know what a resounding defeat it was.

Yet I couldn't help feeling that for all its disasters, Biosphere II was a successful lesson — it provided powerful evidence of how little we understand the natural systems that sustain us, that deliver what are termed the "ecosystem services" of replenishing air, water and soil and removing waste without our ever having to think about them.

Gretchen Daily, an ecologist at Stanford University who investigates the extinction of species, says efforts like Biosphere II are humbling. "It shows some of the good sides of humanity: our curiosity, our determination. And in many ways those are noble qualities. But at the same time, we're like little kids. We've amassed this power, and we've deceived ourselves somewhat. In modern urban societies today, and in the richest and most powerful parts of the world, people are so removed from these ecosystem services that they've all but faded from view."

The failure of Biosphere II is a direct result of a revolutionary change in the human perception of how the natural world works that began about 300 years ago. In the seventeenth century, the French philosopher René Descartes postulated that by stepping outside the world and becoming observers of nature, rather than being part of it, we would be able to see how it really worked. In the following century, Sir Isaac Newton used a scientific approach to discover laws that were universal and timeless. He viewed the world as an immense clockwork mechanism that could be taken apart and its components studied. This methodology is called "scientific reductionism." The scientific method it gave rise to works by pulling things apart and reducing them to their smallest possible components so they can be analyzed under controlled conditions. By measuring input, output and changes within isolated fragments, scientists assume they can determine how each part functions and, by extension, how the whole of nature works. Newton hypothesized that once we knew these secrets, we would be able to use our intellect to harness those functions for our own benefit.

This scientific view of the world sees our species as being at the pinnacle of a steady evolutionary march from simple to complex, from instinctive to intellectual, from a state of nature to civilization. Ever since Descartes, we have considered human intellect — the activity of the mind — to be separate from and superior to the body. As we've become increasingly separated from nature in urban settings, we have come to believe that our intellect, manifested through science, empowers us with the capacity to understand and control the world around us.

As scientific reductionism was applied, our inventive capacity blossomed. Within a hundred years, steam- and coal-powered engines were replacing manual labour and amplifying muscle power. Europeans were able to travel farther and faster than ever before, and to bring back new foods, luxuries and medicines from around the globe — to say nothing of conquering other lands and their inhabitants with powerful weapons. People began to understand how many common diseases spread and how to control them, primarily through better sanitation. We learned to analyze soil, human nutrition and animal breeding, and to adapt them to our own uses.

The technological revolution that scientific reductionism led to has been like one long party. It has brought power and glory. It has enabled us to extend our dominion over the globe and over nature. But as failed experiments like Biosphere II are showing, reductionism provides only part of the whole picture. When we broke aspects of nature down into their component parts — when we took a mosquito out of its surroundings and labelled it a pest, for example — we lost sight of the patterns of nature and the symbiosis within ecosystems, the way every part has a purpose. We lost sight of the patterns the mosquito was part of — its relationships to the fish and the birds it fed, the microorganisms it lived with, the ecosystem in which it played out its life cycle.

We've been trained to look at big creatures as the most noble, the most important, the most pivotal and valuable, with ourselves as the biggest creature of all. We've ignored the relationships all large creatures must have with small ones, like ants, bacteria and fungi, which provide the real fundamentals of survival. But science is always changing. There is a new way of thinking, a fresh view that is beginning to focus on relationships and patterns — and on the role of the most minute, as well as the greatest, creatures in the world around us.

The Meek Inherit the Earth

So far as we know, there is not a single other planet in this universe that has even rudimentary protoplasm. And here we have millions, maybe tens of millions, of unique forms of life that manifest themselves as tigers and polar bears,

thistles, birds and snakes. And we don't know if it's 10
million or 100 million kinds. It's crazy. We don't even have
that basic grasp of what makes our planet tick — let alone
how to keep it ticking.

— NORMAN MYERS, ECOLOGIST

A major reason we're still so far from being able to construct a viable human habitat like Biosphere II, despite all our apparent technological wizardry, is that we really haven't devoted enough attention to the details of the natural world. After all, if we were put in charge of managing a shoe factory, we would at the very least need two important bits of information to do a good job. First, we would need an inventory of every item in the factory. Then we'd have to understand how each of the pieces interact and fit together: if you put soles on before heels, whether you glue or nail first. We need the same kind of information if we intend to interfere with any part of nature's productivity.

So what is the state of our Earth inventory? Although estimates of the number of species range from 2 to 100 million, the consensus among biologists seems to be that there are around 10 million. Globally, the total number of species identified so far is between 1.4 and 1.6 million. The reason for the disparity is that different scientists often mistakenly identify the same species independently. That means that we have names for only 20 percent of all the non-bacterial life forms on Earth. When it comes to bacteria and other microorganisms, we have no idea at all.

How much do we know about how the pieces work together? Edward O. Wilson, a professor of ecology at Harvard, is one of the world's pre-eminent experts on biodiversity, the variety of life on Earth. He uses an ironic example to illustrate how this interdependence works, and how the big and the small organisms typically fit into it: "How can I put this without sounding callous? If all humanity disappeared, the rest of life, except for domestic animals and plants, which represent only a minute fraction of the plants and animals of the world, would benefit enormously." The forests, Wilson says, would gradually grow back, and relative stability would return to the ecosystem services that control global temperature and atmosphere. The fish in the oceans would recover, and most endangered species would slowly come back. Of course, there would be no humans around to enjoy this, but as far as the survival of numbers of species goes, the planet would be better off.

On the other hand, says Wilson, if all members of one of the groups of smaller creatures, such as ants, were to vanish, the results would be close to catastrophic. Ants turn and aerate a very large part of the Earth's soils. They're major predators of other insects, and they're the chief scavengers of small animals, removing and breaking up more than 90 percent of any small, dead creatures as part of the soil-nutrient cycle. They even pollinate many plants. Wilson, who has studied ants all of his professional life, says, "If they were to disappear, there would be major extinctions of other species and probably partial collapse of some ecosystems." The Earth as a whole would suffer. If we go further and imagine the impact of the extinction of a microorganism like the common gut bacterium *Eschercia coli,* or mycorrhysae, the invisible soil fungi that facilitate the uptake of nutrients by plants, we see that the catastrophe would be even worse. The functions of the creatures living in the air we breathe, beneath our feet or in our own bodies are exotic and unimaginable; they are working in concert to keep us alive. As E.O. Wilson says, "We are living on a relatively unexplored planet. And that's why the amazement and the enthusiasm that are invariably aroused when the subject of life on Mars comes up [are] just out of proportion to reality. . . . We are standing on an unexplored world, for the most part, and there are many amazing things still to discover here."

The Whole Is Greater Than the Sum of Its Parts

Newtonian physics was a liberation [at first], but it became a straitjacket by the early twentieth century. Now we have a different kind of liberation. We have the liberation of quantum physics, the liberation of systems theory and the liberation of the Gaia hypothesis, which all help free us from the Newtonian straitjacket.

— FRITJOF CAPRA, PHYSICIST

In the early part of this century, scientists learned to divide an atom into its components — protons, neutrons and electrons. They created a model of the atom that showed it as small, solid objects circling a core, rather like a miniature solar system. Naturally, the scientists believed they were elucidating one of the greatest mysteries of the universe — the nature of energy and matter.

But quantum mechanics reveals that protons, neutrons and electrons do not conform to the solar-system model. As we zero in on such particles, they become fuzzier, or less distinct. The whereabouts of electrons, for example, can be indicated only as a calculated probability. The renowned nuclear physicist Fritjof Capra says, "There are no particles in atoms, such as the balls in the atomic model. There are no hard and solid spheres or objects like grains of sand. A sub-atomic particle is essentially a set of relationships reaching outward to other things, and the other things are again relationships to yet other things."

As the twentieth century progressed, physicists began to make a dramatic shift that reflected this reality, focusing less on discrete objects and more on relationships. We began to realize that the relationships and interactions among creatures, cells and photons were as important to an understanding of the whole they formed as is an analysis of their parts. Systems studies, the new science that has grown up around quantum physics, states it clearly: "The whole is greater than the sum of its parts." Fritjof Capra, one of this discipline's most eloquent spokesmen, says that the traditional or reductionist view of evolution has been that rocks, oceans and the air are the stage on which life plays out its drama. "By an act of creation," he says, "a fluke of chance or some other mystery," life somehow rose up on this stage, evolved from the first cell and has been evolving to "higher forms" ever since. What we are now learning about evolution, however, shows that life is created and shaped by other life, in continuous, interlocking patterns; and as the failure of the Biosphere II project suggests, these patterns aren't easily controlled or knowable. An imbalance in the mixture of soil organisms — microscopic life forms — was enough to topple an entire ecosystem.

A lesson to be drawn from the Biosphere project is that the small, usually overlooked aspects of our ecosystem — the insects and the microorganisms — are in many ways the most important. Insects, for example, make up the most numerous, diverse and successful group of animals on Earth, and only a minute percentage is harmful to or competitive with us. When scientific technology developed powerful weapons like chemical pesticides to use against them, we ended up killing thousands of species just to get at the less than one percent that we find troublesome. We are now beginning to see that insects and microorganisms are vital parts of ecosystems: they form a major portion of the diets of birds, fish, mammals and amphibians, and as predators are still the main force keeping other insects under control.

Similarly, most bacteria are not agents of disease. The vast majority of microorganisms and insects, both invisible and visible, are benign to humans. We're only just learning that if we didn't have them in a natural balance, there wouldn't be many of the other things we like — including ourselves. If biology follows the lead of a hard science like physics, its future will lie in revealing not just bits and pieces of nature but the complex interrelationships that actually make organisms and ecosystems work. The only question is whether we will make this jump into a true analysis of the world around us before the outdated notions of reductionism leave us with few intact systems to study.

Bugs Really Я Us

> The basic pattern of life is a network. Whenever you see life, you see networks. The whole planet, what we can term "Gaia," is a network of processes involving feedback tubes. And the world of bacteria is critical to the details of these feedback processes, because bacteria play a crucial role in the regulation of the whole Gaian system.
>
> — FRITJOF CAPRA

The clockwork approach of scientific reductionism viewed nature as something to be controlled and kept at bay. Nature's most alien forms — the insects and bacteria, long-time intimate guests on the human body — were increasingly seen as being extremely far away from humankind, the apex of creation. When we discovered that some of them carried or caused disease, they were banished, along with nature itself, as something extremely different from civilized humans. Virtually any means to destroy them was considered appropriate, and these attitudes have remained with us in the twentieth century. We crush insects; we develop appallingly dangerous poisons to eradicate them; we invent antiseptics, vaccines and antibiotics to protect "us" from "them." In fact, the difference between what we consider civilized society and degraded or desperate surroundings is sometimes simply the number of visible or invisible bugs.

But for the first 2 billion years of the more than 3.5 billion years that life has existed, bacteria and other microorganisms were the only living things on Earth. Through that long period, they invented all of the fundamental processes of life, from replication to responses to gravity, light and temperature, from fermentation to photosynthesis and mobility. And even today, the total biomass — the weight of living things — of all microorganisms is greater than the biomass of all other creatures put together, including trees and whales and people. It is still a bacterial world. By the time aggregates of cells — multi-celled creatures — appeared, they had no need to reinvent all these basic life properties. Instead, they incorporated bacteria into their own protoplasm to live symbiotically and continue to perform these functions. As Fritjof Capra says, "We owe practically all life to bacteria."

The cells of multi-cellular organisms contain structures called organelles that perform highly specialized roles such as the generation of energy, photosynthesis and chromosome movement. These organelles are evolutionary remnants of bacteria. The mutually beneficial collaboration between organelles and their single-celled hosts is now so profound that host and guest can no longer survive without each other.

Each of us is an aggregate of some 60 trillion cells. Within each cell, there may be hundreds of organelles, the once-independent bacteria. So when you look in the mirror, remember that you are in fact gazing at an immense aggregate of trillions of cells and quadrillions of bacteria. A human being — or a dog or a potted plant, for that matter — is not just an individual. Each one of us is actually a community of organisms.

And just as we are an aggregate of a number of organs, each exquisitely balanced with the others and made up of a diversity of specialized cells, all life forms within the biosphere can be thought of as making up a kind of super-organism. The immensely varied organisms within different ecosystems are held together by the global matrix of air, water, soil and energy from the sun. Collectively, the individuals within a species, as well as the numerous species and the many different ecosystems on the Earth itself, have the properties of a self-regulating entity. The engineer

James Lovelock called this interlocking system of all life on Earth "Gaia," after the Greek goddess of Earth.

Remarkably, all of these levels of variability, from genes to species to ecosystems, have somehow worked in concert to create vast changes in the planet's biophysical makeup and to make the Earth more and more liveable for creatures like us. As Fritjof Capra says, "The environment of life, which we thought of as independent, is itself shaped by life. Not only that, it is shaped in a certain way. The whole system regulates itself and maintains conditions conducive to life. . . . Gaia, like us, maintains her body temperature [over the millennia], and not only overall temperature, but [also] the composition of gases like oxygen and CO_2, the salinity of the oceans — all these processes are maintained at levels that are conducive to life. How does Gaia do this? Through multiple feedback tubes, a network of processes."

The Fish Need the Forest, the Forest Needs the Fish

> *When the forest began to disappear . . . we had flooding, we had erosion . . . and the role of science was misapplied. The Army Corps of Engineers looked at the floods and said, "The answer is to build dams," . . . so now we have 114 dams on the Columbia River. And the relationship between those dams and the salmon is that the temperature of the Columbia and the Snake rivers has permanently risen. It is quite common, in the summer months, to find the Columbia and Snake rivers exceeding 65°F. At 65°F, those waters are lethal to salmon.*
>
> — TED STRONG, YAKIMA TRIBE MEMBER

One example of the complex network of relationships within ecosystems — between their largest and smallest members — can be seen in a controversy raging right now in the Pacific Northwest. Because of the rapid decline of Pacific salmon, oceanographers, botanists, ichthyologists and other scientists have devoted a good deal of time in the last few years to trying to understand more about their life cycle. Up and down the Pacific coast of North America, five species of salmon have spawned in rivers and streams for millennia. But early in this century, human activity, such as the construction of dams, mining, logging, urban development and agriculture, negatively affected salmon habitat and life cycles. Populations plummeted, and human beings intervened in order to restore the salmon stocks.

This work was commenced in a typically reductionist way. It was quickly found that mature adults could be milked of eggs and sperm, and that eggs could be fertilized in containers. The fertilized eggs could then be incubated to hatching. Thus fish hatcheries could be used to vastly increase populations of young salmon. The rather simple assumption was that if more young could be pumped into the system, then somehow, after years at sea, more mature adults would return. When the fry couldn't readily reach the sea from the hatcheries, they were loaded into tankers and trucked downriver.

Lack of knowledge led to incredible blunders. Take as an example what happened to the sockeye salmon, a prolific and highly prized food fish. Sockeye fingerlings were reared and released in rivers close to the ocean on the assumption that this would help them survive by shortening the treacherous journey to the sea. Years later, it was discovered that sockeye fry never go directly to the ocean. Instead, they first spend a year in a freshwater lake. The human attempts to help the sockeye simply ensured that millions perished.

Salmon-breeding programs have cost billions of dollars, but in terms of saving wild races and keeping their numbers high, the investment has not been very successful. In 1994, hundreds of millions of dollars were spent to help salmon in the Snake River in Washington State, for example, but only 800 chinook returned in the fall. The same year, only one adult sockeye made it. Forty-nine wild varieties of salmon in the state have been extirpated. Because the wild populations are dying out, experts have tried to create new genetic strains or bypass the wild part of the animals' life cycle by growing them in net pens. Despite numerous lessons on the hazards of introducing exotic species into new habitats, fish farmers are rearing millions of Atlantic salmon from the east coast in the Pacific. And despite assurances by government bureaucrats that they will not reproduce, the escapees are not only moving into rivers and spawning; their offspring are surviving.

These catastrophic developments have come about because of our truncated and fragmented way of looking at the resource. Management efforts focus on different "resources": terrestrial game, marine life, forests, rivers and estuaries, which are often administered separately by state, federal, international and local bodies. Ted Strong is a member of the Yakima band and the Columbia Inter-Tribal Fish Commission, an organization trying to hammer out a management strategy for the Columbia River basin. He says there's another way to look at the river: "Tribal peoples are often said to be backwards; we look to the past. But if we wanted to impose a value system and order to salmon restoration, we would ask that the scientific community look more to the past than to the future. The recently concluded study by an independent science group on the Columbia River stated that what the salmon needed was 'a complex, interconnected array of wetlands, in-stream flows, gravel beds and so on that are created, manipulated and managed by natural forces.' That's a very fancy way of saying, 'They need a natural river.' And that's what the Indian people propose in our own salmon-restoration plan."

Restoring a dammed, farmed and logged river basin is a pretty tall order. And in any case, many people see nothing wrong with the status quo. Why not try to domesticate salmon? What does it matter if there are fewer species? Pinks and chums never fetched a good price anyway. And, they figure, maybe the Atlantic salmon will replace the native species that have been lost. If species and their environment really were unrelated, if the world existed primarily to fulfil the immediate needs of humans, and if we were able to survive indefinitely in industrialized isolation the way we thought we could back in the 1950s, those might be viable arguments. But when a new breed of scientist decided to look at the totality of the salmon and their habitat, they discovered an amazing relationship between fish and their surroundings that means our reductionist method of trying to help fails to take into account the true nature of a species.

Salmon spend their adult lives at sea, thousands of kilometres from their birthplace in forested and mountain streams. Marine carbon and nitrogen isotopes leave a unique "signature" that scientists can detect, and of course, after years in the ocean, salmon carcasses are full of these two important atomic nutrients. After the adult salmon make the arduous journey from the ocean back to their natal streams, they spawn and die. Various predators — bears, eagles, wolves — catch them and leave their remains on land, where the carcasses are quickly covered with fly eggs, which hatch into maggots that consume the flesh and then pupate.

When the adult flies emerge, they nourish fish, mammals and birds throughout the forest. In the water, the dead salmon are digested by fungus, which in turn nourishes bacteria that sustain insects, copepods and other invertebrates in the stream. And like fallen logs in a forest, their decaying flesh provides nourishment for their own offspring. When the fry emerge from the gravel, a banquet awaits: 25 to 40 percent of the carbon and nitrogen in juvenile salmon comes from the remains of their parents. Isotope studies show that 30 percent of the vital nitrogen and carbon in aquatic algae and insects, and 18 percent in vegetation along the river, comes directly from salmon. So what may seem to be a waste is, in fact, an evolutionary mechanism used to nourish a new generation and to keep the stream itself healthy.

We know that salmon have to have clean, cool, fast-running streams for their habitat. When forests surrounding rivers and streams are clearcut, salmon populations plummet and often disappear. Salmon need the forest to shade the rivers and keep the water cool, to provide nourishment and to prevent soil from silting the gravel of spawning beds. But we are just learning that this relationship is reciprocal — forests need the salmon, too, to remain healthy. University of Victoria biologist Tom Reimchen has shown that in one season, a single bear will carry about 700 partially consumed salmon carcasses into the forest. He has found their remains as far as 200 metres from the river, spanning valley bottoms where the biggest trees grow. After consuming salmon, bears, eagles, wolves and ravens defecate and spread salmon remnants through the forest, providing the largest pulse of nitrogen fertilizer the trees get all year. In fact, you can correlate the amount of growth by the width of tree rings with the amount of marine carbon and nitrogen, which reflects the size of the salmon runs! Grizzly bears were extinguished in Oregon by 1931. Preserved hides of those animals reveal that up to 90 percent of the nitrogen and carbon in their bodies was of marine origin. So the forest and the salmon, the insects and the bears, all need each other — and all are linked through the water and the salmon to the ocean, thousands of kilometres away. When forest, fish, bears and birds are seen this way — as a single living entity, each part of which supports the other — it is clear that our attempts to manage these resources as separate parts are bound to fail.

From Top Down to Bottom Up

The soil is virtually a living organism. It's not just a bunch of grains with bugs walking through them. It is a mass of organic, living material in an inorganic matrix. It's dynamic. It's full of life. And it does not produce anything for human beings unless it's sustained in that living condition.

— E.O. WILSON

One biologist who studies the interrelationships in ecosystems is Orrie Loucks. Field biologists like Loucks are becoming increasingly rare, but it's only through fieldwork that we can access the facts about complex ecosystems. This research simply cannot be done in a laboratory, where scientists can work with only tiny parts of the overall puzzle. "Twenty-five or thirty years ago," Loucks says, "much of the research in ecology was focused on the productivity of ecosystems. We looked at photosynthesis, for example." This approach made sense. After all, in human society, productivity is directly related to the available supply of energy, and the planet's primary source of energy is the sun. So it seemed logical to assume that sunlight and its capture would be limiting factors for the rest of life as well.

But scientists like Loucks have found something quite surprising: energy does influence productivity, but the ultimate regulator of ecosystems is decay. Processes that release nutrients back into the ecosystem for future production are what enable those ecosystems to function. "The breakdown of organic matter," Loucks says, "and the release of the nutrients that are in that organic matter are systems that are vastly more complex than photosynthesis." Decay is more complex than photosynthesis because it involves the co-operation of thousands of species of living organisms, from insects to worms, fungi and bacteria. These species are very sensitive to factors like toxic chemicals, small changes in soil moisture and temperature, and any change in the mix of species that co-operate to break down the organic matter. If anything happens to disrupt the process of decay, then nutrient supplies are curtailed or unavailable to the next season's crop of plants.

Biologists have long studied big things like bears, trees and fish because they are impressive or important to us. The small creatures like insects and bacteria seemed insignificant alongside these lords of the Earth. We could see with our own eyes how wolves, elephants and humans regulated the numbers of the herbivores, plants and so on. For example, when sea otters on the west coast of North Africa were exterminated by fur hunters, their favourite food, sea urchins, exploded in number and drastically diminished the supply of kelp, which is the urchins' main food. Kelp forests provide food and shelter for a bewildering array of organisms, including many species of fish. So as kelp disappeared, so did many fish. When sea otters were reintroduced in California, British Columbia and Alaska, they reinstated "top down" regulation, reducing sea urchins and enabling kelp to return, along with fish.

While we attempt to manage resources by top-down regulation, it has had varying degrees of success. We've devoted far less attention to bottom-up regulation. It wasn't until the early 1980s, for example, that scientists began to realize that soil organisms and their interactions control the extent to which plants grow. Elaine Ingham, a soil pathologist at Oregon State University, describes it best: "Soil is alive. Sand, silt, clay . . . are the mineral fraction of the soil, like the building blocks of a house. The bacteria that grow in that sand, silt and clay, along with some organic material as food, form the tiny bricks. . . . Fungi tie these bricks together into walls, floors and ceilings." These creatures, which Ingham calls the architects, design housing for all the larger organisms, tiny animals and plants, such as microarthropods, earthworms, rotifers, protozoa and nematodes.

These are just a few of the creatures that live in soils. We really don't have a clue how many there are, what each one does or how they work together. In one of the few such descriptive studies ever carried out, scientists in Denmark scooped up a cubic metre of earth in a beech forest and took it into their lab. With the naked eye alone, they found more than 50,000 small earthworms and their relatives, 50,000 different kinds of insects and mites, and 12 million roundworms and their relatives. When they took just a gram from the same soil and put it under the microscope, they found 30,000 protozoa, 50,000 algae, 400,000 fungi and billions of individual bacteria of unknown numbers of species. They identified about 4,000 species of bacteria, almost all completely new to science. When the scientists then took another gram of soil from an estuary not far from the beech forest, they found another 4,000 species of bacteria, almost all different from those in the beech forest and also all new to science!

When such soil organisms are said to be "identified," that simply means that they have been given a name. It doesn't mean that anything is known about what they eat or how long they live, what they all do in concert with each other, what makes one of them flourish in one soil but not in another, or how one soil type becomes home to a copse of oak while another supports white pine. One of the very few things we do know about these unexplored worlds is that without the spaces created by bacteria and microorganisms in the "bricks" of sand and clay, there would be no place for plant roots to move into the soil. They'd have to expend too much energy, as anyone knows who's tried to grow plants in baked clay or the hardpan residue of chemically treated fields. Furthermore, without these spaces, air and water don't infiltrate. Not only does the soil remain barren, but its ability to act as a sponge and watershed purifier is gradually destroyed. Such soil may no longer be conducive to growing the pollinators that enable the area to produce a certain kind of flower or tree, or a species may suffer from huge pest invasions because the nematodes or other tiny predators that kept the pests down are no longer there.

Back in the 1940s and 1950s, in true reductionist fashion, scientists teased soil apart into its mineral, animal and fungal components. They saw soil primarily as an inert matrix that held plants up. To improve productivity for human agriculture, they added water and food in the form of chemical fertilizers, and dealt with pests by blanketing them with poisons. Laboratory soil analysis told them what minerals to add and in what quantities — how much nitrogen, potassium and calcium mix, for example, would give lush dahlias or fields of beans.

The initial results of this approach were spectacular. But now, at the turn of the millennium, we're starting to get some very clear signals that something is wrong with the scientific analysis. In recent years, yields have fallen and researchers are scrambling to invent stronger fertilizers and more high-tech seeds. One of the reasons we're having trouble is that we've converted many agricultural soils into hardpan, leaving none of the spaces that animal and fungal architects kept loose and open. We did that by adding chemicals that are too concentrated and don't contain the complex mixture of leaf litter, dead animals, manure and organic material that provides nutrition for the community of creatures that makes soil so rich for plant crops. Moreover, our fields are soaked in toxic poisons designed to kill whatever we've identified as pests, whether these are plants like dandelions or milkweeds that compete with our crops, insects like corn borers or Colorado potato beetles, or diseases like rust or blight. Unfortunately, these poisons also kill many of the creatures that make the system function in the first place.

Recent evidence shows that all the money spent on these chemical cocktails may be wasted. Despite our arsenal of powerful toxins, most agricultural pests are still controlled by natural enemies like spiders, wasps, birds and other predators that live adjacent to or in the fields. Moreover, in forty years of pesticide use, we have not managed to eradicate a single pest, and we actually have more problems with them than when we started. Even the heavy machinery needed to work large tracts of industrial farms has a negative impact on living, productive soils. As Elaine Ingham says, "You can't keep running your tractors across the surface of the soil, squishing it, [without] destroying all that space, the living room and the dining room and the kitchen, that these organisms need to grow in."

Industrial farming methods — growing single-crop monocultures in huge fields aided by heavy machinery, chemical fertilizers and pesticides — produced double and sometimes triple yields at first, which seemed to prove they were the right thing to do. But as Ingham says, the reason that these heroic methods worked for a generation or so is that nature had built up a reserve in soil: "When you take soil out of a native system, it has accumulated a lot of organic matter. The past lives of all these organisms working on all that organic stuff have built a kind of savings account of nutrients in the soil. For the first forty to sixty years, you're slowly but surely mining out that organic matter, pulling out the material that's in your savings account."

Ingham's economic metaphor is apt. If we use the organic material in soil at the same rate as it is replenished, we can farm indefinitely. If you have a bank account and each year you draw only the interest, you can do that year after year. But if you dip into the capital, as she notes, "You eventually hit bottom, where's there's nothing left in your savings account and you're in serious trouble. And the chemicals won't work, because you don't have the organic matter in the soil; you've mined it out. You don't have any more organisms because there's no food for them." Not only does the soil on hillsides begin to wash away, but fertilizers and toxins run through the soil and end up in surface water and groundwater.

Elaine Ingham and other soil experts who understand that the richness of soil is its biodiversity maintain that the bank account can be filled again. She has had remarkable success overcoming serious hardpan problems by drilling holes in which to insert organic material, compost and manure, and by advocating no-till methods, heavy mulching and careful crop rotation. She even has a business that helps farmers get off the chemical fix. This, she says, is the direction in which we should be moving if we want a real future for soils and crops. Nurturing rotting compost, worms, beetles, slime moulds and funny smells is at the heart of nature's production. It's not clean and tidy and orderly, like petro-chemicals in a lab. But we're finally learning that if we don't pay attention to nature's smallest creatures, to bottom-up intervention and to the role of the tiniest living things in providing for the rest of us, we may find ourselves in a truly frightening place.

Death Takes a Holiday

> *Eleven percent of all bird species are on the verge of extinction as a consequence of what we've done. A report of the world's plants suggests that 12 percent ... are on the brink of extinction, and I suspect that's an underestimate, because there are many of the world's plants that we don't know. It's not just in land and soils; it's in oceans and rivers. A huge fraction of our freshwater clams and mussels are on the verge of extinction. The pattern is ubiquitous. Whenever we have sufficient data, we recognize somewhere between 10 and 40 percent of all the world's species are already on the verge of extinction.*
>
> — STUART PIMM, CONSERVATION BIOLOGIST

Damage to soil doesn't stop with modern agricultural practices. Industrial toxins, the acidic fallout from burning sulphurous fuels like coal, nitrogen oxides from car exhaust, and PCBs and dioxins all end up in forests and streams, as well as on cropland. More than a decade ago, scientists like Orrie Loucks began getting calls from farmers and other people in rural areas around the Ohio River valley who were troubled by the number of dying trees. Loucks and his colleagues set up two test plots. The soils in both plots were carefully matched for mineral type and forest variety; both had the same species of white and black oak and hickory. One site was in southern Ohio, where wind drift and proximity to industry caused very high doses of pollution and a pH level of about 4.1, which indicates very acidic soils. The other site was in southern Illinois, and had low doses of pollution and an average pH of 5.0, a level that enabled the soil to absorb acids and toxins without negative effects. In the southern Illinois soils, the researchers found an average of thirty earthworms per cubic metre. As Loucks says, "That's rich. You can get all the bait you need to go fishing in fifteen minutes." In contrast, the polluted soils of Ohio yielded only one earthworm per cubic metre, and those were of a species that lives in dead wood. No other species were found.

Loucks's group began to track 150 other invertebrates in the two plots of soil. At the polluted Ohio site, the species that still existed in relative abundance were present in populations about 60 to 70 percent of the size of the Illinois populations. And between 40 and 50 percent of the species found at the less polluted site weren't present at all in the Ohio soil. In other words, half of the life forms that sustained the Ohio oak-forest ecosystem had disappeared, and those still remaining were severely depleted. If worm populations reflect the decline of soil micro-organisms, they mirror the toll on larger organisms, too, because the trees in the Ohio plots, reports Loucks, are also dying. Leaf litter under the trees, which normally decomposes between fall and spring every year, is just lying there. In the low-pollution site the litter is about half a centimetre thick, but in the polluted sites it is almost three centimetres. That means that the calcium, nitrogen and all the trace elements that the creatures in the soil — and, ultimately, the trees — need to survive is tied up in the undecayed leaf litter. And as the soil studies on the site have shown, the organisms responsible for decomposing the leaf litter and releasing its nutrients have disappeared, or have become depleted to the point where they can no longer perform their function.

Orrie Loucks's team has developed a keen admiration for the way battalions of different species transform cellulose and putrefying bodies into plant food. Because bacteria cannot easily decompose large pieces of leaves, for example, it is absolutely essential that larger creatures, like earthworms and insects, initially shred the leaves into small pieces. If the sugars in these leaves were just left to the fungi and bacteria, they would devour it all themselves. However, mites eat the bacteria and fungi, like miniature livestock grazing on grass in a pasture, and that keeps the bacteria and fungi under control. The system is held in a dynamic equilibrium, so one part doesn't grow and reproduce too quickly. The raw litter is turned into nutrients at a rate that leaves an optimum amount available to the following year's plants.

As Loucks says, "It's a kind of orchestra, a symphony of different species complementing each other . . . to achieve balance in the breakdown of organic matter." He goes on to ask an important question: "At what point in species impoverishment did ecosystem function become so impaired that we destroyed the capacity of the trees to grow? . . . Every aspect of that system is now dysfunctional. Did the dysfunction start at 20 percent loss of biodiversity? At 10 percent?" Unfortunately, Loucks's team has been unable to get the research funding to find out why. He says, "I can't imagine any question that's more important. If the Earth is threatened, as it is now, with the loss of 30 to 50 percent of its biodiversity, shouldn't we immediately try to understand what has been put at risk?"

Scientific funding these days, however, is aimed at discovering new technological fixes, not at teasing out the intricacies of how nature works or what has gone wrong when productivity drops. Once again, we have to look at our cultural and historical traditions to discover why we have such huge scientific blind spots. Loucks believes that "human observation tends to be directed at events that are big and dramatic, or events that go on over the course of a year, like a major drought. But events that induce profound changes for the Earth and for human prospects, and that stretch over periods of two to three decades, are judged as speculative. And so changes that take place among little organisms over long periods have been just generally discounted. You know, it's only a relatively small audience out there that is able to say, 'Earthworms are king.'"

Destroying the Engines of Life

> *It takes a long time — millions of years — to create species as*
> *fully developed as the ones around us. . . . We are destroying*
> *species a hundred times faster than they could be created, even*
> *if we left the natural environment alone. We are doing the*
> *equivalent of drawing down hard on our bank account; and*
> *you can't be drawing down on your bank account at a*
> *hundred times the rate you're putting new money in without*
> *going broke very fast.*
>
> — E.O. WILSON

Today, we've quickened the pace of extinction to a level never seen before. In tropical rain forests alone, for example, we're eliminating, at a very conservative estimate, about 25,000 entire species every year. Biologists are alarmed by the human-caused acceleration of extinction. We've learned from the past that when major extinction events have occurred, new niches may be opened up for opportunistic species to move in, but it takes long periods of time for the variety of species to be restored.

Norman Myers is a well-known author and lecturer on biodiversity, affiliated with Green College at Oxford University. He says that the great powerhouses of evolution are in the tropics — rain forests, coral reefs and wetlands. They weren't destroyed in the previous great extinctions of species on this planet. And because they were still intact, it took "only" about 5 million years for evolution to refurnish the planet with life forms as complex and diverse as those it had lost. But now, he says, "We're knocking out not only large numbers of species, but also the capacity of evolution to come up with replacement species as readily as it has done in the past. . . . This time, the bounce-back period won't be just 5 million years. It'll be more like 25 million years."

Most of us lack the perspective that would make the extinction crisis seem real. To try to make it clear, let's first note that all organisms of Earth need energy to carry out every life process, from movement and metabolism to growth and reproduction. And that energy comes from the sun. Photosynthesis enables plants to capture photons — packets of energy in sunlight — and convert them into storable chemical energy.

And all the rest of life, from microorganisms to animals, feeds on the sunlight captured by photosynthetic activity to flourish and multiply.

A few years ago, when there were only 5 billion of us, Stuart Pimm, a prominent conservation biologist and professor of ecology at the University of Tennessee in Knoxville, calculated the fraction of all terrestrial photosynthetic activity that human beings take for their own use. We use about 15 million square kilometres for agriculture — most of that is land taken from places that were once forest. We also consume large parts of forests for our fuel and building materials. We graze very large portions of the planet, roughly 60 million square kilometres. About half of the non-frozen land area of the world is some sort of pastureland. Added up, this means that we are already exploiting about 42 percent of the planet's land mass. If you adjust the figures to reflect the fact that there are now 6 billion of us, they will show that we are fully exploiting about half of everything the planet produces annually.

To many people, that may not sound so bad. After all, about half is still left. Indeed, the United Nations Commission on the Environment and Development recommended in 1987 that all countries protect 12 percent of their land base. That target seems to accept that 88 percent of the land is ours to use as we wish. But we are merely one species among perhaps 10 million, and we are still completely dependent on the services performed by all of that biodiversity. By co-opting such a large part of the planet's photosynthetic activity to fuel our energy needs, we deprive many of the other species that would have used it, and thereby drive them to extinction. Because our population has been growing exponentially, we know that the human population could double again, to 10 to 12 billion, in only thirty or forty more years. Will we then take over all available land spaces to grow food for ourselves or our domesticated animals? And Pimm adds a fact that makes the outlook even grimmer. "We, humanity, have highlighted the planet. We have taken the best bits. The forests of Europe, Japan and North America are the bits that are just right. Not too hot, not too cold, not too wet, not too dry. Now, as our population expands, it's moving into areas that are not as good, parts of the planet that are basically indigestible. As a consequence, that other half, that 50 percent of the primary production that is still forests and tundra and grasslands, is not going to support us anywhere as well as the parts we've already used up do."

Our effect on rivers is just as overwhelming. Riparian habitat, the zone along riverbanks, has long been recognized as one of the richest areas of diversity of life on the planet. In harsh desert or tundra regions like Israel or northern Canada, riverbanks shelter almost all the life that exists. That's why dams or river diversions there wreak such environmental havoc. So much water is taken out of the Colorado, the river whose force dug the Grand Canyon, that by the time it reaches the ocean there's none left. The Tennessee is the fifth-largest river in North America, and there isn't one inch of it that hasn't been dammed or channelled. These rivers function as ecological circulatory systems that conduct life's fluid to the land, yet we've altered them so extensively that water shortages are a looming fear for the entire planet in the next few decades. We're only just beginning to realize what our industrial and engineering activity has done to the biological productivity of habitats and nurseries of biodiversity like wetlands and estuaries.

The story of human disruption of complex terrestrial ecosystems is being repeated in the oceans. We're seeing fisheries crash all around the globe as they're overharvested or destroyed in other ways. Shrimp farms and agricultural runoff devastate mangrove swamps and coral reefs that serve as nurseries and habitats for most forms of ocean life. Recent calculations show that we already consume about a third of the biological production of the ocean in a fisheries practice that is on the brink of collapse. As Pimm says, "We're skimming the top level of life out of the ocean — the sharks, sailfish, bluefin tuna — all the top predators, which are the equivalent of the lions, tigers and bears of the terrestrial environment."

Eighty percent of the species for which we have names come from tropical rain forests. We all know what's happening to them. Stuart Pimm says, "If you fly over Haiti, you'll see what looks like an ecosystem haemorrhaging a flow of red blood out into the blue sea." When people cut down a natural forest for fuel or farmland, particularly in a hilly country, soil once held in place by trees is exposed to wind and rain and simply washes out to sea. And in the ocean, soil sediment clogs the rich coral reefs that are incubators for much of the fish population. Forests and reefs made tropical island paradises of ease and plenty. They were the wellsprings of life — all life, including our own — and we're destroying them not just for farms, but also so we can build fancy hotels behind concrete walls along every shoreline. Our culture does not see baby fish and soils and clean water as riches, only the discos and bars of development.

As I said in the introduction to this book, our culture has never before been in the position of having to see the world — the air, the seas, the rivers, our soils — as finite, as something that we could ever use up. For at least a thousand years, Western culture, *our* culture, has believed that when we run out of things in one place, we can just go to another place, we can substitute something else or we can use our inventiveness to create new forms of riches. But we've hit the wall in terms of real riches, the ones you can eat, the ones that sustain lives. Now that we're finally sitting down to take inventory, we're realizing that everything from lions and tigers to earthworms and microbes is disappearing. We can finally compare our numbers and our yearly needs with how much mathematically measurable energy the Earth is capable of producing. The figures are clear.

We have to realize that our culture's old method of dealing with the world — taking all we can and moving on — is not going to work any more. But that's just *our* culture. All over the world, there are remnants of other human cultures that in effect hit the wall of limited resources and saturated populations many, many years ago. Many, but not all, aboriginal cultures have remained the same for thousands of years because they were composed of the people who didn't leave when the resources got scarce. The adventurers among them went off to colonize and exploit new lands. But on every continent, a small core group of people stayed home. They were able to stay because they had figured out the rules of sustaining a finite resource base. They kept their numbers in check, and they kept their exploitation of the resources in check as well. They co-operated in this difficult endeavour by evolving religious beliefs that helped them conserve their own particular piece of the planet, which was to them the whole world.

Only a small fraction of the 6 billion of us who now exist will ever explore anything "out there" again. Of course, there's always the chance that some day, at least a generation from now, hundreds or even thousands of adventurers might try their luck in space. But most of us aren't going anywhere, for the simple reason that there isn't anywhere to go. It may be time, then, to ask a few of the aboriginal people who are still around to give us some advice about how a finite world works. And in the process, we may learn something about all of physical reality.

We Are the Land and the Land Is Us

One of the things that we as Okanagan people know is that our very flesh is our land. Our very breath that we take is our land. Everything that is about us is our land. . . . And so when we call on our spirits in the spirit world, that's how we talk to them. When we refer to everything that is, we have only one word meaning the all, everything, the land, the water, the birds, the insects — everything, including ourselves. We say tamihu. *And that means everything, including us, has that life force in it.*

— JEANETTE ARMSTRONG, OKANAGAN ELDER

What is the life force that Jeanette Armstrong, an elder of the Okanagan people of British Columbia, speaks of? I think it's the same thing that we've been talking about in a scientific way throughout this whole chapter. It's the fundamental interrelatedness of all life on Earth, which we are discovering on the molecular, microscopic and visible-ecosystem levels. She is using only slightly different words to describe the same reality that researchers and scientists like Orrie Loucks, E.O. Wilson and Stuart Pimm have been discovering.

Jeanette Armstrong is a writer, an artist and a community leader on the Okanagan Reserve in Penticton, British Columbia. She is also a critic of modern culture, and her essays have appeared in books such as the Sierra Club's *The Case against the Global Economy*. A grandmother herself, she remembers going out on the land with her own aunts and uncles and grandparents. She recalls, "Going out on the land was like being with members of the family."

Her family taught her about the interrelatedness of life, not through scientific studies, but by speech and example. She says, "When my grandmother would say 'Grandmother' and name a lake, or 'Grandfather' and name a mountain, or refer to 'these grandfather trees' and talk to the wildlife that way, I never used to see the differentiation between human beings and the life forms around us. And I think that perspective, in terms of forming relationships to the land, being in love with the land in the same way that you're in love with people, is an essential part of the human being."

Armstrong lives in British Columbia, where the ancient forests are melting like snow under the advance of modern exploitation. She tries to explain how her people still identify with the land and all the creatures around them. She says, "When those grandmother or grandfather mountains or lakes or rivers or streams are destroyed, it's like your grandparents being hurt. . . . For our people, it's no different than a family member leaving. It's that connection, at that level. And it's more than just an emotional regard for the land, or a love of the land because of its pictorial quality or its beauty. It's an actual relationship with our land in that way. I would hear my grandmother talk about a certain place, and then when we would be there, she would speak and sing to that place. We would share our food with it, and it would share its food with us. . . . In that kind of principle, with that kind of attitude, you can't go out and destroy that land, unless you're insane, no more than you could destroy your own grandparents."

Like Armstrong, people in the vast majority of traditional and indigenous groups believe that the Earth is alive, that it is an organism, like Gaia. And they believe that human beings are as much a part of the natural world as insects or whales or clouds. Most of them believe that humans have a responsibility to take care of the other creatures around them, that calamity will result if we are greedy, wasteful or destructive. They cement this understanding of the physical world not with scientific data, but with emotion and experience.

Brian Swimme is a cosmologist and mathematician teaching at the California Institute for Integral Studies. He's a quantum-mechanics physicist at the cutting edge of modern science. One of the most exciting things we're learning about how the world works, he thinks, is how closely it resembles the pictures painted by traditional peoples and ancient religions. The empirical, scientific way of knowing how the universe works "is simply a new way, one that is powerful and wonderful, but that corroborates much of traditional understanding in often surprising ways." One example Swimme cites is what he calls "the third great discovery of modern science: the realization that the Earth's system is itself self-organizing or self-regulating. And one easy way to capture this is to simply say the Earth is alive. Of course, it's not alive the way a salamander is, it doesn't give birth to baby Earths. But it's alive in the sense that it actually organizes itself so that the complexity of its life forms might continue."

We have scientific data, as opposed to traditional intuition, to back this up. Swimme says, "One easy way of seeing this is that life forms require a particular spectrum of temperatures for their molecules to operate. And the Earth maintains itself in that range. It enables life to come forth. And the reason we know this is that the temperature of the sun has changed drastically over billions of years. It was 25 percent less intense in the beginnings of life. So life itself, the bacteria alive at the time, had to alter clouds to trap heat, to warm the place up for more life. It's a stunning realization, because you can't perceive the Earth as self-regulating in our own local frame of reference."

Ancient and traditional cultures have long taught that the Earth is alive. Swimme says that although we just got these data together, "intuitively, this was something understood by indigenous peoples for about the last 50,000 years. Four hundred years of science have enabled us to begin to approach this intuitive truth from an outer, or empirical, way. Data don't make a truth superior, but they do make it different. Taken together with the old form of knowledge, we have the opportunity for a stronger understanding of the self-regulatory or living nature of Earth."

Swimme believes that this fundamental change in how science views the world will have far-reaching effects on Western culture. He says, "[Now] we begin to see ourselves not just as individuals on planet Earth, but rather as sensing creatures that live within the organized life of Earth. We're part of a whole. And this perspective is, I think, very different from what we've been used to in modern industrial culture." It is scientific reductionism itself that is helping us to see the limitations of our old cultural methods of dealing with the world. If we are to conserve the things we care about, like salmon, like clean air or water or soils full of earthworms, we can no longer see the world as a simple clockwork we can easily take apart with no damage done. We need to come to an understanding of how amazingly complex and delicate the connections that keep life going really are.

We are still enormously ignorant of the complexity and interconnectedness of the world around us. As projects like Biosphere II have reminded us, we have no ability to replicate, let alone improve upon, the natural world. But we do know that the marvellous productivity and regeneration of nature flows from the rich diversity of living things. With extinction cutting out species right and left, we are tearing at the fabric of biodiversity on which we absolutely depend. Modern science is now revealing the depth of our embeddedness in and dependence on nature, as well as the catastrophic changes we are causing. We have to understand all these basic truths. One such truth is that not all bugs are dangerous or dirty; they are in fact part of our family, part of our life history and an integral part of the web of life. We need to respect and accommodate them, and all other life forms, if we are all to go on helping each other to survive.

CHAPTER 2
BIGFOOT

*In 1992, in Rio, all the 100-plus nations said, "Okay, we have
to reduce our impact on the planet." But now, seven years later,
we have more people, more cars, more pollution, more resource
consumption, fewer species, less water, less topsoil. So we are
farther away from sustainability. But how far? We have to
know. If we can't measure that, we will never be able to move
to sustainability. How much nature do we use? And how much
nature do we have left?*

— MATHIAS WACKERNAGEL, CO-DEVELOPER OF THE
ECOLOGICAL FOOTPRINT MEASUREMENT

With stunning speed, humanity has laid claim to every bit of land on the
planet and a wide zone of the oceans along our coastlines. We've even
planted flags on the moon and sent our machines to Mars. The fate of
every ecosystem on the planet is now determined by human activity. We
exploit potentially renewable resources like fish, trees, soil and fresh water
far beyond their rates of replacement. We poison air, water and soil with
toxic effluents. We transform the landscape with cities and farms, dams
and roads. And as we exert our will on the terrain around us, wild things
are pushed out of the way — and out of existence.

We don't seem to worry about this as much as we should, I think
largely because we have an unwarranted faith in the ability of science and
technology to pull us out of the mess that our technological prowess has
created. In my opinion, no more destructive belief exists than the idea that
we have escaped the constraints imposed by nature on all other species.
We assume that by enabling us to exploit and alter our surroundings, our

intellect has freed us from dependence on specific habitats. We believe we are no longer part of nature, because we have acquired the ability to control and manage the forces impinging on us.

This illusion of escape from nature has been reinforced by our extraordinary transformation in this century from country dwellers to city dwellers. In an urban setting, we live in a human-created environment, surrounded by other people plus a few domesticated plants and animals, as well as the pests that have overcome our defences. Living among such a dearth of other species, we no longer recognize our dependence on the rest of life for our well-being and our very survival. It is simpler to assume that the economy delivers our food, clean air, water and energy, and takes away our sewage and waste. We forget that the Earth itself provides all these services, and so makes economists and the economy possible. We are biological beings, as dependent on the biosphere as any other life form, and we forget our animal nature at our peril. As we undermine clean air, water, soil and energy; as we burn fossil fuels beyond the capacity of the Earth to reabsorb the greenhouse molecules thus created; as we use our surroundings as dumping grounds for toxic effluents; and as we degrade pristine areas once teeming with other life and resources, I believe we're embarking on a suicidal path.

Those are pretty strong words, and many people will take issue with them. But having interviewed hundreds of experts and scientists in many parts of the world, I have become convinced that they are true. There are real, measurable limits on the world around us. The resources of our planet are finite; a limited amount of air and water can support a limited number of living creatures, which we need for food and shelter. So what are the limits? Is there any way to calculate how many of us is too many and how much consumption or waste disposal is too much? Once these questions seemed too vast to figure out reliably. But with computers, we have the technical means to find answers.

Bill Rees, a population ecologist at the University of British Columbia, together with Mathias Wackernagel, his former graduate student, has developed one of the first reliable ways to measure how much of the planet's productivity we're already using. They call it our "ecological footprint."

We can already measure the number of organisms other than humans that a given ecosystem can support indefinitely. Ecologists call this the carrying capacity of the ecosystem. Obviously, if there are more individuals feeding on coral or trees than the reef or forest can support, then the habitat will be destroyed over time. Take, as an example, deer in a northwestern forest. As long as there's plenty of food around — plenty of plant biomass — the deer eat and their numbers increase rapidly. "But as they become too numerous," Rees explains, "they overgraze and destroy the very basis of their own existence. And then they crash down to a level that is back in balance with what the now-altered environment can sustain over time."

Throughout the realm of all living organisms, one of the strategies of evolution is reproduction in excess of the number needed to perpetuate a species indefinitely. Other species are able to live off this excess without jeopardizing the prey's long-term survival. Thus numerous species — from puffins to salmon, seals and humans — can take from the lavish abundance of herring in the Pacific Ocean without endangering the herring's survival. But there are still limits that set the carrying capacity of each species.

Rees notes that many economists reject the idea of applying the notion of carrying capacity to human beings. They argue that the planet can sustain our present numbers and more because we aren't like other animals. We're intelligent and inventive, they say, and these qualities have enabled us to go beyond our biological roots. Unlike the deer, we don't have to satisfy our needs from our immediate surroundings. Unlike bears and coral reefs, we can engage in trade. Therefore our population capacity in a given region needn't be limited by the resources in that region. "The idea here," Rees says, "is that almost any place on the planet, any significant region, will have certain things in surplus and other things that may be scarce. But if we're creative, we can trade our surpluses for those things that are locally scarce. And that enables both us and other regions to overcome our local carrying capacity. The population then can rise. The consumption of goods and services can rise far beyond the capacity of the local area to support that population."

Even then, surely, there is a limit; if the numbers everywhere get large enough, eventually the problem will resurface. But those who believe in infinite growth throw in another critical factor: technology. Rees says, "Many people believe that as technology improves, we'll be able to find a substitute for any resource that gets scarce, even scarce everywhere. In other words, human ingenuity can [find a] substitute for any good or service provided by nature. . . . So when you put the whole issue of trade and technological advance in the basket, it seems that carrying capacity is an irrelevant concept for human beings."

If economists don't believe that carrying capacity limits human beings, what is our wealth (i.e., natural wealth, like food and water) based on? Economists believe that human inventiveness can create even natural wealth and will satisfy our every need, including basic ones like food, clean air and shelter. The economist Julian Symon once told me that the more people there are, the better off we'll all be, because there will be more geniuses like Albert Einstein to come up with a never-ending supply of new ideas and inventions. As an ecologist, Bill Rees doesn't think this idea makes much sense. He feels it violates something intrinsic about human beings: "For all our technological wizardry, we're still real animals; we're still organisms dependent on physical processes and physical materials."

Rees and Wackernagel decided to turn the concept of carrying capacity on its head to help apply it to humans. They decided that instead of asking how many people a region could support, they would ask how much land it would take to support the physical needs of each human being. Within any system of trading, regardless of the level of technological development, each person still requires a certain productive area on the surface of the Earth to maintain his or her physical needs and absorb his or her wastes. Rees says, "So all we've done is to invert the traditional carrying-capacity ratio. Instead of asking how many organisms per unit area, it's how much area per organism? Or, if you like, how much area is needed to support a defined population, like a city or a country?" The answer gives you that human's, or that population's, ecological footprint.

Canadians are among the wealthiest people in the world. We have a lavish national lifestyle. We drive big cars. We can eat fresh strawberries all year round. We have big houses full of lots of stuff. It takes a lot of land to provide this lifestyle, to grow fibres for our clothes and provide space and material for our houses, as well as to grow food to feed us and pump water to sustain it all. We also need land to absorb the wastes we create. The carbon dioxide from our cars and the wastes we flush down the toilet or bury in landfills all require a certain amount of water, soil and time before they can be absorbed and made non-toxic. Therefore, as a country, we have a very big ecological footprint. Rees has figured out just how big. "We estimate that the ecological footprint of an average Canadian, taking into account food requirements, fibre requirements, wood requirements, paper requirements and so on, plus just the assimilation of carbon dioxide, would bring us up to about 7 hectares [about 17 acres] per capita. There is a marine component there as well — that includes something on the order of 0.7 hectares [1.7 acres] of productive ocean surface. So . . . the average Canadian needs 7 hectares of biologically productive land of many, many different categories all over the surface of the Earth, dedicated exclusively to [his or her] support."

We have a very big country, so seven hectares each may not sound too bad. We Canadians do not, in fact, use the entire ecological capacity of our country. But Canada isn't alone on the planet, and we do sell our trees, fish and crops. Because of this trade, our forests are in serious decline, our fisheries are collapsing and our agricultural soils are eroding at an extreme rate. As Rees says, "The collapse of our fish stocks is not the result of domestic consumption, but rather the result of our exports. . . . The loss of old-growth [forests] again is not the result of domestic consumption. . . . We export most of our forest products. Most of our grain is exported from Canada, so erosion and other forms of dissipation of our prairie soils have to do with consumption taking place in other countries. Furthermore, such things as atmospheric contamination with, among other things, carbon dioxide . . . is a global problem. It doesn't really matter what we do in this country. If the rest of the world is on an unsustainable path that destroys the atmosphere or upsets climate conditions or makes a hole in the ozone layer, then we all suffer the consequences."

Fair Is Fair

The time has come,
To say fair's fair,
To pay the rent,
To pay our share.

— MIDNIGHT OIL, "BEDS ARE BURNING"

If we Canadians each need seven hectares of productive land mass to be supported in the style to which we've become accustomed, what in fact is the amount of land available to each existing human on this planet, if it were divided up equally? The answer to that question is simple, says Rees. "Anybody can do the math. The reality is that there are . . . just under 6 billion people on the Earth right now. There are only about 8.9 billion hectares [of agricultural land]. So if you divided the total amount of ecologically productive landscape by the human population, . . . we'd each get about a hectare and a half of land." That's 170 metres by 100 metres — equivalent to about a city block.

If you added in everybody's fair share of the productive parts of the ocean, each person would get about two hectares (five acres) of land and water. "That [figure] gives us, right away, a measure of how far [Canadians] would have to move in terms of reducing our consumption to reach our fair Earth-share," Rees says. "Or, conversely, [it tells us] how much we would have to improve our technological efficiency so that we could continue the same level of material consumption. In fact, in order to bring everyone on the planet to the same general level of consumption and well-being of the average Canadian, we would need four or five more Earths — right now! These figures are frightening, but they're real, and they give us a clear idea of how far we have to slim down consumption, population and wastes, as well as readapt technologies, if we are to have a decent future for the majority of humanity. At this point, scientists tell us this is still not an impossible goal."

The ecological footprint measure also gives us some idea of what is possible. We can see just how lavish and excessive Canadian consumption is when we compare it with the per capita consumption of poorer countries like Bangladesh. There, they consume ten to forty times less than we do per capita. The Chinese consume about a seventh of what we do. It follows that if we reduced our consumption, even a little, people in developing countries would have a much better chance of increasing theirs. It also means that any idea of raising the masses of the Third World "up to our level" is impossible, given the scientific and mathematical measurements of the planet's productive capacity. The claim made by economists and corporate leaders that more consumption around the world will benefit the poor is simply untrue. In fact, the opposite is true. All the expansion approach does is use up the future faster, primarily for the benefit of the already excessively rich. According to the United Nations Educational, Scientific, and Cultural Organization (UNESCO), if we divide the world's population into fifths, "in 1990, the richest group received 59 times more than the poorest. Despite growth of almost 3 percent per annum worldwide of per capita GNP over the past three decades, this is almost double the ratio of 30:1 in 1960. In that year, the richest 20 percent already controlled 70.2 percent of global GNP. In 1990 this had climbed to 82.7 percent. In 1960 the poorest 20 percent had to get by with only 2.3 percent, which by 1990 had fallen to 1.4 percent."

Mathias Wackernagel, the co-developer of the ecological footprint concept, is now teaching at the Center for Sustainability Studies in Veracruz, Mexico. He suggests that we are looking in the wrong direction for solutions. "We have been very good at looking at atoms, at plants, animals, even looking at poor people. Because we are rich, we tell the poor people what to do. But we have been very bad at looking at ourselves. . . . We, the world's middle class, are the wealthiest 20 percent of the world. We . . . have the biggest ecological footprint. We have to learn to look at ourselves and see what . . . share of the global pie . . . we occupy."

We've got used to consuming so much of the planet partly because we don't see the connection between our way of life and other parts of the world. The bananas and coffee we have for breakfast weren't grown on our own land base. They came from thousands of kilometres away, but we don't think about that while we're grabbing a bite and reading the morning newspaper. It's as if we're provided with goods and services by servants about whom we never have to think or even notice. Pretending that limitless growth is possible, and that it will benefit the servants because they'll get more too, is just a way of avoiding the reality that we're taking more than our fair share.

Economists often argue that countries with few natural resources and large populations, like Germany or the Netherlands, can nonetheless achieve prosperity because of their ingenuity. The Netherlands is often cited as a model of modern economic development. Despite its proportionately huge population, roughly 434 people per square kilometre, its total land base and natural resources are very limited. Yet Holland has a positive balance of trade and one of the highest per capita gross domestic products (GDPs) on the planet. Instead of natural capital like trees, land and fish, it is argued that Holland's riches are generated through human ingenuity that leads to the production of value-added goods like fancy cheeses and fine electronics.

According to Bill Rees, "Many economists marvel at the fact that sometimes the Netherlands has an export in agricultural produce. But that's a money measure.... Dutch agriculture [actually] requires a land area outside the country about five times larger, some say as much as seven times larger, than the agricultural land within the country." That's because in order to grow their produce, the Dutch have to import petrochemical fertilizers, pesticides, machines and seeds from other countries. But those costs are simply not subtracted from the revenue generated when their flowers and vegetables are sold. Rees says, "The point is, Holland and countries like it, most of the developed nations, for that matter, are often used as models for the Third World to follow. But . . . it's not possible for the Third World to follow these models, because in many respects the Third World is providing the surpluses that these countries exploit in order to have their extremely high standards of living. So for every country that has an ecological deficit, there has to be another part of the Earth that has an ecological surplus. If every country runs an ecological deficit, then we are quite literally consuming the Earth. And in fact . . . that is exactly what we are doing."

This imbalance has begun only very recently. Mathias Wackernagel says, "We now live in an ecologically full world. And that's new. After the Second World War, the ecological footprint, even of rich people, was smaller than the Earth's ecological capacity available on a per capita basis. So expansion was easy. We weren't competing directly with each other. But now the world is overly full, and our research has shown that . . . the ecological footprint of humanity is 35 percent larger than the ecological capacity of the world."

Thirty-five percent larger? How can we be using up more than there is? Wackernagel means that we are now using up natural capital, not just the interest; we are using more than the production that nature provides annually above and beyond what it needs to sustain itself. "It's like an account," he says. "You can use just the interest, or you can use a little more. And what happens? Natural capital disappears. That's what we see. Topsoils vanishing. Deforestation. Water tables going down. Biodiversity loss. So basically, we are depleting our natural capital."

Baby Blues

We certainly have predispositions to do many things, like have [a lot of children]. But one of the most fundamental is the predisposition to learn, and to learn all our lives. The most distinctive human capacity is to modify our behaviour depending on what we see around us. And we can see around us the running out of resources and the risk that our numbers are posing to society. We can learn from that.

— JARAD DIAMOND,
EVOLUTIONARY BIOLOGIST

Like any other species, human beings have always had an ecological footprint. But for 99 percent of our existence, our needs were simple and nature was vast and endlessly self-renewing. That relationship has changed with sudden speed. When I was born in 1936, there were 2 billion people on Earth. There are now 6 billion of us. We have exploded into the age of space travel, computers and global telecommunications. And we have a global economy that is predicated on the need for constant growth.

The problem is that we live in a finite world. Endless growth is an impossibility. Anything that grows steadily over time, whether it's the diameter of a tree, the amount of water we use, the rise in population or the increase in GDP, grows exponentially. Anything that grows exponentially will double in a predictable period of time. Suppose the size of a city grows at a rate of one percent a year. In 70 years, it will have doubled. Growth at 2 percent a year will result in a doubling in 35 years; at 3 percent, in 23 years; at 4 percent, in 17.5 years; and so on.

The University of Colorado physicist Arthur Bartlett once gave me a graphic illustration of the effects of exponential growth. Imagine a test tube full of food for bacteria. Now imagine that we introduce a single bacterium that will proceed to divide every minute. So at the beginning, there's one cell. A minute later, there are two; in two minutes, four; and in three minutes, eight. That's exponential growth. At 60 minutes in this example, the test tube is full of bacteria and all the food is gone. Then when was the test tube half full? The answer, of course, is at 59 minutes.

So at 58 minutes, it was 25 percent full; at 57 minutes, 12.5 percent full. At 55 minutes, the test tube was only 3 percent full.

If, at 55 minutes, some bacterial genius spoke up and said, "I think we have a population problem," the less astute majority would probably retort, "What are you talking about? Ninety-seven percent of the test tube is empty, and we've been around for 55 minutes!" But if the doubling continued, then at 59 minutes most bacteria would probably realize they were in trouble. Suppose they threw money at their scientists and begged for a solution. And suppose that, in less than a minute, those bacterial scientists created three test tubes full of food! Everyone would be saved, right? Well, no. At 60 minutes, the first test tube would be full. At 61 minutes, the second would be full, and at 62 minutes all four would be full. By quadrupling the amount of food and space, they gain only two extra minutes.

Most biologists believe we are long past the fifty-ninth minute with respect to our use of the planet's life-support systems. Fortunately, we aren't living in a test tube. We're living on a planet that can renew itself — but only if we give it a chance. In 1968, Paul Ehrlich, the famous population ecologist from Stanford University, published a blockbuster, a book called *The Population Bomb*. It averred that our numbers were on a collision course with our resources, and it predicted massive famines. Many people now say that book exaggerated the issue and attacked the solution from the wrong angle. After all, we're still managing; our problems didn't get as bad as Ehrlich predicted they would in the ensuing years. Many credit the global economy with the failure of Ehrlich's predictions. However, part of the reason why we haven't come to ruin is that a lot of people did pay attention to Ehrlich's warning.

Over the past year or two, we have, for the first time, seen a drop in the rate of population growth. This phenomenon has to do with more enlightened birth-control policies and populations that are beginning to see for themselves the effects of overcrowding. Moreover, many agencies now working on population issues didn't exist in the seventies. The World Fertility Survey, for example, polled some 500 million women in poor countries around the world. The women told the agency that they didn't want all the children they had, and that they also wanted to space their pregnancies more carefully, but that they lacked the means to do anything about it. If these women were able to have the number of children they really wanted, the Earth's population would stabilize at somewhere around 8 billion, rather than 12 billion, over the next thirty or forty years.

Werner Fornos is a population expert, a former university professor, and, for the past twenty years, president of the Population Institute in Washington, D.C. He says that when he got into population studies in 1972, only 5 percent of couples in the world used modern methods of contraception. That figure is now up to 50 percent. Mexico, once full of huge families, has rapidly declining fertility figures. Brazil has achieved a 60 percent use of contraceptives. Italy, the home of the Vatican, has the lowest fertility rate in the world. And there are many other success stories. But the large cohort of people now passing through their reproductive years means that even in a country like China, which has adopted draconian measures in an effort to stem the tide of babies, the population is still growing at a rate of 21 million people per year. China will soon be surpassed in total population by India, which has reached a billion people and is growing at a rate of 2 million every month. If we do nothing to encourage slower population growth, it will mean, as Fornos says, "the difference between . . . a twenty-first century where we have a hope for a better quality of life, or [one] where the Four Horsemen of the Apocalypse will return, only this time they'll be Global Warming, Ozone Depletion, Famine and Over-Population."

We could help countries like Nicaragua, Honduras and Haiti with simple contraceptive aid so that women can have the number of children they really want. Fornos says that in the United States, "we're currently spending [the equivalent of] roughly a cup of coffee and a donut a year, per person, on international population assistance. I think we can afford to spend half a six-pack of whatever your favourite beverage is." But international population assistance is not just a matter of providing cheap pills or condoms. It's something much more fundamental, as has been proven through a great number of university and United Nations studies over the past ten years. The United Nations–sponsored Conference on Population, held in Cairo in 1993, agreed unanimously on a course of actions to reduce populations.

The first of these is to raise female literacy rates. There is a direct and almost unbreakable connection between the ability of women to read and a lower birth rate, a fact that first came to the attention of researchers through studies unconnected to population. It holds true virtually throughout the world.

The second is to provide more employment opportunities for women, and to give them access to credit, banking and inheritance rights, as well as the kind of training that makes them useful in their societies for reasons other than breeding. An elevation in the social status of women is crucial. Generally, the higher the status of women in society, the lower the birth rate, and vice versa.

The third action suggested at the Cairo Conference is one of the most effective and rewarding ways to reduce the birth rate — lower infant mortality. This can be accomplished by providing clinics for children under the age of five, simple and cheap rehydration powders to save babies from dying of diarrhoea, and hygiene courses for mothers. All these save existing lives and prevent many new births. But some people claim it's counterproductive to save infant lives, because it eliminates natural controls and thereby increases the population. Werner Fornos answers, "I'm involved in population because I love children. And I think we each have an obligation to take care of the children we bring into this world. But also, by reducing infant mortality to its lowest level, you get rid of the compensatory factor." Experience indicates that when women see babies dying, they continue to have them in order to ensure the number of children they really want. When they have some confidence that their first children will live, they immediately cut back on the number of children they bring into the world.

The fourth action to take is to provide universal access to means of fertility control, to prevent unwanted or unintended pregnancies. The main thing to remember about this aspect of a population-control program, says Fornos, is that "universal access to family planning does not mean abortion. I don't understand when our politicians are going to learn that abortion, like war, is a failure of society to come to grips with a much more fundamental problem. And in this case, the fundamental problem is the prevention of unintended pregnancy."

These four steps, according to Fornos, could lead to a future with a stable human population, where our major focus would be to curb consumption enough that it would be possible for the world to share resources more equitably while protecting the pristine wilderness areas left. There are many promising ways to reduce consumption. Already,

Germany requires all manufacturers to take back packaging, obsolete cars, used refrigerators and old computers, and to assume responsibility for the products they make from beginning to end. In Sweden and Denmark, there are industries that recycle their wastes so efficiently that they produce no emissions; every bit of waste is used or returned into natural systems. We could use our vaunted creative energy and ingenuity in these directions, instead of using them to expand markets for clever new gadgets or marketing gimmicks to keep consumption at a fever pitch.

When the population discussion first came up, the perception was that the real problem lay in the Third World, and in general with the poor, who had social customs that demanded and rewarded large families. But we have to remember that while there are far more *people* in poor countries like India, China, Kenya or the Philippines, more than 80 percent of the planet's *resources* are being consumed by countries like the United States, Japan, Germany and Canada. If you're a Canadian or an American with only one child, that child will consume more than forty times what two little Bangladeshis will. The problem of overpopulation is not just numbers. It's a factor of both population and per capita consumption.

Bill McKibben is a journalist famous for an environmental classic, *The End of Nature*. He says we are clearly built for challenge and service. "That we are able to be convinced otherwise, and convinced that our pleasures come from focusing entirely on ourselves, is just one of the great lies that the twentieth century has tried to foist on us." He helps run a project in the northeastern United States called Hundred Dollar Holiday, which is designed to make Christmas a more simple and pleasurable experience while at the same time teaching people to inoculate themselves a bit from the consumerism of the season. When it comes to limiting families, McKibben says we can use the same principles. "You don't have to have only one child simply in order to help save the planet. Do it because it allows you and your spouse to really concentrate your love and affection and time on this one child."

Way Down, Below the Ocean

Worldwide longline fisheries are now extirpating all the top trophic levels of the ocean: the sharks, the sailfish, the bluefish tuna, all these top predators. And as a consequence, the very

nature of our fisheries is changing. We now feed from the
ocean at one trophic level lower than we did thirty years ago.
At this current rate, you can forget swordfish, you can forget
tuna. A generation from now, you'll all be eating anchovies,
and I hope you like them on your pizza.

— STUART PIMM

Our basic environmental problems are overpopulation and overconsumption. We have the ecological footprint to help us measure our individual
and collective impact. But how do we know whether the situation is getting critical? That is, how radically do we have to change and how fast?
Despite 400 years of science, we're still far from having baseline data on
natural systems. Still, and as always in science, we have to go with the best
data we have now. We have to depend on the few experts who actually
have seen what is going on around us.

Seventy-one percent of this planet's surface is covered by oceans.
But for most of human existence, they've been as mysterious as the
moon. The marine biologist Sylvia Earle is the Explorer in Residence for
the National Geographic Society, and she has spent much of the past
twenty-five years underwater, seeing the oceans firsthand. We forget that
they are the basis for all life on Earth. As Earle says, "This planet is governed by the oceans' climate. It's also home for most of life on Earth.
Most of our oxygen comes from the sea. Something like 70 percent of
the oxygen is generated by organisms living in the ocean. Much of the
carbon dioxide is absorbed there. . . . If we dried up the oceans, we would
do away with the cornerstone of our life support."

We are encroaching on this system of life support. The extent of this
devastation was estimated by a marine ecosystem expert, Elliot Norse,
who calculated that the area of ocean floor destroyed annually by draggers, enormous nets that scrape everything off the ocean bottom in huge
swaths, is 150 times the total amount of land cleared by logging in the
world's forests! Right off the coast of Canada and the northern United
States, says Earle, underwater robots have provided us with an underwater view of George's Bank and the Grand Banks, "and where people
have been with scallop dredges, it looks like a superhighway. It's like a
bulldozer has just gone by. If you go to places where they haven't been
scraping the sea floor, it looks hauntingly like a coral reef. There are

sponges. There are . . . soft corals. They are beautiful with diverse life —
crabs, starfish and various kinds of fish."

One of the worst aspects of this type of "fishing" is the waste. Only a
few targeted species — scallops, for example — are kept. The others are
thrown away. "It's like going through the streets of Toronto and knocking down the buildings and trees and picking out a few pedestrians that
you might like to munch on," says Earle. The scale of fishing that is now
permitted with new technologies only increases such wasteful fishing
practices. Fishing boats are like immense factories equipped with processing facilities and freezers, satellite positioning and sonar locators. They
can stay at sea for weeks and pinpoint their prey with deadly accuracy.
The weapons they deploy — longlines, dredges, nets — are massive.
"Some nets are [big] enough to engulf something as large as a dozen
giant jets in a single swoop through the ocean," says Earle. "In one bite,
you could take the equivalent of twelve Boeing 747 aircraft, for example.
These are being applied in the ocean in a way that takes everything. I
liken it to using bulldozers to catch songbirds and squirrels."

Again, there are many things that can be done; limits on fisheries and
protection of coral reefs are already legislated in many parts of the world.
As Earle says, "We are in a peculiar position right now, in our lifetime.
We're at a turning point. We have the power to protect the sea, and to
change, in ways that will benefit not just the fish, the whales, the phytoplankton and all the rest of ocean life, but that will directly have a positive
benefit on our future: our health, our wealth, our survival."

No one sets out deliberately to trash the very things we need for our
survival. But our ability to focus on a challenge — especially one that
brings money and prosperity, whether it's catching fish or farming the
land — can blind us to the links that connect all parts of the planet.
Oceans are connected to air and land, and the things we do to each of
them have repercussions for the others. Our ecological footprint is now
so massive that even the vast expanses of the oceans are showing it. Earle
observes, "Taking care of the ocean starts at the tops of mountains. What
we do upstream affects everything downstream. . . . What we put on our
backyards, on our farms or what we allow to go into the atmosphere
flows onto the land and finally into the sea. Ultimately the sea is the sewer
for the whole of civilization. Wherever we live on the planet, we are
affecting the oceans of the world."

Losing Our Skin

We've created the situation with these huge fires or floods or insect epidemics [that] are overtaking us. We've been trying to industrialize forests. We've been trying to make them meet human dreams and expectations of completely efficient, productive, simplified landscapes. And what we need to do right now is just give that up completely. Let's recognize that there are real constraints on how much wood or grass or water we can take out. These are not closed systems. It's still possible for us to do some work. We just need to work with the forest instead of against it.

— NANCY LANGSTON, FORESTER

We've become aware only gradually of what's happening to another cornerstone of our life support system — forests. Alan Durning, a colleague of mine and an environmentalist known for an important book, *How Much Is Enough?* has devised a visual image to help illustrate both the speed and the severity of human pressures on Earth, as well as their astonishing escalation in the last few decades. He asks us to imagine a time-lapse film of Earth taken from space. "Play back the last 10,000 years sped up, so that a millennium passes by every minute. For more than seven minutes, the screen displays what looks like a still photograph — the blue planet Earth, its lands swathed in a mantle of trees. After seven and a half minutes, there's a tiny clearing of forest around Athens. This is the flowering of classical Greece. Little else changes. At nine minutes — one thousand years ago — the forest gets thinner in parts of Europe, Central America, China and India. Twelve seconds from the end, two centuries ago, the thinning spreads a little farther in Europe and China. Six seconds from the end, eastern North America is deforested. This is the Industrial Revolution. Little else has changed.

"In the final three seconds, after 1950, the change accelerates explosively. Vast tracts of forest vanish from Japan, the Philippines, the mainland of Southeast Asia, most of Central America, the Horn of Africa, western North America and eastern South America, the Indian subcontinent and sub-Saharan Africa. Fires rage in the Amazon basin, where they never have before. Central Europe's forests die, poisoned by the air and the rain. Southeast Asia looks like a dog with mange. Malaysian Borneo is shaved. In the final fractions of a second, the clearings spread to Siberia and the Canadian North. Forest disappears so quickly from so many places that it looks like a plague of locusts has landed on the Earth."

The forest industry says that there are more trees growing in the United States now than in 1920. That may be true, since the twenties saw the end of a timber rampage that denuded the entire eastern seaboard. But they are also counting as trees the millions of sickly, chemically supported seedlings (also known as plantation forests) planted around North America by timber and paper companies. These plants are part of a massive monoculture, and bear little resemblance to the functioning, diverse-species ecosystems that deliver all the services we expect from a forest. Our original natural forest cover is being either destroyed or replaced by these simplified systems, which are merely uniform stands of trees of the same age and species; other plants attempting to grow in such a system are generally cleared or killed with herbicides. This is very different from the complex interaction of natural species in a real forest.

The World Resources Institute (WRI) in Washington, D.C., a research group trying to promote sustainable development, has published a groundbreaking report on the current state of the Earth's forests. Nigel Sizer, the head of the team that created this survey, says, "Most of the forests that you would drive through in the United States, and even in a significant part of Canada, are no longer natural, fully functioning forests. A lot of them are plantation forests, . . . very highly managed and manipulated by man. They've lost significant components of their biological diversity." Sizer says that not only are forests degraded, but, significantly, they are highly fragmented. "They are no longer able to withstand catastrophic disturbances . . . like hurricanes or massive flooding episodes. To a large extent, they're dependent now upon human intervention and human management to maintain them as functioning ecosystems."

How much of what we used to have is left? Sizer and his team estimate that four-fifths of our great natural forests are gone. And the 20 percent that is left is concentrated in three countries: Brazil, Canada and Russia. Forest disappearance is a new phenomenon, and it is directly related to our ecological footprint. We've logged forests for pulp, fibre and lumber, and to make room for agriculture and support our ever-increasing material demands. Now there are so few untouched forests left that there's a kind of gold rush for the remaining trees.

We think that Canada is a modern, industrialized nation, yet in terms of the way we deal with our forests we behave like a developing country. For example, during the early 1990s, the Government of Alberta's premier, Donald Getty, sought to diversify the province's economy. The government saw the province's boreal forest as an under-utilized resource and invited major transnational logging companies to exploit it. Like a typical developing country, Alberta offered massive financial incentives to foreign companies. The Getty government underwrote the cost of immense pulp mills, guaranteed access to vast tracts of land for next to no stumpage costs, failed to respond satisfactorily to the land claims of the First Nations of the territory and seemed to pay no attention to the ecological consequences of the massive clearcuts that would occur.

Most Canadians are surprised to find that their country is the target of this Third World type of resource exploitation. They shouldn't be. Canada is one of the few countries in the world with much of its original forest cover left. The boreal forest lies just south of the Arctic tundra. It's not as lush or diverse as a tropical rain forest, but it's a vast system that is just as important for removing carbon dioxide from the atmosphere and pumping out oxygen. Sizer says the Canadian government and its bureaucracy are no different from those he encountered in Brazil or Africa. "We see a very tight connection between the political system, politicians and [their] campaign financing, and the operations interests of the large pulp-and-paper and timber companies in [Canada]. We see very limited public access to objective information about the state of Canada's forests."

Furthermore, Sizer says, "Canada is one of the countries with the poorest national statistics on the state of [its] forests, which is very striking when you consider that the forest industry is one of the largest industries in Canada, and that this is a country with the expertise, the ability and the resources to collect better statistics than just about anywhere else. This is a striking situation, and I don't think it's a coincidence. In our work mapping out global forest conditions, the country where we received the most conflicting information, and the most concerted pressure to ensure that we reflected this or that point of view, was Canada — more than Brazil, more than Indonesia, more than Russia. I think that that says a lot."

Of course, it's not just Canadians who have to worry about how we treat our forests. One of the special characteristics of the boreal forests that you find in Canada and Russia is that they store vast amounts of carbon in the soil below the surface of the ground. And with forest clearance, that carbon is released into the atmosphere, adding to the gases that cause global warming. With more warming, the northern forests will degenerate simply because of rising temperatures. This could begin what's called a positive feedback loop: forests cut or dying will release more carbon from their soils; more warming will cause still more carbon emissions; and the situation could spiral out of control.

Can anything be done to protect the remaining forests? Despite the lure of billions of dollars and the unprotected status of most of the remaining forests in the world, there is some hope for protection and even reconstruction. Sizer has some hopeful stories even from a poor country like Surinam. After the WRI released a report about rapacious Asian loggers who were about to move into that country, the people of Surinam objected to the selling off of their forests, and the international community offered assistance to Surinamese citizens' groups. And, says Sizer, "The government of Surinam did not sign the massive and highly lucrative contracts that the Asians were offering. In fact, the previous government lost the elections partly because they were proposing to sign those contracts. The people of Surinam objected strongly, especially the indigenous people in the hinterland, who do have a vote in that country."

We could take a lesson from the Surinamese. For large multinational corporations, the ultimate goal is to maximize profit in the shortest possible time and give investors the highest possible return on investment. These companies do not — indeed, their shareholders will not allow them to — consider the well-being of local ecosystems or communities. To gain access to forests, companies will do whatever they can, and are not above bribery, deceit or threats. In an industrialized area like British Columbia, companies routinely threaten to move their plants, lay off employees or pull out of the province in order to win concessions. Through the 1970s and 1980s, as the volume of wood being cut climbed steadily, the number of jobs in the forest industry dropped steeply. The reason, of course, was greater mechanization and automation that replaced employees, yet the industry and many workers blamed environmentalists. In a recent book, the forest expert Patricia Marchak has indicated that the province's system of stewardship over the forests must undergo a radical shift away from large companies and towards local community-controlled forests. The annual volume of wood being cut in British Columbia's forests exceeds by a large margin the amount that can be removed sustainably while still protecting the diverse values of the forest.

In seventeenth-century Europe, trees were considered unsightly, gloomy weeds, obstructions to healthful fresh air, agriculture and human activities. Trees weren't allowed in gardens or cities. But at that time, there were still enormous, untouched forests spreading out over the rest of the planet. Today we know how vital trees are and how badly we need them, yet we still treat them as if they're obstructions to human progress or, at best, a source of fuel or cash. Today our ecological footprint hovers over every tree on Earth. Without making major changes in the way we live, we'll all come crashing down together.

Atmospheric Pressures

> *What this climate problem has become is much less of a science issue than an ideological battleground between those people who believe in protecting the commons and those people who believe that anything that interferes with private entrepreneurial rights is worse than whatever might happen at the collective level. This is all unconscious; nobody ever says it outright.*
>
> — STEPHEN SCHNEIDER, CLIMATOLOGIST

The atmosphere is a very complex mixture of gases that acts like an immense blanket that envelops the world. This blanket maintains a temperature conducive to life; it also gives us our weather and climate. Trees and air are inextricably linked: what we do to one affects the other. Among other things, forests act as a "carbon sink" for the atmosphere, absorbing carbon dioxide. But in addition to losing this carbon sink because of the destruction of forests, the atmosphere is sustaining other assaults. Stephen Schneider, a climatologist who spent twenty years at the National Center for Atmospheric Research in Boulder, Colorado, and is currently a professor at Stanford University, says there is absolutely no doubt that the world is warming up. But if you read the mainstream papers or watch the news on television, you might be under the impression that climate change through global warming is still controversial and needs verification.

Schneider says, "The words 'global warming' have become almost a battle-cry for various factions in the world who 'believe' or 'don't believe,' who think it's serious or not serious. Yet despite a . . . number of uncertainties surrounding the climate-change debate, the actual existence of global warming is a fact established virtually beyond doubt. If we look at the thermometers of the world and see what they've done over the last century, [we see that] the world is about a half-degree Celsius or so warmer than it was a century ago. Mountain glaciers have receded virtually all around the world, and many are disappearing at a rapid rate. And finally, the sea levels have risen something on the order of 10 to 20 centimetres. Those are all consistent with warming. In fact, looks at historical records convince us that the last two decades were the warmest in the past one thousand years."

Schneider says the real issue about which scientists disagree is what's causing the warming. "The debate is whether that warming is just a perverse act of nature or whether this is something that humans have done through increasing numbers of people demanding higher standards of living and using technologies that change the land surface and dump pollutants in the atmosphere. What created it? That's the controversy among the knowledgeable scientific community, not whether the warming itself exists, which is a virtual fact."

Schneider spends a lot of time advising the Intergovernmental Panel on Climate Change. That panel was set up by the World Meteorological Organization and the United Nations Environment Program to establish a global consensus about what is well known and what is speculative about all aspects of climate change. More than 2,000 scientists contribute to this panel. After reviewing more than 20,000 scientific papers on weather and climate, it has now concluded that there is overwhelming evidence that human activity is a major cause of global warming.

Bill McKibben's famous environmental best-seller *The End of Nature* is about global warming. He says, "This is no longer a scientific issue that's in dispute. That doesn't mean that you can't find a few people who will say otherwise. You could also find people who don't believe in evolution. And you can find people who don't believe in the Holocaust, and you can find all sorts of things. But this is as solid a physical fact as we have around us. . . . Tens of thousands of scientists have produced airplane hangars full of reports and studies and graphs and charts. We now know, beyond any reasonable doubt, what is taking place and what's likely to take place in the next one hundred years. We don't know exactly what's going to happen down to the last tenth of a degree or down to the last inch of sea level or something like that. But we do know that we've raised the temperature of the planet. Nineteen ninety-eight was by far the warmest year, and that made nine of the ten warmest years on record within the last decade."

It doesn't take a rocket scientist — or a panel of experts — to see the links between the warming of the planet, the thinning of the ozone layer and human activity. So-called greenhouse gases are produced by natural processes of metabolism, decay, fire, transpiration and evaporation. We're increasing their production by chopping down trees and disturbing phytoplankton in the oceans. We know the fuels we've been burning since the Industrial Revolution — oil, coal, gas and wood — release carbon dioxide in the atmosphere, and there is now 25 to 30 percent more carbon dioxide in the atmosphere than there was before the Industrial Revolution. We're also adding to the mix human-made greenhouse gases like CFCs, which have been used in refrigerator coolants and aerosols. Besides reflecting heat, CFCs also deplete the ozone layer, which protects us from dangerous ultraviolet rays. The thinning of the ozone layer has been implicated as the cause of increases in skin cancers and deformities in sensitive creatures like frogs. Clearly, the twentieth century bears discernible evidence of human activity on the composition of the atmosphere. And now the vast majority of climate experts believes this activity has had a significant effect on the temperature of the Earth.

Of course, human beings have always made changes to the world. We've had to to survive. We've built houses, ploughed fields, dammed rivers, cut trees. But as Bill McKibben says, there was always a border, an edge where our disruption ended. There were always mountaintops, seabeds, the Antarctic, places where there was no human footprint. McKibben was motivated to write *The End of Nature* because of the terrifying implications of human intervention on the composition of our global atmosphere. "It occurred to me as I began to read the early science about global warming, about climate change, that finally we were affecting everything. That one species on this planet now had its thumb utterly on the scale, and was changing everything around us."

What does the future hold? Scientists really don't know how much the temperature will rise. Steve Schneider says the best estimates are that we can expect somewhere between one and four degrees of warming in the next century. He says, "By and large, most of us can adapt to one degree. But four degrees is virtually the difference between an ice age and a warm epoch like we're in now. It takes nature ten thousand years to make those kinds of changes, and we're talking about changes like that on the order of a century. There isn't an ecologist anywhere who thinks that we can adapt to that without dramatic dislocation to the species in the world, and to agriculture and other patterns of living that depend on the climate."

These changes go beyond a simple rise in temperature. These per-turbations to the entire envelope of gases that sustains life have all kinds of other effects, from strange weather to localized crop failures or ecosystem collapses. "Then you have the speculative stuff," Schneider says. "What happens to hurricanes? What surprises might be triggered with ocean currents? What happens to ecosystems? Where will species flourish and where will species go extinct?" We're now experiencing an increase in the number of record-breaking hot days. We're not getting an overall increase in rainfall, but we are getting more of a phenomenon called rain dumps, when the rain falls all at once and does real damage. Insurance payments for catastrophic weather events in the 1990s exceed all payments made during the previous three decades. All these things have driven the insurance industry to support action against fossil fuels and CFCs.

And there's more to worry about. "Could what we're doing now cause something irreversible, something we can't say, 'Oops, let's back out of that'?" asks Schneider. "Well, unfortunately, the answer is very definitely yes. Climatologists call these surprise scenarios." There are plenty of candidates for such surprises. The Gulf Stream could change direction or stop, so that while the world was warming, Europe would freeze. The destruction of the West Antarctic ice sheet could raise sea levels by many metres, flooding coastlines and inundating island nations. It might take a few generations for that scenario to play out, but once it starts we won't be able to stop it.

Many respond to experts like Schneider by saying that one of the most unpredictable processes in our world is climate, and that there have been many extreme events in the past that we and our ecosystems have all survived. But, Bill McKibben points out, "climate changes all the time, but it changes slowly. We're doing it at an enormous rate of speed — by most estimates, something between ten and sixty times faster than it changes normally. That has real consequences. . . . Natural systems can't adapt to that sort of speed of change." And he adds, "With the ability to change the climate, you change everything. You change the flora and the fauna that live at a particular place. You change the rate at which the rain falls and at which the rain evaporates. You change the speed of the wind. You may change the very ocean currents. . . . Nothing that we've ever done as a species is as large in its effect as this. An all-out nuclear war . . . would have been a consequence of the same magnitude. But happily, we stepped back from that brink. Unhappily, we're not stepping back from this one."

How can we step back? Well, everyone agrees that we must reduce the burning of fossil fuels as quickly as possible. This is entirely feasible with the technology we have now — solar energy, wind harnessed by windmills, fuels like alcohol and methane from fermentation, even used vegetable oils. Indeed, Denmark already generates 7 percent of its energy by wind and has plans to make that 50 percent by the year 2010. Globally, wind and solar energy are the fastest-growing sectors in the energy industry. We also need to reinvent trains and other comfortable forms of mass transit, to lure people out of their private cars.

Even big oil companies like British Petroleum and Shell have seen the writing on the wall. They are hedging their bets with major investments in alternative energy. PetroCanada has invested in an ethanol-producing business to reduce emissions from gasohol. Greenpeace International has developed a "green" refrigerator that is extremely energy efficient and doesn't use ozone-depleting CFCs. It is available all over the world, except in North America, where inefficient ozone-damaging fridges still rule the roost.

When there is a conflict between an available clean technology and an entrenched dirty one, the challenge is politics and the need for legislative action, not technology. Governments in Canada and the United States continue to subsidize fossil-fuel energy to the tune of billions of dollars annually and then plead a lack of money to support alternative energy or public transit. We can do it, we just have to want to.

Poison in the Well

In 1976, somebody made a decision at Love Canal when they did a cost/benefit analysis. They put a dollar on my head. They put a dollar on the potential for my children. They put a dollar on my husband's head, based on what he was making, which at the time was $10,000 a year. And they decided that we were not worthy of a $20 million clean-up. They thought, for $20 million, that it was perfectly okay to kill not only my children, but the 900 families that were living at Love Canal.... And that's wrong.

— LOIS GIBBS, FOUNDER OF THE CENTER FOR HEALTH,
ENVIRONMENT AND JUSTICE

One of my biggest heroes is Lois Gibbs. She's an environmental activist who emerged from the grass-roots and founded the Center for Health, Environment and Justice, one of the most effective environmental groups in North America. She has been called the Mother of the Superfund because her efforts helped create a mechanism in the United States for licensing, evaluating and cleaning up toxic-waste dumps. Her story is a graphic and frightening illustration of the effect that toxic waste has on our ecological footprint. It is also an inspiring story of how ordinary citizens can work together for change.

When Lois Gibbs was a young housewife back in the 1970s, she lived with her husband and two young children in a suburb called Love Canal, near Niagara Falls in Upstate New York. The new subdivision had been built over a former industrial site and landfill, and 90 percent of the residents worked at nearby chemical companies that manufactured pesticides and solvents. Nobody thought anything about it until a lot of the residents, especially the children, began to experience health problems. Gibbs had two small children at the time. Her son, Michael, was a perfectly healthy one-year-old when the family moved to Love Canal. After living there for four years, he developed asthma, epilepsy, a urinary-tract problem that required two operations to correct and an immune-system problem very similar to AIDS. Gibbs's daughter, Melissa, who was conceived and carried at Love Canal, developed a rare blood disease that caused internal haemorrhaging and left her with a very high risk of developing leukemia.

Very frightened, and at a loss to understand her children's health problems, Gibbs stumbled upon a newspaper story that described workplace diseases and symptoms resulting from exposure to the same chemicals that were in the landfill at Love Canal. Gibbs says, "I'm reading this newspaper and I see epilepsy, asthma, depressed immune system, blood disorders, leukemia. And I'm checking off my kids' problems, and it was like, 'Whoa. This is really scary.'"

It wasn't in Gibbs's nature to make a fuss. Like most of us, she assumed someone in charge would know what to do. She figured that if she was scared, then so were other people. So she waited for somebody smarter and more skilled to show up and tell her what to do. "But nobody came knocking on my door. And so Michael got very sick, and he was in the hospital. And that was sort of the turning point for me." Gibbs remembers thinking, "'You know, the reason he's here sick is not just Love Canal. It's not the city's and the government's fault. It's *my* fault. I made a decision that I would sit back and wait for somebody else to come and do this. And when they didn't come, I didn't do anything. What kind of responsible mother could I possibly be if I sat back, knowing my children were being poisoned?' And that's when I got up enough courage to go to the very first door and begin to talk to people."

Her neighbours, equally scared, were also waiting. When Gibbs made contact with them, they began to compare notes and to organize. They found that their homes and playgrounds had been built over 20,000 tons of mixed chemicals, mostly solvents and pesticides that had been buried there by Hooker Chemical Corporation, a division of Occidental Petroleum. Doing their own research, they discovered that among the 240 chemicals in their environment was the highly toxic lindane, which has been banned in the United States and Canada for decades. This poison, 100 percent pure, was lying on the surface of the ground, a ubiquitous yellow dust no one had really noticed before.

Gibbs determined that her own problems were not the worst. "We had statistics that showed that 56 percent of the children ... were born with birth defects ranging from three ears to extra rows of teeth, extra fingers, extra toes or mental retardation. We found that the women at Love Canal gave birth at statistically higher rates to low-birthweight babies than [did women] in other communities. We had more miscarriages and stillborn children than other communities. And central-nervous-system problems and so on."

Gibbs was transformed into an environmental activist. She says the collective effort of 500 of the community's families changed her life. "Some people were just brilliant, smart people who could pronounce all the silly chemicals, could look at the technical reports. Some were just so creative [that] they came up with these ideas that were fun, media-worthy and focused on politicians. Other people were great at things like typing and cutting newspaper clippings. That's what makes organizations run. That's what creates power. And that's how we won at Love Canal." With Gibbs as a major spokesperson, they protested the lack of responsible dumping and demanded that the government do something. After years of fighting, they won. There was an investigation, followed by a clean-up. And all 900 families in the community received enough money to move away from Love Canal.

After all that, Gibbs launched the Citizens' Clearinghouse on Hazardous Waste, whose name was later changed to the Center for Health, Environment and Justice. The organization has been successful in stopping every single proposal for a commercial hazardous-waste landfill in the United States since 1980! Not one has been sited in the United States since Gibbs got to work. The disposal sites are legal to build — you need double-liners, leak-detection systems, monitoring programs, and then you can build them — but people have said no. "When they go out and they try to site these things, ... people literally come out and link their arms with their kids, with their husbands, with their cows, with their tractors, and they just stand up and refuse it. And corporations cannot fight that."

When I recently interviewed Gibbs, she had just returned from Rochester, New York, where Kodak's headquarters are located. She told me about the alarming number of families living near the Kodak facility whose children have been diagnosed with brain cancer. The parents, and other concerned community residents, allege that the number of local cases of nervous system cancers in children is unusually high, and together-er constitute a "cancer cluster" that they fear is linked to the emissions from the Kodak facility. Kodak denies any connection between its incin-erator and the cancers. New York state agencies have so far not been able to show a link; a new federal study is trying to assess the situation, but it has always been very difficult to prove the exact connections between toxic emissions and human disease.

Things aren't much different in Canada. Elizabeth May of the Sierra Club of Canada has been helping out the community of Sydney, Nova Scotia; its inhabitants are living adjacent to the largest toxic-waste site in Canada and possibly all of North America. She says, "Within a commu-nity that includes tens of thousands of people, there are families living along a street who have toxic waste in a ditch running through their backyards, . . . people with arsenic pooling on their basement floors. They're sick every day, and the government says, 'We don't think there's any risk to your health. The kinds of illnesses you're having are complete-ly consistent with the bacteriological, viral infections such as Canadians get every winter.' This is outrageous."

The source of the contamination was a provincially and federally operated steel mill and coking plant. While the most polluting elements of these operations have closed down for economic reasons, the legacy is an enormous amount of toxic wastes — 700,000 tons of sludge contami-nated with polyaromatic hydrocarbons (PAHs), of which 45,000 tons are PCB-contaminated and located in an estuary now known as the Tar Ponds. That's more than *twenty-three times* the amount of toxins buried at Love Canal. There are also more than 125 acres of land, the former site of the coke oven, that are saturated to depths of eighty feet with PAHs such as naphthalene, benzene, toluene and benzopyrene, as well as arsenic, cyanide and other heavy metals, all of which are incredibly dan-gerous carcinogens and poisons. As May says, "Cancer and birth-defect rates are far above the national average in Sydney. The site looks like something out of Eastern Europe. You have to understand, this is far worse than comparable steel sites in the rest of North America. [People's] backyards have eighteen times the Canadian Council of Ministers of the Environment guideline for arsenic for residential and parkland areas. Eighteen times! And the government is saying, 'Well, you're not going to run into trouble unless you go back out there and eat the soil.'" May acknowledges that the government is finally throwing money at the Tar Ponds, but she says that so far almost all has gone for "more studies, not to move people away or begin a clean-up."

In both Canada and the United States, when communities ask for a simple health study to establish facts about their illnesses, they are told the same thing: "The health problems are just a random clustering." Lois Gibbs heard it twenty years ago, and it's the same line that governments use today. When our ecological footprint gets so huge that our babies contract leukemia and are born without brains or eyes, when we've poisoned our wells and crops and animals, it ought to be time to ask what it costs Earth to have photographs and pesticides and car tires and the myriad other products that are so very toxic. And for people who say that we have come to need these products, and that we also need the jobs they create, Lois Gibbs has a very clear answer: we can have almost all of our products, and our health — if we want to.

One thing we can do is to make the cheap disposal of hazardous wastes more difficult. We also can force businesses to take responsibility for their products through legislation. Many countries have done it already. If waste-disposal costs were part of production costs, they would have to be added into the costs each company would have to deduct before it realized its profits, just as is done in Sweden and Germany. If the prices of products reflected their real costs to society, and if manufacturers couldn't just offload their garbage onto the community or the government, these companies would soon find ways to dispose of or substitute for the really hazardous substances.

Lois Gibbs's husband worked in a chemical plant back in the 1970s. She says, "He was a chemical operator. He made it, they dumped it, I yelled about it. Our dinner table [conversation] was very interesting." But workers often know how to make better products. She says, "My husband could have gone [to his bosses] . . . and made six suggestions about what they could do to keep [for example, vinyl chloride] from going out the stack into the community, [to keep] the workers safe. It's really not always an either/or situation. It's a matter of whether the corporations are made to invest in protecting their workers and their communities or not." And if proper waste disposal cuts too deep into a product's costs for that product to remain viable, well, it's supposed to be a free-market system, without subsidies given to losing operations.

Ironically, toxics are one of our easiest environmental problems. We have the technology to eliminate, replace or contain them, and we even have an economic system that can guide our decisions about which substances simply aren't worth having around, like DDT, lindane or dioxins. But the best news of all is that the clean-ups work. Since Lois Gibbs won her fight with the government, her children have largely recovered. Melissa's blood count is within normal limits, and all of Michael's problems are gone, except for his asthma. Gibbs says that although the government has never bothered to run any follow-up studies, many Love Canal families report the same thing. Michael's urinary-tract problem was supposed to be lifelong, but Gibbs says it disappeared a year after they got away from Love Canal. At first, she thought it might have been a coincidence. "But when you looked at the hematology clinic results for Melissa's blood, you actually could see the levels of platelets increasing over time. And if you looked at the brainwave test from Michael's epilepsy, you could see his epilepsy actually disappearing. It isn't coincidence. The body is an amazing instrument. And if we can remove ourselves from these chemicals, we can heal."

Lois Gibbs runs a true NIMBY organization. That's the acronym coined by corporations and their PR firms to belittle environmentalists for their "not in my backyard" attitudes. The idea is that toxic waste, even if it robs babies of eyes, has to go somewhere, and that it's selfish to want to partake of the benefits of modern life, like steel mills, computer chips and weedkillers, if we are unwilling to accept the consequences. Lois Gibbs says she wears the acronym as a badge of honour. "It means that people are unwilling to accept somebody else's poison in their backyard for somebody else's profit." She says corporate spokesmen often argue, "'It's got to go somewhere, Ms. Gibbs. If we don't put it in your backyard, then whose backyard do we put it in?' And our answer is: 'It's not an either/or. It's not either your backyard or my backyard.' In today's technology, we know how to take care of hazardous waste. We know how to take care of garbage. We know how to take care of most of the stuff that we produce. What we are unwilling to do, what corporations are unwilling to do, is pay the cost to deal with their waste at the front end."

So we have to make them. And when we do, everybody's footprint will be a lot smaller.

CHAPTER 3
SEZ WHO?

We, the undersigned, senior members of the world's scientific community, hereby warn all humanity of what lies ahead. A great change in our stewardship of the Earth and the life on it is required if vast human misery is to be avoided and our global home on this planet is not to be irretrievably mutilated.
— "WORLD SCIENTISTS' WARNING TO HUMANITY," NOVEMBER 1992

From Tuktoyuktuk to St. John's, from Seoul to Rio, Shanghai and Bombay, the Age of Information is touted as our route to the future. We are told that the revolution in information that has occurred during the past fifty years has aided the spread of democracy and will continue to empower people everywhere. That's the reason we turn to the purveyors of information, the media, whenever we feel that an issue must be brought to public attention. That's why people like me, who are concerned with specific issues, like the environment, depend on the media to spread the word.

The media have indeed informed the public about threats to our air, water and food. Ever since 1962, when Rachel Carson published *Silent Spring,* more and more information has been made available. And the public has responded. About ten years ago, public interest in the environment reached its height. In 1988, George Bush promised that, if elected, he would be an environmental president. In the same year, Prime Minister Brian Mulroney was re-elected, and to indicate his ecological concern he moved the minister of the environment into the inner Cabinet. Newly created environment departments around the world were poised to cut back on fossil-fuel use, monitor the effects of acid rain and other pollutants, clean up toxic wastes, and protect plant and animal species. Information about our troubled environment had reached a large number of people, and that information, as expected, led to civic and political action. In 1992, it all reached its apex as the largest-ever gathering of heads of state in human history met at the Earth Summit in Rio de Janeiro. "Sustainable development" was the rallying cry, and politicians and business leaders promised to take a new path. Henceforth, they said, the environment would be weighed in every political, social and economic decision.

Yet only two weeks after all the fine statements of purpose and government commitments were signed in Rio, the Group of Seven industrialized nations met in Munich and not a word was mentioned about the environment. The main topic was the global economy. The environment, it was said, had fallen off the list of public concerns, and environmentalism had been relegated to a transitory fad.

Something even more portentous happened a few months after the Earth Summit. A remarkable document called "World Scientists' Warning to Humanity" was released. It was signed by more than 1,600 senior scientists from all over the world, including more than half of all living Nobel Prize winners. Here's part of what it said:

> Human beings and the natural world are on a collision course. . . .
> Many of our current practices put at serious risk the future for
> human society . . . and may so alter the living world that it will be
> unable to sustain life in the manner that we know. Fundamental
> changes are urgent. . . . No more than one or a few years remain
> before the chance to avert the threats we now confront will be
> lost and the prospects for humanity immeasurably diminished.

Since scientists are usually extremely cautious about making public statements, it was remarkable that so many eminent scientists would sign such a strongly worded document. It was therefore a real shock to me that no one — not Canada's national newspaper, or its national television network, or any major American television network — bothered to report the "Warning to Humanity." Two of the most prestigious North American newspapers, the *New York Times* and the *Washington Post*, pronounced the warning "not newsworthy."

What has happened to move environmental stories from the front page to the waste bin? Were the pundits right to have turned their attention elsewhere? Have the problems gone away? Could our informed demand for action have moved us all so far along a road to recovery that the need to heed the "Warning to Humanity" is no longer urgent? Or could it be that having access to enormous amounts of information doesn't always mean that we're really informed? Is it possible that even with all the wondrous new ways to access information, we're not always able to learn about and analyze the issues that are most crucial to our lives? Could it be that although we live in the Age of Information, we receive insufficient, misleading or even no information at all about issues that ought to be of extreme importance to every one of us?

Finger-Lickin' Good

> *In North America, some of the protections, like the First Amendment for a free press, are being used by commercial interests to inhibit speech or to protect commercial speech. Here it's a matter of catching up with the techniques and providing the laws and regulations that will make sure that people are not intimidated, and cannot be shut down because they can't afford to defend themselves.*
>
> — LAWRENCE GROSSMAN, FORMER PRESIDENT OF
> NBC NEWS AND PBS

If you live within reach of any form of North American media, you probably remember this story: Oprah Winfrey, the famous talk-show host, was taken to court by some angry cattlemen who accused her of defaming their product, U.S. beef. This story was played out in the centre ring of a media circus for weeks. Winfrey even took her show down to Texas, where she was being tried. Crowds of emotional supporters, as well as a lot of journalists, gathered on the courthouse steps every day until she was acquitted. What the audience to this spectacle took away was some vague idea of the trials and tribulations of the incredibly famous. But unless you saw the particular "Oprah" episode on which the lawsuit was based, you might not have known that the court case was actually about something of far more direct concern to each of us.

Howard Lyman, a former Montana cattle rancher and current activist with the Society for the Prevention of Cruelty to Animals, was the subject of that "Oprah" episode. He told millions of viewers some simple and verifiable facts about modern meat production. Lyman explained that herbivorous food animals like cows and sheep have been turned into carnivores and cannibals by being fed the ground-up and cooked-down flesh and blood of their own and other animal species. He says, "We started doing this after the Second World War. Remember, about half of the volume of . . . beef animals is not sellable to humans. You either have to pay to put it in a landfill, or find a way to turn it into a product that is sellable. The solution that they've come up with is to render it. Grind it. Cook it. Turn it into meal [that's] high in protein. [And] feed it back to other animals."

We're putting this grey, sugary-looking, rendered protein into our pets' food, and ultimately into our own bodies as well because we feed it to animals we eat — cows, sheep, pigs, chickens, turkeys. "Old spent laying hens have very little value," says Lyman. "To take those old hens and put them into a cage and load them on a truck is to get almost no economic return from them. It is much easier to take them and suck them out with a big vacuum cleaner into a grinder. We're grinding up live chickens and feeding them back to other chickens. We collect the manure and feed it back to them, too. It's a whole new meaning to [the phrase] 'finger-licking good.'" Such practices are not done everywhere, but they're considered normal by the industry and are widespread in North America.

Howard Lyman's specific attacks on beef centred around the fear of bovine spongiform encephalopathy, or mad cow disease. During the British epidemic of this disease, it was found that feeding rendered sheep to cows can pass on a terrible brain infection called scrapie. And when humans eat the infected cows, they can get it too, dying horribly of Creutzfeldt-Jakob disease (CJD) as their brains gradually fill with holes, like sponges. Although there have been no officially documented cases of mad cow disease in the United States, the same type of feed was being used there. In Canada, where food-industry practices are similar to those in Britain, there have been several documented cases of the disease. Lyman concluded by saying, "We should clean up the way we're producing our food. And maybe we should be eating much different food than what we are."

After Oprah Winfrey heard all this, she announced, "Stop me cold from eatin' another burger!" It was riveting television, and the people who saw it demanded changes, which they got within a year. Lyman says, "The [public] response . . . was overwhelming." As a result, in August 1997 the Food and Drug Administration and United States Department of Agriculture passed regulations against feeding ruminant animals to ruminants. It was a baby step, since it did not stop cows from being fed to pigs or pigs to cows, but as Lyman says, "At least we ended up with a lot more people understanding the issue, responding, educating themselves, . . . finding out what the facts are."

It looks like a happy ending after all. But the satisfying story of how important information was brought to the public so that citizens could take steps to protect themselves is not what made that "Oprah" episode a big media event. Something else happened. The Cattlemen's Association sued both Oprah Winfrey and Howard Lyman, claiming $20 million under a new state law prohibiting anyone from making disparaging remarks about food. In the end, Winfrey won. But because she did, the law was never challenged in a higher court. It's still on the books, ready to chill the hearts of any of us who might want to discuss publicly our concerns about the industrial food chain. Despite the media circus surrounding Winfrey's trial, there was almost no mention of the implications of the Food Disparagement Act, and what it means to people who might fall victims to bad beef. Perhaps reporters were afraid of being sued.

The question remains whether the public would ever have heard about this particular story unless people like Oprah Winfrey and Howard Lyman were willing to accept the risk of an enormous lawsuit. In all likelihood, the United States would still be feeding sheep to cows. The reporters who congregated on the courthouse steps didn't talk about the service the show had performed for the public, or about the truth or falseness of the accusations. And they certainly didn't go into the social implications of this kind of legal chill. In fact, they were at the court only because a big celebrity was on trial.

Oprah Winfrey can afford to defend herself from a $20 million lawsuit. But Howard Lyman, a typical environmental activist, is not a rich man. He incurred thousands of dollars in legal fees, as well as the loss of his time, simply for trying to inform the public about how the food industry works. And he's become a pariah with the media. He told me he's no longer invited to appear on high-profile talk shows, nor is he interviewed by big-circulation magazines. As a result, his message is being suppressed by media self-censorship. It's called libel chill.

So the basic concept — that information will help people in a democracy protect themselves — proved partly true. But we heard about the story mainly because of its entertainment value. Most reports focused on the scandal — a big celebrity gets sued — and on the sensational ending of a big celebrity triumphing. How did the information media lose sight of their major reason for existing?

Bread and Circuses

> *Let's face it, television news is increasingly becoming*
> *entertainment. There's a complete blurring between what's*
> *significant as a global event and what's basically salacious gossip.*
> — ELIZABETH MAY, EXECUTIVE DIRECTOR,
> SIERRA CLUB OF CANADA

It's important to know what's going on around us. Such knowledge allows us to form opinions about issues and then to act on them. In fact, it's axiomatic that a democratic government is impossible to sustain without a free press. And these days it has become the accepted wisdom that the more kinds of media we have, the better it will be for society. We now have the Internet and are approaching the 500-channel universe. It is hoped that with access to all this information, we'll have more power to control our lives.

Lawrence Grossman, past president of both NBC News and PBS, has thought deeply about the nature of information and public discourse. He says, "Most people get most of their information now in the United States from local television newscasts. And local television newscasts, as every study has shown, are filled with nothing but crime and happy talk and sports and weather and very little else. So while there is a great opportunity for an informed public to act in [its] own interest, there are questions as to whether we're really getting an informed public. And while everybody talks about this great new age as the Information Age, what we're really saying is [that] it's not the Information Age coming upon us as much as the Entertainment Age."

News shows on television and the radio are more about distraction and amusement than they are about discourse on serious issues. People don't want serious issues — or so we are told by those who run the media — they want entertainment and celebrities and sports and spectacles. And since mainstream media organizations thrive on ratings, they pander to their perceptions of what the public wants. "There's a great tendency to blame the people: why aren't they interested in things that affect their own lives?" says Grossman. "But at the same time we aren't doing anything about encouraging that interest, stimulating that interest, providing what is necessary to make sure that they get well informed. And the one thing we know about democracy is that we cannot just leave it to chance. And it's certainly unwise to leave it to a medium that is dominated by entertainment, diversion and the need for profits."

With the glaring exception of the United States, virtually every democracy in the world has publicly funded television and radio channels. But the very idea of subsidizing information this way is under profound attack, especially here in North America. The one U.S. public broadcaster, PBS, has been stripped of nearly all the public funding it once enjoyed. It now runs what amount to commercials for corporate sponsors between desperate pleas for viewer funding. In Canada, the CBC has been subjected to cut after cut, not to eliminate fat, as is claimed, but to make the organization less of a public broadcaster and more of a profit-centred corporation. At the beginning of the new millennium, it seems it's no longer appropriate to spend tax money on information. It's supposed to fund itself.

Lawrence Grossman ran both NBC and PBS, one commercially funded and the other supported with public money. He says that in our new era of telecommunications, with the convergence of satellites, computers and television, the race to broadcast is being "entirely driven by and won by commercial interests — understandably, because there's a huge amount of money to be made." We entrust these public airwaves to the free market because it is widely believed that money-making corporations are efficient and will do the best job. But Grossman says, "The marketplace fails in certain areas — not in entertainment, in sports, in commercial data distribution, but in areas like providing fair-minded, intelligent, full civic information and education." He says the marketplace also fails when it comes to providing education for "an increasingly older and maturing society that requires . . . job retraining, continuing education. The marketplace fails when it comes to providing culture and arts, particularly for minority audiences. The marketplace fails when it comes to quality children's programming. And so, if society values those, something has to be done to make sure that they are provided."

But who will provide them? Certainly not the current system of private networks. When it comes to providing objective economic analysis or civic information on justice issues and environmental problems, commercial television pays little serious attention. Most commercial broadcasters don't produce or broadcast the serious documentary programming that deals with such issues. Neil Postman, a professor at New York University, a famous media analyst and the author of best-sellers like *Amusing Ourselves to Death* and *The Disappearance of Childhood*, calls television the "command centre of our culture" because it is our primary source of news and information. The problem, Postman says, is that "as a visual medium, television is good for fast-moving, exciting, exotic images. It is not good for serious public discourse," and that's a major reason why there's so little of it on the air.

Postman says a television news director knows what the medium is good for. So when he or she has to choose between footage of a man committing suicide in some small American city and a discussion of the country's annual budget, guess which one gets the most air time? Matters that require talk, detailed explanation, complex concepts and language, and historical perspective just don't work as well as those exciting visuals.

Use What You Got

Electronic media can be used to exploit people, to exploit issues and to put the wrong focus on priorities. But so can words in a book. And yes, it's more of an emotional than a rational medium. But the important thing is not to wring your hands over whether people are smart enough to be able to see through it. The important thing is to have a set of policies that enables these media to be used for civic and democratic purposes, and not just for superficial, bad or money-making purposes.

— LAWRENCE GROSSMAN

Lawrence Grossman says we have alternatives. He says that the kind of intelligent, fair-minded commentary we need is not the responsibility of the commercial broadcasters. Their responsibility is "to their owners and stockholders, to maximize profit. And that's a perfectly legitimate and reasonable objective. But it has *nothing* to do with the public interest. Nor should it be confused with the public interest."

So what can we do? We can increase support for public broadcasters while we still have them. And we can even let in some new players. Grossman points out that we already have great respect for certain institutions in our society. "The universities, the museums, the libraries have all been totally bypassed by the television and radio era. We should make sure that they are not bypassed by the telecommunications era. They have a lot to offer. It would be relatively inexpensive for them to provide the content. Then people will have a choice. . . . When it's important to them, and when there are issues of real national or even personal and local interest, they will have a place to turn to get the legitimate facts and information that they need."

In a sense, with access to the Internet, some of this is already happening. But real broadcasting needs funding, and Grossman says that's not an insurmountable obstacle. "In my judgement, the money should come from the commercial enterprises [that] are exploiting the publicly owned spectrum. The airwaves are incredibly valuable, and commercial enterprises pay nothing for them. Some of their huge profits, a thin slice, should be taken off the top to provide a public freeway that serves people, connects to every home, every hospital, every school, every library, every museum, every prison. [This could] provide the kinds of material that society values and needs for its survival, and that democracy in particular requires, but that the marketplace, understandably and for very good reasons, is not providing."

This plan is far from being hopelessly idealistic. A hundred years ago, there were no public libraries in most of North America, but a combination of public will — local funding and staffing — and philanthropy — such as the millions endowed by industrialist Andrew Carnegie — made free access to books a reality across the continent. We simply have to apply what we have done before to new methods of delivering information. Grossman says, "Never underestimate . . . people's ability to figure out their own self-interest. We have a lot of problems . . . with public participation in civic activities. One major reason is there's much more entertainment and diversion and amusement than there used to be. It's a lot easier to spend your time on that. But when people really feel that something is important to them, whether it's jobs or social security or pension protection or health care, they'll get on the case."

To bring about change, loud, explicit demand is essential. We cannot leave these matters, as Grossman says, "to serendipity or accident, or to corporations that have . . . a bottom-line interest. We've got to make provision for a public freeway in which the major issues can be discussed, through programs with documentaries, through printouts, CD-ROMs or courses, where you can have town meetings and public discussion of issues. . . . You cannot force people to attend or to listen or participate, but you sure can take the steps required to make this stuff available, so that people will have nobody to blame but themselves if they make the wrong decision."

Real Time vs. Fast Forward

When you watch a subject like climate change in the news, it's never treated as climate change. It's floods in China, or fires burning out of control in Florida, or people dying of a massive heat wave in the Midwest. But generally speaking, those short, fast stories aren't presented as what they are: one long, slow, compelling story of how human behaviour is changing the climate of the world we live in.

— ELIZABETH MAY

In 1989, my family and I had the wonderful privilege of spending ten days in the Kayapo village of Aucre, deep in the Amazon rain forest, some fourteen days by dugout canoe from the nearest town. It was a humbling experience, as it made me to realize how limited my academic knowledge was for day-to-day survival. Walking into the forest each day to gather food, I often paused, overwhelmed by the complexity of the surroundings, the immensity of my ignorance and the vast store of information my Kayapo hosts possess for their survival.

The community of creatures making up that forest was also constantly receiving information from the world around it, information that flowed through the air, water and soil. The most obvious information was the day and night cycle, which signalled the nocturnal and diurnal responses of activity or rest. Even on the equator, plants know when to germinate and flower, and animals regulate their behaviour in tune with the vegetation. The flashes of colour in birds offered information, both to their own kind and to other species. The colour patterns of flowers were informative to potential pollinators, and the different shades, patterns and shapes of butterflies and caterpillars gave signals to both mates and potential predators.

I was aware of the cacophony of sound, but I couldn't decipher the information contained within all that insect and bird noise. Indeed, much of the information coursing through the forest — such as minute quantities of molecules functioning as pheromones, territorial markers or indicators of food or predators — was beyond my sensory capacity. I couldn't hear the sounds of insects and bats that lay beyond my aural detection. But even if I couldn't detect or decipher it all, I knew that the forest community was awash with information vital to life.

As I was led through the forest and along the rivers, I watched the way my Kayapo hosts "read" the information contained in their surroundings. Animal tracks, specific plants, the type of soil — all told the Kayapo of hazards or sources of food or useful materials. These forest people possessed knowledge that was generations old, and that had been painstakingly acquired through acute observation and trial-and-error experience. That vast quantity of information formed a knowledge base that not only helped the Kayapo survive, but also informed them of who they are as a people, what their history is, and their very reason for being.

The media expert Neil Postman says that as biological beings, we evolved sense organs — eyes, tongue, ears, skin, nose — that inform us about the physical world around us. What we see, taste, hear, touch or smell is immensely important to our survival. He says that, as is the case in the Kayapo world, "there was a time when the purpose of information was to solve specific problems, in either the physical or symbolic environment. People sought information because they needed it to do something in the world." But beginning in the 1840s, according to Postman, with the invention of telegraphy and photography, this began to change. By the time we got radio and television, to say nothing of the Internet, we had become inundated with information from all over the world. The information that comes to our senses today is fundamentally different from that received when we had to pay attention to nature. Rather than impelling us to action — as the smell of smoke, the crack of a twig or the stripes of a tiger used to do — information today pacifies us. Now, although there's a huge quantity of sensory input, there's little demand for output. As Postman says, "There's nothing we can do. I mean, we now can watch a murder, or a story about a murder, on television, or something just as lurid and awful, and continue to eat our chicken sandwich. We don't even get upset by it. We're not invited to do anything in any case. . . . This [passive observation] may have created the sense of impotence that people feel. After all, if you're constantly getting information about which you can do nothing, or very little, it tends to suggest that you're a rather impotent person. I mean, I have no plans to do anything about the troubles in Northern Ireland. Or the troubles in the Middle East."

This sense of impotence may explain why the public often seems unable to act in response to those stories that seem so central to our well-being, to our very survival. "Maybe this accounts in some part for the surprising indifference that many people have toward toxicity in the physical environment," Postman says. "One may wonder, wouldn't people be interested in global warming, or in what's happening to the rain forest? I mean, what could be more interesting? But it's possible that we've simply been conditioned to think that information has nothing to do with us. It's just a kind of commodity."

Moreover, Postman adds, information often comes to us in a form that is composed mostly of "ands," as in "This happened, and then this happened, and then this happened. You have a news show, and you tell people the budget was passed today. A man committed suicide. There's an earthquake in Chile. No one would even ask, 'Did the earthquake in Chile happen because this man in Oklahoma City committed suicide? Did this man commit suicide because the budget was passed?' There is no cause and effect. This is a significant difference between a visual medium, like television, and language."

There's something else about the way we get information today that's very different from the way we got it in the past. Telecommunications have become so sophisticated that the images created are difficult to distinguish from real-life pictures. We can speed up time and destroy space. We can even ignore our place in reality by entering the virtual world of cyberspace, where we can have the kinkiest sex without worrying about AIDS or getting caught; we can have the spine-tingling thrill of a car race, crash into a wall and still walk away; we can take part in a gunfight, lose and live to fight again. Virtual reality is better than the messiness and complexity of real life.

As a journalist, I had always thought that my own programs allowed the viewers to experience nature in a way that would inspire them to love it. But now I realize that my programs, too, are a creation, not a reflection, of reality. To make a film about the Arctic or the Amazon rain forest, a photographer spends many lonely months in a blind or laboriously lugging gear in search of exquisite shots. Back in the editing room, hours of this hard-earned film are boiled down to sequences of sensational shot after sensational shot. As a result, the film is filled with colour and activity that will thrill and amaze the audience. But anyone who has ever travelled to the Arctic or to a tropical rain forest knows that the constant flurry of activity is not what the wilderness is like at all. Even in a species-rich rain forest, most of the activity goes on at night or high above ground in the forest canopy. You can wait a long time and see very few animals.

The difference between the film and reality isn't truth; the animals are really there, and in a responsible documentary they're behaving naturally. What's missing in the filmed version of nature is *time*. Nature must have time, but television cannot tolerate it. So we create a virtual reality, a collage of images that conveys a distorted sense of what a real wilderness is like. The destructive aspect of what we create is the implicit message that nature functions at a faster pace than it really does. And the further we humans get from the natural pace of nature, the less we realize what Earth time is. In cities, surrounded by technologies like cellphones and fast-paced videos, working in offices to serve an economy that demands constant, rapid growth, it's easy to assume that nature can deliver the things we want at a similar pace. Fish, trees or soil microorganisms don't grow fast enough for our speedy time-frame. But if the programs we create give an impression of a hopped-up nature, we might expect it to be able to meet our ever-faster modern needs.

Time is the one ingredient that is absolutely vital for nature. It is the vast sweep of evolutionary time that has allowed life to flourish and huge changes to occur. In the 4 billion years that life has existed, the sun has increased in intensity by 25 percent, magnetic poles have switched and reversed back, continents have smashed into each other and then pulled apart, ice ages and warm periods have come and gone, and the atmosphere has been transformed from a non-oxygen to an oxygen-rich one. Yet life has persisted, simply because of the immense periods of time it has had to make adjustments.

Today, the rate at which we are extracting trees, fish, topsoil and clean water, as well as creating pollutants and greenhouse gases, may match the speed of information technology and the economy, but it is not in synch with the reproductive rates of natural systems. More and more, our sources of information are no longer connected to the natural world and its limits. Politics, civic action and participatory democracy need time too. Democratic groups like PTAs and other voluntary human institutions take time to do their work.

Until we slow down the rate of growth in information and technology and learn to pay attention to the true pace of the non-technological planet, we'll keep making unrealistic demands that can't be fulfilled. At the very least, we need to understand that our accelerated rates of production and use of human-made technical information function at a completely different pace from that of the natural rates of information exchange, like those I experienced in the Brazilian rain forest.

Life in the Fast Lane

> *Computers ... change the way children's minds process information and affect not only what they know but what they are capable of knowing — that is, computers alter the pathways of children's cognition. Newly immersed in data-based forms of knowledge and limited to information transmissible in digital form, our culture is sacrificing the subtle, contextual and memory-based knowledge gleaned from living in a nature-based culture, meaningful interactive learning with other humans, and an ecologically based value system.*
>
> — C.A. BOWERS, AUTHOR OF *EDUCATION, CULTURAL MYTHS, AND THE ECOLOGICAL CRISIS*

David Shenk is a young computer enthusiast who revelled in the birth of the so-called Information Revolution. He's still enthusiastic, but now, after ten years of surfing the Net, he's starting to have second thoughts. He wrote about them in a best-seller called *Data Smog*. "Information is a resource," he says. "It is something that we all need. But there is a point beyond which the speed of information, and even the amount of information, starts to diminish the quality of our lives. We always want to get more information, and to learn more and more. But we need to distinguish between information and knowledge. The point is always converting that raw data into knowledge and wisdom. I think we live in an age now where it's very easy to get caught up in the thrill of getting the information, and forget that it's all about taking that information and turning it into something interesting inside your brain."

Although he's barely thirty, Shenk has realized that we have to "take the time and make sure that all the other parts of our lives are in place, so we can turn information into knowledge. We need to communicate that knowledge and wisdom [to] people we know, love, respect and spend time with. We need to live richer lives as a result of that information — not just amass it and bombard ourselves with it."

To make matters even worse, the clamour for our attention grows steadily more strident and outrageous. Shenk says, "There's kind of a vicious spiral that results from this, in that the more people who are competing for our attention, the more outrageous things they have to do to get our attention. . . . And so the neon signs become bigger and the ads on television become louder, more shocking and more vulgar, and so do the shows between the ads."

Coping with not just two or three but the hundreds of ideas that shoot by our eyes and ears every day may be far more damaging to our ability to concentrate and make judgements than we think. When I worked in the lab as a full-time scientist, I'd wake up in the morning thinking about a single research idea. Then I'd go to work and think and read and talk *only* about that idea. I'd often go back to the lab at night to keep working on it. And this could go on for days and weeks. It was the most exhilarating, creative time of my life. But today I find that my time is fragmented by more and more demands: faxes, voicemail, e-mail and letters; the insistent pull of television, newspapers and radio; not to mention my family and friends.

"Part of this vicious spiral is that we get distracted. . . . And when we get distracted, we can't concentrate as well," Shenk maintains. "And we don't communicate as well, and so forth. As information speeds up, it gets to a point where it's literally impossible to think sceptically. The way we think sceptically is that first we examine a claim, and then we accept it tentatively. And then, a millisecond later, we ask ourselves whether or not that is a true or false thing. Well, information is moving so quickly that we don't get to that second part. We tend to accept things much less critically, and I think that is a terrible thing — not just for consumers, but for society. I think it's going to have all sorts of repercussions, some of which we don't even understand."

Dying for Attention

The most significant events happening on the face of the Earth today do not make the evening news. The evening news is predictably about plane crashes or murders or political shenanigans. It's not about how 30,000 children died today because they lacked clean drinking water. That happens every day, so it's not news. We don't hear on the weather station about the retreat of glaciers due to a climate that is changing so dramatically and fundamentally that we no longer can predict anything.

— ELIZABETH MAY

Physiologists have long known about an interesting property of neurons. When a nerve cell is stimulated, it gives a measurable electrical response. But if the neuron is repeatedly stimulated, the intensity of the response gradually diminishes until it no longer registers. This is called habituation. You notice it if a loud bell goes off. You are startled at first, but very soon, if the ringing continues, it recedes in your awareness until you hardly notice it. In many ways, we have an analogous response to stories about the environment. Many environmental problems, like global warming, are what I call slow-motion catastrophes. We don't see blood and people dying right away, so after a while we become habituated to the warnings. Like everybody else, environmentalists need ever more spectacular stunts to garner attention.

As described earlier, Lois Gibbs runs one of the most effective grass-roots citizens' groups in the world, the Center for Health, Environment and Justice, out of Maryland. They fight waste dumps and the spread of dangerous toxins like dioxin in the environment. She says, "Some media are our allies. But the other side of [the coin] is that the corporations, the polluters, can buy as much media as they want. So for us to get media, we have to do something — I call it performing for the media — to get their attention. But it's a Catch-22. If you behave outside the ordinary in order to be newsworthy, you can be dismissed as a bunch of crazy, hysterical radicals, whereas the governor, health commissioner and corporations can get serious coverage or just run ads. So it has to be very fine-line organizing that we do. We take people who are outside the norm and get them jumping around to get the media's attention, and then we have the other folks — the moms, the dads, the straight, conservative people — give the presentation."

Paul Watson is arguably the most radical of environmentalists. He was a founding member of Greenpeace, but he left twenty years ago to form the Sea Shepherd Society, an organization dedicated to the protection of marine mammals. Watson is probably best known for leading the fight against the slaughter of baby seals in Quebec and Newfoundland. More recently, he sank the entire Icelandic whaling fleet, an act for which he was put in prison. He's out now, and he claims he does these things not because he's angry, but because of the way our media culture has developed. Watson tells a story about calling the foreign editor of the *Los Angeles Times* not long ago. The paper had carried a piece on the whaling industry which suggested that since people weren't protesting any more, they had become receptive to the idea that whaling would be resurrected. "I called him up and I said, 'That's absolutely ridiculous. People aren't supportive of whaling,'" Watson recalls. "And his answer to me was very telling about how the media view these things. He said, 'Well, you'll just have to go out and sink another whaling boat, won't ya?' In other words, that's the only way they're going to pay attention to us. They're not going to give you the time of day if you're trying to talk about something based on information and statistics or whatever. They're only interested in dramatics."

Watson has studied the media, and he claims that most reporters and their bosses are interested in only four things: sex, scandal, violence and celebrity. A story isn't a story unless it has at least one of these elements, and when you have all four, as the O.J. Simpson trial did, you have a super-story. When it comes to his type of activism, Watson says, "We just play the game. When I did a campaign against aerial shooting of wolves in British Columbia in 1984, we had a story that carried the headlines across Canada for two weeks. The reason is that we had all four elements: sex, scandal, violence and celebrity. We had the violence of them shooting the wolves. We had the violence of the threats against us. We had the scandal of [a provincial] environment minister [forced to resign after being accused of] taking a bribe from a big game–hunting organization in return for giving them what they wanted. And to round that all [off], I simply recruited Bo Derek as our spokesperson.

"And I remember at the press conference a reporter saying to me, 'Oh, come on now. What's Bo Derek know about wolves? I mean, what do you have her here for? . . . She's an actress, for God's sake.' And I said, 'Yes. You make the rules. And we play the game. You must have just graduated from journalism school or something, because if I had the best wolf biologist in the world and called this press conference, there'd be an empty room. But because Bo Derek is our spokesperson, it'll be the headline of your newspaper tomorrow and there's nothing you can do about it.' "

Watson says his theatrics work "like an acupuncture needle. We stimulate responses to try to get people thinking. My role as a conservationist is to say things that people don't want to hear and do things that people don't want to do. I'm here to rock the boat. To sink the ship, if necessary. But my main focus is to make people think, 'Why is he doing that?' Because there's a problem, that's why."

Manufacturing Consent

> *The Earth Summit itself was greenwash on a grand scale,*
> *because it gave the false impression that important, positive*
> *change was occurring, and it failed to alert the world to the*
> *root causes of environment and development problems.*
>
> — JED GREER AND KENNY BRUNO, IN *GREENWASH:*
> *THE REALITY BEHIND CORPORATE ENVIRONMENTALISM*

There's another obstacle to getting heard — it's called greenwashing.

It involves using the rhetoric of the environmental movement to cloak ecologically damaging activities. Elizabeth May, head of the Sierra Club of Canada, one of our country's most vital environmental watchdogs, says that there is a deliberate effort to play on public exhaustion and distraction. "Nobody has energy for outrage when you're trying to raise kids, hold down a job, pay your mortgage. Maintaining that extra thing in your life — wondering when the government is going to do something to protect us from pesticides, radioactive fallout or whatever — is a strain." She says that when politicians are pressured by the voting public, a very clever government, industry and corporate approach is to say, "We heard you. Uncle! We're so sorry! *Mea culpa!* Now we're all going to be environmentalists together. There's no difference between Sierra Club and Monsanto; we're all just so concerned about the environment. We are parents too, after all."

May got into environmental issues back in the late sixties and early seventies, when as a college student she tried to stop the spraying program to kill the spruce budworm in Nova Scotia. The practice has been linked to the destruction of salmon streams, as well as to Reye's syndrome, a deadly brain swelling in children. She says that when governments began to create the environmental departments and international agreements that were supposed to protect biodiversity, stabilize carbon emissions and regulate polluters, most of us breathed a sigh of relief and went back to worrying about our mortgages. The problem is that a lot of it was just talk. Information without action.

"It's not that it was nonsense at some level. Sometimes, with political will, these globally agreed-upon treaties could do something. But a very good way to shut down public outrage is to say, 'We've dealt with it. We're on top of it now.' The public goes back to sleep, which they wouldn't do if the media stayed on the case. The media have to say, 'Right, the government says they're committed to this; they've said they're going to take action. Let's see what happens when the rubber hits the road.'"

Perhaps because, as Neil Postman contends, there is little indication of cause and effect in today's information, there seems to be very little demand in newsrooms for follow-up stories to see whether people really act on what they espouse. And information without an invitation to action is ultimately disempowering.

Besides all the inertia, babble and entertainment working against informing the public about vital issues like environmental degradation, despite the empty promises and inaction, there is also a conscious and commercially supported effort to create *disinformation*. Today, there's a whole industry devoted to selling messages, whether the message is to buy some consumer item or to vote for a certain politician. The industry is called public relations, and its employees now considerably outnumber actual journalists.

So if a product has negative environmental repercussions, a company doesn't have to change the product so much as it has to change the information getting out about it. Josh Karlinger, head of the Transnational Resource and Action Center (TRAC) in San Francisco, is also author of *The Corporate Planet*. He contends that PR firms went into high gear when environmentalists started to threaten the way their clients did business. "The environmental movement has put a tremendous amount of pressure on [those in] the corporate world. It has cost them billions of dollars. It's forced them to change some of what they've produced and how they produce it. And there's a potential that the environmental movement will foster even more thorough-going change. So the public-relations counsellors of these big, global, public-relations corporations have counselled their corporate clients to sit down at the table and make friends with the environmentalists, and promote a joint approach to solving some of these problems."

It all goes back to the 1980s again, when public pressure for change was at its height. "These corporations," Karlinger explains, "at the behest of their public-relations firms, began to pour hundreds of thousands of dollars into the environmental movement. This new approach was summed up in the slogan Cooperation, Not Confrontation, and it seemed to augur a new age of harmony, with responsible corporations working out compromises with sophisticated and economically realistic environmentalists. But when the information superhighway and the global economy superseded the environment in people's minds, there were big changes. . . . Suddenly, all these same corporations that [had been] . . . talking about sustainable development were lobbying the halls of Congress to completely gut the environmental regulations of the country."

We have to remember that corporations, especially global ones, are in the business of making it as easy and as profitable as possible to produce their goods. They cannot have the environment and the public good as a central concern because those matters can conflict with their primary goal: realizing bigger profits. Corporations must do battle with anyone and anything that threatens their bottom line, and that includes environmental groups. And the only weapon environmental groups have is to reveal the PR spin ecologically destructive industries are using.

Lies, Damn Lies and the Public-Relations Industry

No one talks about the fact that there's an international, $35-billion-a-year propaganda-for-hire industry. And what I learned in writing the book is that even our most exaggerated parody of this industry couldn't anticipate how cynical and pervasive it really is.

— JOHN STAUBER

John Stauber is a lifelong environmental activist and the director of the Center for Media and Democracy in Madison, Wisconsin. He and his colleague Sheldon Rampton recently co-authored a wonderfully arresting and blackly funny book called *Toxic Sludge Is Good for You*. Stauber says that after years of trying to figure out why the environmental message was so hard to get out and so often got twisted, "it dawned on me that every issue I cared about or worked on — whether it was an environment or a community issue, a peace and social-justice issue — every time, on the other side of that issue, was a vested interest, usually somebody making a profit off the status quo."

He decided to do some serious research into how these interests were protecting themselves from the various civic movements designed to legislate, regulate or otherwise change the way they were doing business. He says that using the Freedom of Information Act, he found "a motherlode of insider public-relations documents that revealed how the propaganda-for-hire industry works." This industry is worth about $35 billion globally, and it employs 150,000 paid practitioners in the United States alone. Its mandate is well summed up in a brochure produced by the PR giant Burson-Marsteller. "The role of communications is to manage perceptions which motivate behaviours and create business results," the company explains. "We are totally focused on this idea as our mission. Burson-Marsteller helps clients manage issues by influencing, in the right combination, public attitudes, public perceptions, public behaviour, and public policy."

Josh Karliner, who runs a monthly magazine called PR Watch, says, "[Burson-Marsteller is] a subsidiary of Young and Rubicam, which is one of the largest advertising firms in the world. They have offices in dozens of countries around the planet. They serve as spin-doctors, public-relations counsellors, to large transnational corporations. And they even have a department that provides emergency response. They advertise themselves as the ones [who] will help corporations with image problems, [especially] if they've got consumer activists, labour activists or environmental activists breathing down their necks." A list of Burson-Marsteller clients is extremely revealing. "They worked with Union Carbide during the Bhopal gas disaster," says Karliner. "They worked with Exxon during the Exxon Valdez disaster. In the 1970s they worked for the dictatorship in Argentina. They worked for Ceauşescu in Romania. They worked for the Mexican government in the NAFTA negotiations. And recently they worked for the United States oil and chemical industry in their efforts to roll back the Clean Air Act in Congress." In Canada, they worked for Hydro-Quebec, promoting the James Bay Two Project, and they formed the British Columbia Forest Alliance, a group that campaigns against restrictions on logging and actively works to discredit environmentalists.

Other public-relations companies like Montgovern, Duchin and Bisco even maintain dossiers on social activists, people who might be, as John Stauber says, "working to stop an incinerator from being built in their community, or it might be people concerned about the health effects of factory farming or dioxin-contaminated products."

A few years ago, Ron Duchin, head of Montgovern, Duchin and Bisco, addressed the National Cattlemen's Association (the same organization that sued Howard Lyman and Oprah Winfrey) on how to divide and conquer environmental and social grass-roots activists. He said, "Activists essentially fall into categories — the radicals, the opportunists, the realists and the idealists." Duchin described the "radicals" as people who want to change the system. They "have underlying socio-political motives, and see multinational corporations as inherently evil. These people do not trust the federal, state and local governments to protect them and to safeguard the environment. They believe rather that individuals and local groups should have direct power over industry. . . . Their principle aims right now are social justice and political empowerment." These are the people Duchin wants to stop, because their objectives clearly threaten those of his corporate clients. In Duchin's prescription, "The way to stop these people is to isolate them from the other activists."

The "idealists" also get involved in civic, justice and environmental issues, but they are very different. Duchin says they "want a perfect world, and find it easy to brand any product or practice which can be shown to mar that perfection as evil. Because of their intrinsic altruism, however, because they have nothing perceptible to gain by holding their position, they're easily believed by both the media and the public, and sometimes even politicians." But Duchin believes these people are vulnerable. "If idealists can be shown that their position and their opposition to an industry or its products causes harm to others and cannot be ethically justified," he explains, "they're forced to change their position." He goes on to say, "They need to be educated." And generally this education process "requires great sensitivity and understanding on the part of the educator."

John Stauber, who quotes extensively from Duchin's speech in his book, gives an example of how this education might take place. "A typical corporate rap might be to sit down with a church group or other concerned [group of] people and say, 'Look, you know no one is more concerned than the people at XYZ corporation about chemicals in the environment. After all, we have kids too. And we live in this community, and we're just like you. You've got to understand — if these radicals have their way, we'll be put out of business. And if we're put out of business, we can't provide jobs to the community. And if we can't provide jobs to the community, then there's going to be a depression in this town. Everybody's going to suffer. Nobody wants that. So let's sit down and work for a common solution.'" Sounds reasonable. Except that there will still be pollution. Or an incinerator, albeit a smaller one. Or something else that the group didn't want.

The third category of people comprises those Duchin calls the "realists." These are people who "can live with trade-offs, are willing to work within the system and aren't interested in radical change." Duchin adds, "The realists should always receive the highest priority in any strategy dealing with the issue. . . . The credibility of the radicals will [then] be lost." This is because Duchin's realists will strike a deal, some kind of compromise favourable to industry, that will end up making the radicals, however rational and just their demands, look extreme.

The final group is made up of the so-called opportunists. Duchin says they become involved with an issue for fame or glory or personal aggrandizement, and they, of course, are the easiest of all to deal with. "Radicals" like Lois Gibbs can't be bought with money or thrown off track by disinformation. They can only be discredited. And, to a degree far beyond even my own understanding, as both a journalist and an environmentalist, they often are.

Looking for the Terrorists

Environmentalists fall into two categories: socialists and enviro-religious fanatics.
— RUSH LIMBAUGH, IN *THE WAY THINGS OUGHT TO BE*

When Holly Dressel and I started the radio series on which this book is based, we wanted to look at all sides of the environment issue. We thought it would be a good idea to get in touch with radical environmentalists, groups like Paul Watson's Sea Shepherd Society or the loose confederation of "tree huggers" known as EarthFirst! We'd heard in the media about tree spiking and other acts of "environmental terrorism," and so we pictured these groups in camouflage outfits, monkey-wrenching power lines and spiking trees. What we found was by and large rather different.

Josh Karliner, of TRAC, says we are all victims of a strategy to "marginalize some of the most progressive elements of the environmental movement, to divide and conquer the environmental movement, and to make the progressive groups look extreme." There's a name for this strategy: brownwashing. Paul Watson, who has been called an environmental terrorist, knows all about it. He says, "We do . . . target property. We sink whaling ships. We confiscate drift nets. Our targets are all material that is being used to illegally destroy life, and I have no problem with that at all. Martin Luther King once said, 'You cannot commit an act of violence against a non-sentient object.' And that's where our values come into conflict. Society at large puts more value on private property than [it does] upon life." He tells a story to illustrate this point. "A ranger in Zimbabwe a couple of years ago was severely criticized by human-rights groups for shooting a poacher who was about to kill a black rhino, the reasoning being 'How dare you take the life of a human being, just to protect an animal?' And his answer, I thought, really summed it up and exposed our hypocrisy. He said, 'If I were a police officer in Harare, and a man ran out of Barclay's Bank with a bag of money and I shot him in the head and killed him on the spot, you'd call me a hero. You'd pin a medal on me, and say, 'Good boy!'" As Watson points out, we will kill to protect property. We will kill even to protect paper money. And we are honoured for doing it. But protecting the natural heritage of the nation for the benefit of future generations is not considered as valuable as a bag of money.

This is not to say that people in the environmental movement condone killing of any kind. Quite the contrary. "One of the things that I'm most proud of in the conservation movement is the fact that no conservationist, of any non-government organization that I ever heard of, has been responsible for killing or injuring another human being," says Watson. "It's an unblemished record of non-violence. But the media call us violent and terrorists and extremists. And when environmentalists get killed, which is often, [people say,] 'Well, they shouldn't have been in the way.'"

Watson points out that Chico Mendez was murdered for trying to protect the rain forest. Dian Fossey was murdered for her efforts to save mountain gorillas. Francisco Perrera was murdered by agents of the French government when they blew up the *Rainbow Warrior,* which was protesting atomic-bomb tests. Yet nobody condemned those acts as terrorism. Organizations like EarthFirst! are classic, direct-action, non-violent protest groups that organize sit-ins or sing songs while blocking logging roads. They do not resist the police, even when being beaten or pepper-sprayed. Their members are regular people, most of them women, from all walks of life: teachers, firefighters, librarians, you name it. In short, they are the progressives that the PR people worry about.

"I don't know of any environmental terrorist organizations," Watson asserts. "Never heard of such a thing. To me, Exxon or Union Carbide are environmental terrorists. But you know, the language gets polluted through media probably just as much as the air and water do. Anyway, what is a radical conservationist? It's a contradiction in terms. A conservationist is a conservative. So I am a conservative. And probably an arch-conservative because I'm a more aggressive conservationist than most. I represent the majority, because I represent all of those untold numbers of children that have yet to be born. And I am not about to give in to the so-called majority rule of the minority [who] happen to be alive today."

Watson invented something that most environmentalists are reluctant to claim as their own: tree spiking. But he says this act, too, is the victim of disinformation. "We first did it in 1982 on the south base of Grouse Mountain, facing the city of Vancouver, B.C. We spiked 2,000 trees and informed the sawmills. Those trees are still there because the sawmills wouldn't buy them. It costs too much money to remove the spikes." Watson claims the tactic is safe because there's no point in spiking unless you warn the loggers — and besides, chainsaws have guards to protect loggers from hitting bits of metal (which are often embedded in trees in any case). But the most convincing reason for claiming it's safe is that, to date, no one's been hurt by it.

"The one case that's trotted out is George Alexander, at the Louisiana-Pacific plant in northern California, who was almost killed by a fragment of shrapnel in a tree," says Watson. "What they don't tell you is that it wasn't a tree spike, it was a piece of metal, which is not that uncommon — a nail, gunshot, that kind of thing. And it was Louisiana-Pacific's negligence that resulted in the injury. They refused to put up a proper shield to protect their workers. George Alexander himself agreed with me when I talked to him about it."

Watson also says he doesn't advocate tree-spiking to hurt or terrify loggers. Tree-spiking means downtime in the sawmills, which can cost the industry big money, anywhere from $20,000 to $50,000 an hour. "When you cut into their profits, they notice. But of course, they get Burson-Marsteller and the PR companies to put forth a volume of information about how this is terrorism. I'll tell you what terrorism is. Terrorism is destroying forests. Terrorism is destroying the carrying capacity of thousands upon thousands of species. Terrorism is depriving our children of their heritage. That, to me, is what terrorism is."

The Monkey-Wrench Gang

We use all the tools in the toolbox, short of violence.
                                                    — EARTHFIRST! CREDO

Most people do not condone destruction of property. Many feel uncomfortable even with direct action, and believe that civil protest should be organized within the system. But the fact remains that the word "eco-terrorism" has been used freely to describe small citizens' groups organizing petitions and engaging in boycotts; peaceful, legal, public demonstrations; and sit-ins. Many participants in such activities have been beaten, gassed and pepper-sprayed for their attempts to protect the environment or to fight for civil rights. But members of the media don't always tell that story.

When the airwaves, the networks, the newspapers and the vast advertising industry are all controlled by vested interests that must protect their ways of doing business, citizen protest becomes difficult and easily slandered. Chad Hanson is a national director of the biggest American environmental group, the Sierra Club, a very conservative organization with a large number of Republican members. He says, "The message that's been promoted by industry in the media — that somehow there are all these radical and violent environmental organizations out there — is absolutely ridiculous. Completely untrue. Most so-called radical groups are just promoting positions that the public already supports. This includes EarthFirst! I have never seen any EarthFirst! activist engage in anything that could possibly be construed as violent behaviour. Ever. This is an absolutely peaceful, non-violent community. The only violence that goes on out there is violence perpetrated against citizens, of all types, by industry and often government. . . . And I would like to see the media cover this more."

A perfect example of Hanson's claim is the Headwaters Campaign in northern California. For years, EarthFirst! and other citizens' groups have been trying to save the last acres of ancient redwoods and old-growth forest in the region from a corporate raider that began liquidating the forest about ten years ago. EarthFirst! lobbied, circulated petitions and wrote letters. Finally, last year, a group of mostly young women went to the offices of the local senator and the company itself. Karen Pickett, a fifteen-year veteran of EarthFirst!, was with them. She says that this was a classic demonstration, with signs and banners. Once in the offices, the women sat in a small circle and then "locked themselves down," as they call it, with a length of steel pipe and a bracelet so they would be very difficult to move and so the demonstration could be prolonged in order to attract the media attention they needed so badly.

When the sheriff's men came in, the women continued singing and chanting. The police warned they were going to use pepper spray. There have been eighty recorded deaths from pepper spray; it can be dangerous for asthmatics, and it can cause permanent eye damage. When the women didn't unlock themselves from the pipe, the police didn't just spray them from aerosol cans. "They actually took Q-tips full of the stuff and swabbed it directly into the protesters' eyes," recounts Pickett. "They took a video of themselves doing it, while the young women cried and screamed and begged them not to do it any more." The women, who were still locked together, were helpless even to put up a hand. Although the local media picked up the story, no one else in North America heard much about this particular display of violence. And the police still maintain that their actions were necessary to "defend themselves" against the dangerous demonstrators.

Who Do You Trust?

> *The real key is information, getting the right information so you can make decisions today about yourself, your family and your community. Should you or should you not drink that water? Should you or should you not allow your children to play in that yard? You need to know these things.*
>
> — LOIS GIBBS

Organizations that are trying to get vital information out to the citizenry have to use information technologies, but these technologies often have other priorities. Increasingly, ownership of print and electronic media is concentrated in the hands of a few tycoons, who determine the perspective and output of their property. Environmental and human-rights groups must also run the gauntlet of the public's boredom, distraction and media overload. On top of that, media outlets themselves may not want to carry information that could antagonize advertisers, program sponsors or owners.

I know from firsthand experience how rough the private sector can be when anything critical is broadcast or printed. A few years ago, "The Nature of Things" was to carry a special look at Canada's forestry practices. Before the program had even been completed or pre-screened, the forest industry took out newspaper ads condemning it and calling for public support. At the same time, the CBC found itself under enormous pressure to have the program cut or watered down. The Canadian Imperial Bank of Commerce announced that it would not advertise on "The Nature of Things" because of the episode. It was crude hardball, but to the CBC's credit, the program was not modified and was broadcast to wide public acclaim.

Who should you believe? If programs that discuss an issue like global warming are sponsored by gas or car companies, we might want to think twice. If a scientist makes a declaration about the safety or hazard of genetically modified food, a new drug, the burning of fossil fuels or clearcutting forests, we should find out the primary source of support for that expert. Often an organization that seems to be grass-roots has, in fact, been set up and funded by industry, so it's important to see who funds such organizations and who's on their board of directors. On the other hand, a group that has little or nothing to gain monetarily by its stance, and that raises concerns about children, quality of life or health issues, just might be what it says it is.

And there are a lot of groups like that. Many activists will tell you that there is nothing that frightens polluters more than a little old lady with a sign at a demo. Lois Gibbs says, "Corporations are scared to death of us because they can't deal with us, . . . we will not compromise. We will not give up on our children. We will not give up on our homes. We will not give up on our schools and our communities for somebody else's profit. So they just walk away from the table, saying, 'You're unreasonable, hysterical, radical people.' But we really aren't."

She says most communities, even the most disadvantaged or impoverished ones, can win many of these fights. "This isn't a legal battle, because it's perfectly legal to poison people and poison the environment. It's not a scientific battle, because you can have lots of scientists arguing about whether grey is grey or whether it's really black and white or something in between. These are *political* fights." And they're fought, like most political battles, at the level of information. To illustrate this point, Gibbs recounts the story of a member of her centre, a PTA mom in Texas, who introduced a resolution at her local elementary school to support efforts to eliminate the release of the dangerous and

ubiquitous carcinogen dioxin into the environment. At the very next
PTA meeting, people from the oil and chemical industries showed up to
state their side of the issue. Nevertheless, the resolution still passed. The
woman then took it on to a state convention of the PTA, where she again
planned to introduce the resolution. "The petrochemical industry went
crazy," Gibbs recalls. "They called all of their plants, all of their workers,
all of their managers, to tell them to get their own wives off to the PTA
to vote against the resolution."

At the convention, the industry bought space to set up an exhibit,
which was rather unusual at a PTA convention. On the floor, a battle
ensued when industry supporters argued that the resolution would
wreck the Texas economy. But the resolution passed, and the members
of the Texas PTA voted to support programs to eliminate dioxin dis-
charges. The expensive, frenzied effort of the chemical industry to control a non-binding PTA resolution gives some idea of the extent to
which people will go to attempt to control information in our society.
That's why information is still so important, even if so much of it is
banal, silly or superficial.

The Centre of the Universe

> *The message you get from the consumer world of television all*
> *the time is: "You are the most important thing on Earth.*
> *Nothing is more important than you." If we don't get past*
> *that idea, ... then we're unlikely to ever deal clearly with either*
> *environmental or social-justice issues.*

> — BILL MCKIBBEN, AUTHOR OF
> THE END OF NATURE

If we are to use information in a way that empowers us to make
informed decisions, we have to understand the current nature of information and the technology that has been developed to bring it to us.
Information has always been the key to our survival. But today, as never
before in our evolutionary history, the information reaching our brains
is filtered, fabricated, shaped and controlled by powerful human forces
with agendas that differ from the common good. Information dissemination is not something we can leave to the marketplace, to commercial

interests or even to Hollywood. On some level, we all have to make sure that genuine survival information continues to be freely available, alongside all the diversion and entertainment.

Paul Watson asks, "Why do I sink ships? Because nobody will listen to me if I don't. And I'm trying to convey a message. That message is, 'We're in some very serious trouble.' The possibility of losing biodiversity, and therefore the ability of the environment to sustain us, is very, very real. In 200 years, the human species could be extinct, unless we take action now and stop worrying about whether we're going to get a new car or whether the new 'Roseanne' show is going to come up again in the fall. We're so engrossed in trivialities, we never get down to thinking about what is real in this world."

What is real in this world is the human impact on it. We're moving too fast and demanding too much. Our extraordinary technologies could do a lot to help us and the world's biodiversity survive, but we're not very good at predicting and controlling their effects. They take us down paths that distance us from understanding the kind of planet we need to live on, and they have nothing to do with the productivity rates of the natural services we need to survive. "We had no control about where we came from, but we certainly do have control about where we're going," says Paul Watson. "The world that is being shaped now is the . . . world of the future. Will there be elephants here 2,000 years from now? We have to make that decision. Will there be redwood trees? It's up to us. We spend most of our time entertaining ourselves and trying to avoid reality. But the reality is, we've become gods. We are making these god-like decisions as to whether the planet will survive, whether our own species will survive. And that is an awesome responsibility. It's one we should be facing up to, instead of involving ourselves in circuses and trying to entertain ourselves."

CHAPTER 4
UNNATURAL SELECTIONS

*We've taken flounder genes and put them into tomatoes. We've
taken human genes and put them into salmon. We've taken
the fluorescent genes from fireflies and put them into tobacco
plants. It is very important to understand that we are crossing
species boundaries at will. There is no time in history, that I'm
aware of, where flounders mated with tomatoes, where humans
mated with mice, where salmon mated with chickens. This is a
completely new arena.*

— ANDY KIMBRELL, THE INTERNATIONAL CENTER
FOR TECHNOLOGY ASSESSMENT

Genes could be called the pre-packaged destiny of every living being.
Every detail of the hereditary makeup of each of the Earth's organisms
has been honed by natural selection so that it can adapt to its environment. Whether it's the camouflage of a zebra's stripes, the sensuous floral
structures of an orchid, the social behaviour of ants or the humming-
bird's extensive tongue, all of life's characteristics have been refined
through evolution to achieve an exquisite balance with the organism's
surroundings. As biological beings, we too are products of evolution;
every aspect of our physical makeup, as well as much of our behaviour, is
the result of hundreds of thousands of years of selection and adaptation,
and enables us to survive in the places and circumstances in which we
find ourselves.

When, about 10,000 to 12,000 years ago, some people discovered
the efficacy of domesticating plants and animals, they began a revolution
that transformed us from nomadic hunter-gatherers to farmers. Very

quickly, those ancient farmers recognized one of the most basic principles in genetics — like begets like. By applying that principle, people learned to breed animals and plants for desirable traits, such as bigger kernels on corn, thicker wool on sheep or greater speed in horses. Human tinkering with genetic destiny has been going on all over the world for millennia, and it has been making gradual but sweeping changes.

However, in recent years a transformation of this process has occurred. It began with the recognition that genes could be identified as a molecule within cells. That molecule was deoxyribonucleic acid, or DNA. The basic structure of DNA was proposed by Francis Crick and James Watson in 1953. Their elegant model, which explains how DNA can encode information, replicate and mutate, is a double helix in which pairs of four kinds of structures called "bases" are arranged in a linear sequence. The four bases can be thought of as letters in a four-symbol alphabet. The words in the biological language are spelled out three letters at a time, thereby giving us sixty-four possible arrangements of the four letters. (In other words, four possible letters at each of the three positions, or $4 \times 4 \times 4 = 64$ different combinations.) Hundreds of such triplets strung together make up a sentence, or a gene. A simplified form of life like a virus may have as few as ten genes, while a fruit fly has 10,000 and a human being, 100,000. The total human DNA makeup is called the human genome and contains 3 billion genetic letters, or bases, from each parent.

The definition of a species is that individuals belonging to it can breed only with other members of the species. They cannot interbreed with other species. Two creatures that seem basically alike — say, a red-headed and a downy woodpecker — cannot breed and produce viable offspring, even if they should mate. The reason is that each one evolved under different circumstances, and therefore has its own private genetic code, like no other species'. It means that each species has its own habits, mating dances, nests, diet and ecological niche. It also means it has viruses, bacteria, parasites and other symbiotic guests specific to its own genetic makeup. Other species may share them too, but viruses or other infective agents that have evolved specifically to infect, say, a sheep or a chimpanzee, do not readily infect another species. Over time, viruses and their hosts evolve a relationship; the host can tolerate the virus without being quickly overwhelmed, while the virus tempers its effects so that the host isn't killed off too quickly. The species barrier, which has kept different species from mixing their genes, has also restricted the range of hosts for disease bacteria and parasites. We don't know exactly why this barrier exists, or all the details about how it works, but it is the foundation on which life's complexity rests.

In the past twenty-five years, genetic tinkering has jumped from breeding into an entirely new realm. We have not only acquired an understanding of how genes are structured and function but also gained tools to manipulate DNA. DNA can be chemically extracted from virtually any organism, specific sequences can be isolated and the sequential arrangement of letters in those fragments determined. Those DNA pieces can be replicated millions of times, attached to DNA from any other organism, then inserted into yet another life form.

For billions of years, life has followed the principle that each living organism exchanged DNA only with others of its kind. But today, scientists can deliberately bypass species barriers and introduce foreign DNA into an organism at will. This is called horizontal gene transfer. Mae Wan Ho's book *Genetic Engineering: Dream or Nightmare?* voices the growing concern within the scientific community over this practice. She says, "Genetic engineering, or biotechnology, is based on recombining genes from very widely different sources. And also transferring genes between organisms that are not just different species, but are in different kingdoms. . . . So that species that had no possibility of interbreeding, and very, very, very low probability of exchanging genes in nature, are now unrestricted due to these new laboratory operations." That is the basis of biotechnology. We already live in a world where new life forms created by human beings are replicating among us.

Over the past two decades, the fantastic benefits promised by genetic engineering seem to be on the verge of coming true. Scientists propose to put pharmaceuticals, such as a vaccine against childhood dysentery, into common foods like bananas, thereby saving millions of lives. Fish or cows that grow bigger and faster on less food are another research area. A lab just outside Montreal has spliced spider genes into goats in an effort to create new, super-strong fibres that will be expressed by the genes in the milk. Food could be designed to contain more nutrients — like vitamin A — and fewer "bad things" — like cholesterol. Mice have been genetically engineered to grow human ears, and pigs are being bred to grow human organs for transplants. Scientists are even isolating DNA from species now extinct, such as mastodons, Neanderthal people and the killer flu virus of 1918. These are just a few of the coming miracles, and they've been chosen from an enormous list. It sounds as if the future is limited only by scientific imagination and daring. And because of the incredible promises, stocks in biotech companies have been the darling of speculators, who have invested billions of dollars. When the big biotech firm Genentech went public, its stock price rose by 30 percent in the first day.

Those are a few of the spectacular stories that have been covered extensively. But they've also been accompanied by disturbing developments, such as the report that scientists have created headless tadpoles as a kind of prelude to generating other headless animals for use as organ and tissue banks. Israel and Iraq are reported to have been trying to develop weapons designed to home in on specific genetic targets. Today, even though the packaging doesn't inform us of this, as much as 70 percent of our modern, processed foods contains parts of modified organisms, new genetic inventions. And some of these organisms are having "unexpected effects"; corn that was genetically engineered to carry its own selective insecticide, for example, is now threatening to inadvertently wipe out the monarch butterfly population of North America.

The technological dexterity of biotechnology is truly awesome, but the manipulations are carried out in complex, living creatures that we understand at only the crudest level. The reasons why genetic engineering is proving to be so problematical are the basis for this chapter.

A Personal Declaration

> *The point is not that* science *is bad — the charge that is too often made by the green movement and by journalists in the popular media — but that there can be* bad *science that ill serves humanity.*
>
> — MAE WAN HO, GENETICIST

There are those among my colleagues who suggest that I am a heretic because I was once deeply involved in genetic research but have since raised questions about much of what is being pursued today. The practice of genetic research was the great joy of my life for twenty-five years, a period when I ate, slept and dreamed about experiments and ideas in genetics. At one time, my lab was the largest genetics-research group in Canada, and I am proud of the work that we did. It continues to be a great source of satisfaction that a genetics book I co-wrote with Tony Griffiths has become the most widely used introductory genetics text in the world. Genetics has been my passion, the source of my friends and colleagues, and the most challenging and rewarding intellectual activity of my career.

It is precisely because genetics has been my life's passion that I also care about its future. As a science that goes to the very heart of all life's forms and functions, genetics has enormous implications; it is full of promise to benefit and improve human lives, but equally heavy with potential to destroy and cause untold suffering. For those who care for the long-term flourishing of genetics, it is vital to raise questions and anticipate problems, as well as proclaiming the potential benefits.

Val Geddings is also a geneticist. He specialized in the area of evolution, and he has worked as a genetics adviser for the United States Department of Agriculture, the World Bank and the Office of Technology Assessment of the U.S. Congress. He once represented the United States at the biosafety negotiations of the United Nations' Biodiversity Convention, the body that is trying to hammer out international regulations on genetically engineered organisms. Today, Geddings represents private industry, as a vice-president of the Biotechnology Industry Organization, an umbrella group for more than 700 biotech corporations worldwide. He says public fears about the safety of biotech are misplaced, because DNA, the material we're splicing from one organism to another, is the same chemical substance throughout the living kingdom.

Geddings says, "What's a gene? A gene is a stretch of DNA. What we know from genetic analyses of chimpanzees and humans is that 98.6 percent of the nucleotide-base sequences in chimpanzees are identical to those you find in humans. Why is this? That's a function of our descent from a common ancestor. It illustrates the degree to which different species are related to one another. And that's the beauty of this part of genetics — that we're all related. There isn't any violation of the natural order, taking a gene from one place and putting it someplace else. It might have come from there in the first place, and it's just going home! There's a vast amount of genetic similarity, in a very high degree, between any organism and many, many, many other organisms. It doesn't make any biological sense to talk about moving a gene from one species to another as a violation of natural order. . . . Everything's related to everything else. We're all united by descent from a common ancestor."

That sounds convincing, even inspiring, and of course it is true that all living things are related by a shared evolutionary history. But human genes won't make a chimpanzee, even though most of them are identical to the chimp's. What Geddings's statement ignores is any recognition of *context*. Natural selection doesn't act on each and every gene we carry. Selection is based on the phenotype, the ultimate expression of all the genes acting in concert to create an organism that functions in its surroundings. Individual genes are like the separate instruments in an orchestra. Each plays its part according to the score, and taken together, they can make beautiful music. Music is music, you may say, but what would happen if you stuck Elvis Presley into the middle of a Beethoven sonata? Or substituted a twelve-year-old playing marching-band trumpet for Louis Armstrong playing jazz? That's what genetic engineering does. Technically speaking, a trumpet *is* a trumpet. A gene *is* a gene. But taking a gene from one species and sticking it into another is placing it into an entirely different genetic context. What biotechnologists do represents a fundamentally different way of making new genetic combinations. And it *is* unnatural.

The Most Elegant Science

Information coding, decoding and storage, that was all beautifully and simply stated by Watson and Crick. And that paradigm of what a gene does, how it stores information and is replicated and so on, that problem is pretty much solved. But what's gone on now is the illegitimate application of that paradigm, that legitimate notion of genetics, to this illegitimate area, of reducing complex behaviours to single genes. It's just a mistake of the first order. . . . It's great science. It's absolutely great science. But it's flawed. It's the wrong assumption.

— RICHARD STROHMAN, EMERITUS PROFESSOR OF MICROBIOLOGY

The word "engineering" conjures up images of roads and bridges and buildings, all designed and constructed to precise specifications. But as a geneticist, I can assure you that *genetic* engineering is based on trial and error, rather than on precision. For instance, if I want to insert a gene from a fruit fly into a daffodil, I can't pluck out just that gene and set it down exactly where I want it to go in its new home. The technique just doesn't work like that. Some geneticists even use a kind of molecular shotgun to blast the genes into cells. And they never know exactly where they'll end up.

Christine von Weizsaecker, a molecular biologist who is also the president of a German environmental group called Ecoropa, thinks that one reason biotechnology is dangerous is its imprecision. She uses a metaphor to describe the crudeness of gene splicing: "These genes . . . are thrown like sand on a piece of paper. . . . So let's say you have a favourite poem — and the genes of plants and animals and humans work together in the same consistent and forged way as a good poem. Now, if you say, 'I have a favourite poem, but one of the words that I really like is lacking from that poem.' So you cut out the new word you want from somewhere else, and say, 'I want to insert it into that poem.' What genetic engineering allows you to do is to make fifty copies of the word, let's say 'love' or 'wind' or 'flower.' And you throw them on the page of your favourite poem. Now, what are the chances that you really have a better poem? It may even be that that piece of word obliterates one of the words that is essential to the poem. Or that they come into completely different context. Like, you wanted the word 'love' included in the poem, and all of a sudden it reads, 'There is no love,' because it's contextualized. So there is no control over the genetic context in the gene, or over the environmental context in which it finds itself."

That means that for every genetic-engineering success — a plant that expresses the gene you wanted to introduce into it, like the luminescence of a firefly in a tobacco plant — there are thousands and thousands of failures. There are so many failures because of the imprecision in positioning the added genes.

Brian Goodwin, a theoretical biologist teaching at Schumacher College in Devon, England, says, "The assumption is that a characteristic can be transferred from one species to another simply by moving the gene. The problem is that genes are defined by context. For example, a gene that in a mouse produces a hormone regulating growth will have one effect in the mouse; but [the same] gene producing the hormone in a human being will have a very different effect. So as we move genes from one species to another, we will keep getting unpredictable effects which simply could not have been anticipated."

That sounds surprisingly pessimistic, given all we hear about this wonderful new science. After all, genetics *does* allow us to predict the pattern of inheritance of genes, describe how they're expressed and transfer characters from one genetic strain to another — but all *within* a species. Once we cross species barriers, we're in brand-new territory. We have absolutely no idea what might happen. Goodwin explains, "The problem is, this is experimenting as you go along. Nobody has any confidence any more that they can exactly predict the consequences. They just *hope* that they're only going to get small effects, the effects they want, and that they're not going to propagate really serious changes in the other constituents of that organism, that could be damaging to human health or dangerous for ecological systems."

Goodwin believes that when it comes to biotechnology, there's a time-lag in our thinking. Most of science has moved away from a focus on isolated elements to the analysis of complex patterns. Biology, and especially commercial gene technology, is an exception. In the ultimate expression of scientific reductionism, biotechnology views a gene as an isolated unit. Biotechnologists believe that a gene will express itself in exactly the same way, no matter where we choose to put it. But one of the great lessons of twentieth-century biology is that at every level — subatomic particles, molecules, genes, cells, organs and individuals — there are interactions that confound reductionist expectations. For example, cotton plants have been genetically engineered to produce a protein from a species called *Bacillis thuringensis*, or Bt, which acts as a natural insecticide. The gene was supposed to confer immunity from that great scourge of cotton plants, the boll weevil. However, in many cases, farmers who bought and planted the engineered seeds found that not only did they still have to spray against pests but the plants also showed deformities like twisting, few leaves and impossibly tall heights. Other plants had deformed and unusable cotton bolls. The engineered cotton plants yielded shocking monsters. The gene obviously functioned in its new surroundings in unpredictable ways.

Why do eminent private and public researchers keep developing genetically engineered products if they so often fail? Simply because acknowledging the failures is not in their interests. More and more, genetics- and biology-research projects, and even entire university departments, are dependent on private industry to keep going. Even government grants demand promises of "practical applications" for every bit of research in a very short time-frame. Dr. Richard Strohman is a renowned molecular biologist who is now an emeritus professor and past chair of the prestigious department of molecular biology at the University of California at Berkeley. In his retirement, he has begun to lend his reputation and expertise to the analysis of the hazards and pitfalls of the practice of genetic engineering. He says flatly, "Academic and corporate researchers have become indistinguishable. Every country in the post-industrial world now requires scientists to show that their work is going to be useful in the day-to-day world. This insistence that everything be greeted with immediate usefulness is counterproductive beyond measure."

This approach is incredibly short-sighted, and is sure to mean that important insights are ignored because they don't seem useful at the time. When I was a graduate student, we had to read difficult but beautifully documented papers on "jumping genes" by Barbara McClintock. We all believed the phenomena she was studying were a quirk of the special properties of the corn seed. Only decades later was it shown that in fact jumping genes can be found in most organisms, and they are now a standard tool of genetic engineers. If the current criteria for practical results were used decades ago, McClintock's research on jumping genes would never have been funded.

Strohman goes even further: "The problem is that in order for the application to be profitable, which it has to be in this culture, you've got to have your eye on magic bullets. You've got to be able to boil down some very complex behaviour — let's say a human disease or some ability for corn to produce more protein per ear — to a single entity that you can identify, isolate, and then put in a bottle or into a feed-bag or whatever. That's how you make money. And when it works, it's wonderful. But the trouble is that it often doesn't work. And when you put a biological entity out into the environment, or into a human being, and you're not completely certain — and you can never be certain in this business, in my opinion — your ability to do damage is very, very high."

Jumping Genes

Fears that genes for antibiotic resistance could jump from genetically modified foods to bacteria in the gut may be fueled by new research from the Netherlands. The results show that DNA lingers in the intestine, and confirm that genetically modified (GM) bacteria can transfer their antibiotic-resistance genes to bacteria in the gut.

— DEBORA MACKENZIE, "CAN WE REALLY STOMACH GM FOODS?" *NEW SCIENTIST*, JANUARY 30, 1999

The fact that genetic engineering, as it is being practised for the marketplace, appears to be built on faulty assumptions is deeply disturbing. Equally worrisome are the actual dangers inherent in gene-splicing techniques. The heart of biotechnology is the ability to work with pure DNA in a test tube. DNA is the primary building block of life, and it doesn't matter, in a test tube, where it comes from. So scientists can snip a bit of DNA from any living source and then insert it into another organism. Geneticists do this under controlled conditions to try to achieve a predictable result: an engineered organism that has new and, they hope, useful properties. But even DNA isolated in laboratories doesn't always travel alone. It can include what Mae Wan Ho calls genetic parasites, elements of DNA such as viruses, plasmids (rings of DNA that are separate from a cell's chromosome) and transposable elements (sequences of DNA that can change position in the genome). When we snip a bit of DNA out of an organism, we can also include the parasites — about which we know very little.

Mae Wan Ho says, "Natural genetic parasites, like viruses and other transposable elements, proteins and plasmids, are naturally specific to certain species. They have species barriers, genetic barriers. A virus from a pig will not generally attack humans, and so on. What genetic engineering does is to destroy these species barriers. So when you join these viruses and transposable elements from widely different sources, you create similarities to all these different species. You're levelling the gene-transfer barriers that naturally exist. I really am worried about this, because since 1993 an increasing number of publications [have reported] that horizontal gene transfer is responsible for new and bold pathogens arising."

Horizontal gene transfer, the tool on which biotechnology is built, can also happen in nature, but very rarely. It's a good thing it's rare, because it can be dangerous. In December 1997, officials in Hong Kong panicked over a deadly infection spread by a virus found in birds. They exterminated more than a million chickens because the chicken virus had horizontally transferred to humans. Many new flus originate in Asia because in some Asian countries, especially China, pigs, ducks and chickens are raised in close proximity. As a result, viruses specific to different species can infect the same animal simultaneously. When that happens, the genes of the different viruses can be shuffled to create a brand-new disease, which can infect the people living in the barnyard as well. Such pathogens can be extremely dangerous, since the host to the new virus has not built up any defences to temper the attack. The flu pandemic of 1918, which killed more than 22 million people worldwide, was probably such a disease. AIDS is now known to be a virus that originated in chimpanzees and jumped to humans who ate the chimps or accidentally exchanged blood with them. Mad cow disease is almost certainly the result of horizontal transfer of an infectious protein long known to kill sheep.

Seen in this context, genetic engineering, whose entire intent is to increase horizontal gene transfer, creates more and more opportunities for these kinds of unwanted species jumps. Mae Wan Ho says, "What makes me so worried about the whole thing is that, within the past twenty-five years, we have . . . at least thirty new diseases arising, including ebola, AIDS, hepatitis C, Lyme disease, hantavirus and so on. And we didn't know where they came from. But . . . within the past three or four years, they have now been attributed to horizontal gene transfer; that is, they come from other species and have jumped to us. . . . Now there may be no connection between the commercialization of genetic engineering and this escalation in new diseases that have jumped species, but I think we need a proper public enquiry to look into it." Her fears are not without foundation. Just a few months after Ho and I spoke, scientists reported in a prestigious journal, *The Proceedings of the National Academy of Sciences U.S.A.*, that a genetic parasite belonging to yeast, a favourite subject for genetic engineers, has suddenly jumped into many unrelated species of higher plants. Obviously, if parasites of yeast are making jumps into entirely new phyla, many other kinds of genetic parasites can as well.

In the early 1970s, geneticists, including me, were enthralled by their new-found abilities to create novel gene combinations. One scientist proposed removing a gene from a cancer-causing virus and inserting it into *Escherichia coli,* a common gut bacterium found in our intestines. He wanted to study the virus gene's expression away from the other genes in the virus. At some point, a colleague wondered whether such a bacterium might become a cancer-causing organism that posed a hazard to human beings. Suddenly, scientists were confronted with the very real possibility that they might create a nightmarish organism. It led them to what I believe was their finest hour: all geneticists voluntarily suspended such potentially dangerous experiments until there had been a wide discussion of hazards and ways to avoid risks. Eminent scientists, politicians and members of the public met under a blaze of media interest. Eventually, it was decided that potential escapes of hazardous organisms could be minimized by categorizing experiments into different levels of hazard and prescribing containment facilities that became more stringent at each level, rather like nuclear-containment facilities. As well, viruses and bacteria were deliberately "crippled" with defective genes to reduce their ability to survive outside lab conditions.

In those days, Mae Wan Ho was the biosafety officer in her recombinant DNA lab at the Open University. She says, "We never thought it was safe just to dump everything down the drain, or even in the bin. We had to incinerate everything. We had to autoclave all the waste. We had to do everything in a flow hood. ... And my colleagues who are still working in human genetics are still carrying out these procedures very carefully in the recombinant DNA lab. Meanwhile, private biotech companies are releasing these things into the environment in field trials and out of their labs."

So what happened to the moratorium? As new tools and techniques were developed and refined, the potential for exploration of new areas and commercial opportunities escalated. Scientists began to put pressure on governments to ease off on the safety measures because they were cumbersome and expensive. The media began to focus on the incredible benefits and economic opportunities to be realized from biotechnology. At around the same time, in the late 1970s, genetic engineering went from scientific research to product output. The biotech commercialization drive began in earnest. Once private industry saw a potential for making money, they began to fund huge labs and large-scale projects.

And when they did, the moratorium just kind of trickled away.

Meanwhile, public fears and scientists' worries subsided or were ignored, and most genetic engineers convinced themselves that the hazards were conjectural or imaginary. At one public meeting that I attended in Cambridge, Massachusetts, in the 1970s, the eminent Harvard molecular biologist Marc Ptashne testified that recombinant DNA technology posed less of a hazard than owning a pet dog. It was an astounding statement given the totally new status of the technology and our complete ignorance of gene manipulation at that time. Unfortunately, Mae Wan Ho and her colleagues have some bad news. She says, "Evidence has come to light within the past three or four years that these so-called crippled strains can actually sometimes survive quite well in the environment. Or they can go dormant for a while and then reappear, having acquired the new genes from their friends out there in the environment to enable them to live. The ideology of competition, the 'survival of the fittest' that you have in reductionist science is nowhere more inaccurate than in the microbial world. Members of the microbial world are very good at sharing their genes."

Seduced by the Lab

Scientists devote their lives to making conditions predictable, stable and harmonized. They just don't have a clue of the conditions in other parts of the world. They never think of what a biotech lab might be like in the hands of a desperate, totalitarian government. In a way, science trains people to be naive. And in a way, it's touching and loveable. But it's not very good for taking precautions and anticipating risks.
— CHRISTINE VON WEIZSAECKER

Back in the late 1980s and early 1990s, Ricarda Steinbrecher was a young geneticist working in a prestigious King's College lab in London on the genes that control hemophilia. Just as I did more than twenty-five years ago, Steinbrecher found her research mesmerizing and a joy to perform. But like me, she couldn't ignore niggling questions and concerns about how this science was being applied. She became particularly worried about how genetically modified organisms were being released into open fields with little or no investigation into their impact on the health of the environment and the diverse web of life they would find there. Eventually, Steinbrecher left the lab and offered her considerable knowledge and expertise to various non-governmental and environmental organizations that are trying to find out more about the possible effects of genetic engineering. Today she helps them analyze and evaluate data, as well as educating the public on the issues. She misses the joy of lab research and says, "Genetics is a fascinating field and it's beautiful, and I'd love to learn more about it and so would a lot of others. But that doesn't mean we should produce something we do not know much about yet and put it into the open environment. That's just the opposite of what all logic and science says."

So why have scientists embarked so enthusiastically on the path of corporate genetic engineering? The allure of money cannot be the full explanation. In part, it's because of scientific attitudes and enthusiasm. And it's because of human curiosity. There is a wonderful sense of community in a lab — a collective of talented people sharing an interest and feeling the thrill and power of probing nature's secrets. It's seductive and addictive, but it's also sometimes so much fun that you can actually forget the implications of what you're doing. When I was a geneticist studying heredity in fruitflies, we would refer to the insects as "bags of chromosomes." We bred them only to follow genes and chromosomes, and we seldom looked at them as whole, living organisms. To study gene expression, we bred them so that legs grew out of their heads and wings out of their eyes. I have filmed in labs where human organs were being grown in mice, and where rats were sewn together so they could exchange blood through criss-crossed arteries. Ricarda Steinbrecher says, "Where does a scientist draw the boundary? When should you stop being fascinated and experimental, and when should morals come into play? This is why constant interaction and checking with society is so crucial, so vital. Because, as a scientist, it's very easy to be so into one's own experiments that there's no boundary left. The only boundary is the boundary of imagination."

The kind of genetic engineering going on today would benefit from more societal scrutiny. In their obsession with specific goals and fascination with their technical dexterity, scientists seldom reflect seriously on the social or environmental ramifications of their work. Christine von

Weizsaecker is a molecular biologist with laboratory experience. She says the scientists who play with ebola vectors and antibiotic-resistance genes and dump their failures in the food supply don't see things the way the general public might. "I think it has to do with one-track minds. People think of risks in their own contexts. [Scientists] work in labs with Petri dishes; with a homogeneous environment; with exactly the same temperature, standardized nutrient broth and mono-cellular organisms, not several types of them, but just one type. And in this [environment], all the normal accidents, changes, unpredictable things that the future may bring just don't come to their mind."

Brian Goodwin concurs. "The education of biotechnologists is one of the narrowest in the world," he says. Biological education has been getting more and more specialized over the years, but with the introduction of recombinant DNA technology, the situation has worsened. Industrialized countries have put a lot of money into training scientists in this area because it's seen as the technology of the twenty-first century. "The scientists are extremely creative and very competent within an extraordinarily narrow range," explains Goodwin. "But often they don't know about organismic physiology. They don't know about whole organisms. And they certainly don't know about the ecosystems that they are potentially threatening."

So the problem for society is that even though these are "good" scientists, they have become more like technicians. Their training is so specialized that they really are, as Goodwin says, "simply unable to see the potential consequences of the sorts of products they're producing. And they are not required, within the conventions of science, to take responsibility for their actions." Goodwin goes on to argue that it's absolutely essential that laws, liability and insurance are devised to make scientists in these fields more directly responsible for what they create. That is the only way that the training will be forced to come in contact with the real world it affects.

Genetic Pollution

Scientists from the government-funded National Institute of Agricultural Botany have discovered the first genetically modified (GM) superweeds in Britain, following the spread of

pollen from a genetically modified trial crop to wild turnip
plants. The hybrids were produced after plants in a field of
wild turnip crossed with a nearby test-site of genetically
engineered oilseed rape. Some of the "Frankenstein" plants,
which had inherited their GM parents' herbicide-resistant
genes, were able to breed.
— MARIE WOOLF, *THE INDEPENDENT,* APRIL 18, 1999

Scientists like Mae Wan Ho, Brian Goodwin, Ricarda Steinbrecher and
Christine von Weizsaecker are worried about unexpected risks, such as
the inadvertent introduction of a virus from one species into another,
that could have devastating consequences. But there's a longer-term
potential with deliberate experiments that is even more disturbing.
Genetically engineered organisms are not just kept in a lab or in growth
chambers; they are being intentionally released into the environment,
mostly as agricultural crops.

Jeremy Rifkin, an economist by training, is the founder of the
Foundation on Economic Trends, a Washington-based think-tank that
tries to analyze the effects of new technologies on society. He's also the
author of several best-sellers, including *The Biotechnology Century.* He
says, "We are embarking on what is surely going to be the most radical
experiment on the Earth's systems in all of history. What we're talking
about over the next ten years is the release of thousands and thousands of
novel organisms, transgenic plants and animals proliferating all over the
world. This really is a second genesis, artificially designed in the laboratory and placed out into the ecosystems."

Rifkin's greatest concern is that genetically engineered products are
fundamentally different from other man-made pollutants that are already
causing us so much trouble. He says, "Genetically engineered products
are *alive,* so they're inherently more unpredictable. Because they're alive,
they can reproduce. And they can mutate. They can proliferate. They can
spread quickly across the world. How can you recall a virus, a bacterium
or even a transgenic plant or insect [which carries genes of another species]
back to the laboratory? Even if a small percentage of these transgenic creatures become pests, we're talking about enormous genetic pollution."

This is not hyperbole. We have ample evidence about the hazards
of exotic organisms in a new environment. Rabbits in Australia, zebra

mussels in the Great Lakes, cats on tropical islands, purple loosestrife spreading across North American waterways — all these species were benign or useful in the places in the world where they belonged, but out of the surroundings in which they evolved, where they existed along with other organisms to keep them in check, they have become pests that are devastating local native wildlife and costing billions of dollars a year in lost crops, eradication programs and restoration. If that's what wild creatures that are displaced from their natural habitats can do, what can be expected from life forms with genes spanning species barriers, life forms that are therefore exotic anywhere on Earth?

There already exist genetically engineered products designed to help farmers live weed-free. "Roundup Ready" soybean, canola, corn and potatoes are genetically engineered to resist Monsanto's patented weedkiller, Roundup. This is a clever ploy by Monsanto and other chemical companies to keep farmers hooked on company products. The expensive, patented seed and the herbicide are sold as a package.

Roundup destroys all green, leafy plants. Before the genetic engineers developed Roundup Ready seed, the pesticide had to be applied early in the season, before the emergence of the main crop, so it wouldn't kill those plants. Now farmers can drench their food crops with herbicide all season long, and the food plants won't die — though the crabgrass and milkweed and lamb's quarters that surround the crop will. Many so-called weeds are crucial food for other species, as milkweed is for monarch butterflies.

We're destabilizing nature's balance to accommodate a sophisticated but, one can argue, largely unnecessary technology. There are simpler mechanical ways to deal with weeds, including no-till farming, mulching and companion cropping. But none of these Earth-friendly methods can be patented to make big money. They're not splashy, high-tech, instant fixes. They evolve over years and generations because methods have to be developed at a local level by individuals who care about and observe the crops, soils and wild plants of each locality.

Industrial farmers may think of weeds as competitors for sunlight, space and nutrients, but one person's weed can be another person's, or species', food. Vandana Shiva is a physicist from India. She heads two agencies concerned with agricultural crops and food production and also works with the Third World Network on environmental and justice issues. She has written many books and articles on the politics of food and on biotechnology. She points out that many people get their nutrition from so-called weed species: "In India, at least 80 to 90 percent of the nutrition comes from what the agricultural industry terms 'weeds.' . . . [Industrial agriculturalists] have this attitude that the weeds are stealing from them, so they spray [herbicides like Roundup] on a field which has sometimes 200 species that the women of the area would normally use in various ways as food, medicinal plants or fodder. At the moment, about 40,000 children in India are going blind for lack of vitamin A, only because industrial farming has destroyed so many wild field plants, the sources of vitamin A that were available to the poorest person in the rural areas. With biotechnology, they will increase this lunacy."

Herbicides and pesticides are powerful metabolic inhibitors — that's why they are used. And most have also been shown to be carcinogenic. Roundup is supposed to be a relatively mild compound, but it has been shown to be associated with illness, poisonings, and serious allergic reactions, and it is highly toxic to fish. In fact, it's rated the third most poisonous agrochemical in California. The crops engineered to be resistant to this herbicide are repeatedly dosed with it throughout their growing period; conventional plants would die if they were sprayed with such chemicals. So we are now eating, in our soy and canola, season-long residues of this herbicide, and no tests have ever been performed to find out if that's safe.

We have to ask ourselves, and quickly, if we are getting benefits from these new technologies that are in any way commensurate with their risks. Vandana Shiva says, "There's really a struggle going on between the view that imagines the whole world is a marketplace, and the thousands of cultures that think that we are part of an Earth family. It could be called the web of life. It could be called a democracy of all beings. But once you're able to recognize that you're in that democracy of life, and you accept the fact that all beings have to live, then you shape a whole different set of alternatives and technologies. If you assume you can push every troublesome boll worm to extinction, every troublesome beetle into extinction, then you shape the technologies that you think will make them extinct.

"But of course they're more hardy than we are. They're more resilient than we are. And as is being said more and more, it's the small beasts and the small organisms, especially the microorganisms, that are going to prove to be much more superior in the silly war we have declared on them. The best we can do is accommodate. The best we can do is give each other space. And through that giving of space, we create the sustainable systems that also look after our needs."

Feeding the World

Biotechnology is one of tomorrow's tools in our hands today. Slowing its acceptance is a luxury our hungry world cannot afford.
— MONSANTO PUBLIC-RELATIONS STATEMENT,
REPORTED BY THE AFRICA NEWS SERVICE

[This] monopoly of agricultural-development funds by a narrow set of technologies is dangerous and irresponsible. . . . It is only too obvious to concerned scientists, farmers and citizens . . . that we are about to repeat the mistakes of the insecticide era, even before it is behind us.
— HANS HERREN, DIRECTOR OF THE INTERNATIONAL CENTER
OF INSECT PHYSIOLOGY AND ECOLOGY, NAIROBI, KENYA

Throughout human history, we have used new technologies to increase food yields, always seeking more food for less input and less effort, whether it was a horse to replace human muscle power or a plough as an alternative to sticks. After the Second World War, a revolutionary new kind of farming was developed, one based on the wide use of petrochemical fertilizers, herbicides and pesticides. It also depended on growing large fields of single crops — or monocultures — and the use of heavy machinery. At first, the results seemed miraculous: yields per hectare were doubled and tripled. By the 1960s, it was hailed as the answer to world hunger; it was called the Green Revolution. But by the 1980s, those miracles had begun to evaporate. The increased yields, particularly in the Third World, were illusory.

Vandana Shiva has spent many years studying the legacy of the Green Revolution, and she says, "The issue of more food through the Green Revolution is a construction. It's an illusion. If you reduce food to just wheat and rice — and more and more land has been converted to just growing wheat and rice — and you define rice and wheat as food, then of course you've grown more food, because you have stopped seeing the millets that fed the people, the legumes that fed the people, the oilseeds and the straw that fed the cattle and the soil."

Shiva continues, "You actually have lower biomass production in the monoculture fields of the Green Revolution than [on] a typical polyculture farm of indigenous agriculture. When you get rid of your straw and it stops being edible by cattle, sooner or later you have to use other lands to claim that much fodder. So if your land used to be providing enough fodder for your animals, and food for the family, you now have to use two or three times the amount of land to grow the same amount of food, plus that fodder, for that same unit of a farming family, which has to include its animals. Over time, it means that people stop producing fodder for their cattle. Over time, it leads to the cycle that we've seen take place in England, where farm production of fodder shifted to off-farm purchase of cattle feed. The last round of that was rendered meat, ground up from infected carcasses of sheep and cows, being fed back to the cattle. And we get the mad cow disease. That's how the food-security system of industrial agriculture works." The Green Revolution was expensive. It required costly, energy-guzzling machinery, chemical fertilizers and pesticides. And the ecological cost of degraded soil, resistant pests, toxic pollution and lost biodiversity are yet to be reckoned.

Today around the world, as human populations explode, genetic engineering is touted as the only means of averting mass starvation. Dick Goddown was the vice-president in charge of food and agriculture for the Biotechnology Industry Organization (BIO) when we interviewed him for our radio series in 1997. He stated the promise of biotechnology: "I think that it's the best hope we have, as denizens of this planet, of being able to feed the people who are going to be on it. I don't see anything else on the horizon, and I do see a real, very definite promise in biotechnology. I see very definite evidence of the increased yields that come from genetically engineering plants. And producing more, particularly more of a staple crop, is going to be a subject that we're all going to have to deal with as the population of the Earth increases, perhaps doubles, in the next forty years, and goes from the more than

5 billion people [who] are on the planet right now to somewhere between 8 and 10 billion. Therefore, the potential for agriculture is just phenomenal. Biotechnology will be agriculture and agriculture will be biotechnology in the very short future."

This type of rhetoric stops many well-meaning First World environmentalists in their tracks. How can we stand in the way of feeding starving and desperate people, even if the only solution being offered has so much potential for environmental and health problems? This is Vandana Shiva's response: "Oh, my God, the charity argument! That's on every level a deception. First of all, the kinds of things they're producing don't feed the Third World. Tomatoes don't feed the hungry. Not even soybeans. Soybean goes to feed the pigs and the cattle of the North. It's not the staple of Third World people who are going hungry. Most of the research is not about increasing production. All the investments in agriculture are about increasing chemical sales and increasing monopoly control."

If we look at the major products of biotechnology that are currently on the market, we find agricultural crops like corn, soybeans, cotton and potatoes that have been engineered to resist expensive, patented herbicides, or that have encoded the Bt insecticide so that the whole plant is poisonous to insects. These are crops for northern nations, and they require heavy machinery, huge fields and copious chemical fertilizers, all of which are beyond the means of farmers subsisting on small landholdings. Third World staples that primarily benefit the poor are not primary targets of the biotech industry. "There's another important reason why this would not solve the hunger problem," Shiva explains. "All this is taking place in the private domain, by corporations that are not in the business of charity. They are in the business of selling. The food they will produce will be even more costly. It will not reach the entitlements of the poor."

She continues: "The fiction of population is amazing. Because every time we are told that we need to shift to new forms of producing food, nobody informs the public that the methods being proposed will use more resources to produce the same amount of food. And therefore, we'll actually create a deeper crisis, in terms of poorer populations. If you take the Green Revolution in industrial agriculture, 300 units of input — that is, energy from fertilizers, machines, pesticides and so forth — were used to produce 100 units of food. For organic, biodiversity-intensive agriculture, internal-input agriculture, you need only *five* units of inputs for the same 100 units of food."

Many find it hard to believe that traditional systems — recycling waste back into small, multi-species fields, for example — could be more efficient than modern methods. But all energy, whether in food, muscle power or fuel, represents stored sunlight. And much more stored sunlight is used up by burning petrochemicals for transportation, creating fertilizer and running heavy machinery than in companion cropping, composting and mulching. So when the total amount of energy used to grow and move a crop is weighed against the amount of energy actually in the food, modern agriculture is lavishly inefficient compared with traditional small-scale farming. Perhaps the lesson is that to get at the roots of hunger, we have to examine sociology and politics, not buy into another dubious and potentially disastrous quick technological fix.

Assessing the Risks

It's easy to be carried away by a wonderful idea, especially one that can make a lot of money.
— BETH BURROWS, PRESIDENT OF THE EDMONDS INSTITUTE

The revolution in gene technology is happening extremely quickly. Even though I'm a geneticist, I was unaware of the number of gene-engineered products that had already reached the market until I started working on this radio series and book. If you eat packaged breakfast cereal, ice cream, baby food, canola oil or non-organic soy in any form, you're most likely ingesting genetically modified organisms (GMOs) every day. That means the GMOs are replicating around us and are being absorbed by our bodies as we eat them. And they can't be avoided easily, because in Canada and the United States, there are no labelling requirements to indicate what we're ingesting or what creatures they came from in the first place. Common engineered products include tomatoes with a fish gene, soy and corn with cauliflower viruses and petunia genes, enzymes made by genetically engineered bacteria and yeasts in our breads, prepared foods and soaps, and the increased risks of pesticide ingestion in all Roundup Ready products.

When people realized that genetically modified foods weren't being labelled in Europe, a furore ensued until labelling laws were implemented. Now, huge supermarket chains and food giants like the European branches of Nestlé, Unilever and Burger King have promised to ban genetically engineered products. But none of this has happened in North America. Ironically, if genetically modified foods do have deleterious health effects, the rest of the world can watch North America for signs of what these might be.

Jeremy Rifkin reports, "We know that 2 percent of adults and 8 percent of children around the world have allergies to commonly known foods. We don't know what their allergenic reaction might be to eating foods that have genes from organisms that we have never consumed in all of evolution. The possibility of millions of people around the world being subjected . . . to allergenic reactions to genetic foods . . . is a very real proposition in the next few years."

Christine von Weizsaecker adds, "We will be eating new things. We always have tried new things, but at a completely different pace. . . . If over a few years, you flood whole continents with new substances, you are going to pay a hell of a high price for your learning. If everything is flooded, who will then be able to prove what the cause is? And you know how much suffering came from the time-lag between the first signs of endocrine disrupters, or thalidomide, and the real, final scientific proof." In other words, the risks are huge as we perform a massive global experiment, using ourselves as guinea-pigs.

A chilling example of just how risky things are getting ecologically happened just a few years ago, when a German biotech company engineered a bacterium to get rid of rotting crop wastes on farms. The bacterium was a common soil microorganism called *Klebsiella planticula,* and it brought an unexpected bonus. The engineered bacterium produced a by-product — ethanol — that can be used as a fuel that is far less polluting than gasoline. It seemed like a win-win creation — it would eliminate rotting wastes and decrease greenhouse-gas output when ethanol was used instead of gas. The company applied to field test the bacterium in the United States, and the Environmental Protection Agency (EPA) assigned the research to a small university, Oregon State. Labs routinely test organisms in sterile soil so the variables are under rigid control, but Michael Holmes, the doctoral student assigned to do the experiments, thought that testing in sterile soils didn't make much sense.

He decided to carry out the tests in different kinds of "living" soils, that is, ones with naturally occurring soil organisms in them. To his amazement, he found that every plant that was put into soil with the engineered *Klebsiella* died.

Why did they die? Well, most plants get their nourishment with the help of organisms called mycorrhysal fungi. The fungi live just below the surface of the soil and help make nutrients available to plant roots. When the genetically engineered *Klebsiella* was introduced into living soils, it interfered with this process in a variety of ways, sometimes simply killing the fungi outright. And without mycorrhysal fungi in soils, no plants of any kind can survive. As Beth Burrows, the founder of the Edmonds Institute, an environmental think-tank near Seattle, Washington, says, "Without plants, you don't get animals. And without animals, there are none of us, either. . . . So if we add something into a soil that kills [mycorrhysae], we're essentially cutting our own throats. And if we test in *sterile* soils, we'll never know. Because there's no mycorrhysal fungi in a sterile soil."

It's easy to forget that the living world is far more complex than we know. As Burrows says, "A funny thing happens on farmers' fields. These microorganisms move around. Birds land on soil, and they pick up all kinds of things from the surface. And they get up and they fly off, and they take what they touched with them. As do tractors. As do the feet of farmers. As do cars. As do particles, just dirt particles that fly into the air. You can't contain it. . . . So if I decide I'm going to have *Klebsiella* in my fields, I've made a decision for my neighbour as well. And I might have made a decision for the guy in the next county. And if we get really good birds, I might have made a decision for all America."

The genetically engineered *Klebsiella* could have ended all plant life on this continent. The implications of this single case are nothing short of terrifying. And there are literally thousands of independent biotech labs around the world, industriously developing new living creatures for commercial exploitation without adequate testing.

Don't Worry, Be Happy

> *Could we learn from past experience? Please? [Could we learn] that you don't trust the company that's making the product to tell you about the problems it has? How many times*

do we have to beat our heads against this brick wall before
society in general learns that this is not a good way to do
business? Yes, it may cost a few dollars right now, but down
the line, it could save your life.
— ELAINE INGHAM, SOIL PATHOLOGIST

All kinds of genetically modified organisms like *Klebsiella* are on the market or waiting in the wings. How do we know they're safe? We don't, and won't for years after they are being widely used. How are they licensed? By government agencies that often make their decisions without public input or inspection, and often after heavy lobbying by biotech industries. Who does the testing? Mostly the companies that are developing the products. Testing by the company with the most at stake in marketing the product is the way it has been done for years; only when a government suspects a problem, or is invited to investigate by the company, does it conduct its own tests. And since government downsizing started in the 1980s, fewer and fewer labs and scientists do this work outside private industry.

Elaine Ingham is the soil pathologist at Oregon State University who directed Michael Holmes's research on the *Klebsiella*. She thinks there are serious problems with the testing regimes in most countries. "The testing systems are inadequate. It's a conflict of interest. We're expecting the people who are going to gain profit from these organisms to be honest about the dangers and the difficulties of those products. If they do want to make a huge, enormous profit, it's an immense conflict of interest to expect that they're going to be honest about it. We're all human beings, and we know we don't function that way. . . . We need independent testing agencies to carry out all of this kind of testing. You know, you'd think we would learn from the chemical industry."

Back in the 1940s and 1950s, we were told that all the new petro-chemical fertilizers — herbicides and pesticides like lindane and DDT — were safe. "All these chemical companies said, 'Oh, we've tested it. Don't worry, there are no negative effects,'" says Ingham. Of course, now, fifty years later, countless people, especially children, have suffered cancer and deformities, and we've spent billions on toxic-waste clean-ups. Today the companies that assure us that biotechnology is safe are often the same ones that gave us DDT, PCBs, Agent Orange and all of the other toxins that created health problems as they leaked out of landfills and into water courses.

What about the government institutions that are already set up? In 1998, a scandal shook the United Kingdom when a researcher went public with the dramatic results he got from early tests of genetically engineered potatoes on rats. He found their growth was affected, some developed tumours and some showed significant shrinkage of the brain after only ten days of feeding on genetically modified potatoes. A protein or common virus used in the gene-splicing technique in the engineered potatoes was implicated. Dr. Arpad Pusztai announced his findings to the public because he felt it was his duty as a scientist working for a tax-supported institute. He was immediately forced to "retire" by the government and his institute.

Eventually, the government, faced with citizens who were outraged to discover that they had no idea at all what they were eating, had to take remedial action. Pusztai was reinstated and a ban was imposed on growing genetically engineered crops of any kind in the United Kingdom for three years. There are now laws requiring the labelling of genetically modified foods that come from abroad. Almost every major food chain in the United Kingdom has pledged not to buy them — to be "gene-free" — which has severely affected American grain and soy farmers. And more research is being carried out on the effects of these crops on insects, normal crops and the wild environment.

Canada, the United States, Europe — we're all signatories to documents prepared at the Earth Summit in Rio de Janeiro in 1992. Embodied in those documents was a concept called the Precautionary Principle. Brian Goodwin says, "The Precautionary Principle says that you don't use a technology unless you have very firm safeguards and reasons to believe that there is no real hazard associated with that technology." In other words, the onus would be on companies developing products that have potential repercussions to *prove* that their new addition to the biosphere is not dangerous. At the moment, most of the regulatory agencies that are supposed to protect us leave the burden of proof with the casualties of our new technologies — the victims of Minamata or Love Canal or Bhopal, to say nothing of the destroyed plants, animals and ecosystems all around us.

A Transcalculational World

If you introduce a foreign gene into any genome, then your
first assumption is that something unexpected is going to
happen. You'll be extremely lucky if you have an effect that's
restricted to the particular character you're after — say, . . . a
protein that produces a certain effect on the organism, such as
producing an insecticide and therefore protecting it from
insect attack. You'll be extraordinarily lucky . . . because
genomes are integrated. They're organized. You have to
understand them as wholes, not just as collections of parts.
— BRIAN GOODWIN, THEORETICAL BIOLOGIST

So far, biotechnology hasn't come close to living up to its PR claims. Medical gene therapy is admitted to be an almost complete failure so far. Even the poster child of genetic engineering, bacterially produced human insulin for diabetes, according to British reports, appears to cause comas and other life-threatening problems in around 10 percent of diabetics. Far more worrisome is the fact that reports of these side-effects appear to have been energetically suppressed by the industry. Genetically engineered products that are present in everything from packaged foods to detergents have recently been linked to serious allergies. And virtually *all* genetically engineered agricultural products have been accompanied by problems and failures. Non-pest insects like lacewings, ladybugs and monarchs are being killed by the Bt-engineered crops. Pollen carried away from crop fields by bees and wind is transferring genes to weedy relatives of genetically engineered canola, such as wild turnip. The controversy surrounding these and other products has become so widespread and serious that it has adversely affected stock values and set off a chain of lawsuits against Monsanto and other manufacturers.

Dr. Richard Strohman thinks there's a fundamental problem that underlies the entire application of genetic technology, and that is that genes don't exist in a vacuum. "Crudely put, it's garbage in, garbage out. It's garbage because the assumptions are wrong," he says. What Strohman means is that genetic engineers are not only trying to apply hereditary laws derived from studies *within* species to the transfer of genes *between* species, they also assume the laws that apply to conditions determined by single genes apply to all hereditary diseases or traits. Strohman discusses specifically the work on human diseases, but his ideas apply across the board to all areas of biotechnology.

Monogenic diseases (diseases caused by one gene only), like Huntington's chorea or cystic fibrosis, are very rare. But because genetic fixes may work with monogenic diseases, it has been assumed that they could also be applied to diseases in general. Strohman says, "Why doesn't this single-gene analysis work for complex things like most common cancers or most heart diseases or most cardiovascular problems — the big premature killers and the diseases that take the quality of life away from people in a premature way? Because these are all what we call multifactorial disorders. They have many causes. They utilize many genes, and they're not caused by any one gene. . . . It's impossible to follow the effect of one gene in this matrix of interaction. We say such things are *transcalculational* — that is to say, hopelessly complex."

When interviewed, most of the scientists quoted in this chapter expressed a variety of concerns that at the time were still speculative and unsubstantiated by data. In fact, what has actually happened since those interviews has been far more dramatic. Every single conjectural possibility has come true. The commercial products of genetic engineering, released with increasing rapidity, have turned out to be even more virulent and dangerous than the scientists had imagined. There is now substantial evidence of exactly the type of instability and environmental pollution that critics warned might occur if genetically engineered products were released. The warnings that were raised are being verified in the real world, showing once again that the one-gene, one-trait, reductionist assumptions of commercial biotechnology are dangerously out of date. It may be time to call for a moratorium on genetic releases until more workable paradigms and institutions are in place to assess them.

We need to cast off the simplified models of living organisms proposed by reductionist science, and to realize that they are only caricatures of the real world. Strohman says, "Molecular biologists and cell biologists are revealing to us a level of complexity in life that we never dreamt was there. We're seeing connections and interconnections and complexity that is mind-boggling. It's stupendous. It's transcalculational. It means that the whole science is going to have to change. And this reductionist biology of trying to locate complex things in a single anything . . . is not going to work. We're going to have to accept the challenge of complexity. We're going to need to train scientists differently. We're going to need to mix biologists with engineers and mathematicians with ecologists. They're going to have to learn about the world in which organisms live."

Billions of dollars have now been invested in biotechnology corporations, and their products are beginning to flood the markets. The challenge now is to bring informed critical voices to the discussion about the future of this crucially important area. It is precisely because the technique is so powerful that unhurried, serious debate must counter the headlong rush to apply these new tools.

CHAPTER 5
YOUR MONEY OR
YOUR LIFE FORMS

Genes are the green gold of the twenty-first century, every bit as important to power in the next era as oil and rare metals and minerals were to the Industrial Revolution.

— JEREMY RIFKIN, HEAD OF THE
FOUNDATION ON ECONOMIC TRENDS

When a private or public biotechnology company isolates a gene and then inserts it into another organism, it can then claim ownership of the resulting "new" gene and start making money. That means all of life — every bird and dog and bee, every bit of tissue inside our bodies — is up for sale. Genetically modified mice, sheep, fish, insects, plants and bacteria have already been patented, and companies are claiming royalties on them whenever they're used. Even people are fair game — the government of Iceland recently sold the DNA sequences of all 70,000 Icelanders to a private company.

Jeremy Rifkin, head of the Foundation on Economic Trends in Washington, D.C., and author of fourteen books analyzing the impact of science and technology on our culture, says, "All over the world, global companies are scouting for rare genes in microorganisms, plants, animals and the human population that may be of some value commercially in agriculture, in energy, in bioremediation, in material development, in pharmacy, in medicine. There's a great struggle going on around the world as to who will control these genetic resources, this rich reservoir of genetic information that took millions of years to evolve."

The search for DNA resources doesn't end with plants and other animals. Now we're prospecting for gold inside ourselves. The Human Genome Project has been called the Holy Grail of molecular biology. Scientists from many countries have embarked on a massive undertaking: to map all 3 billion letters in the 100,000 genes that make up the blueprint of our species. This is more than just a scientific breakthrough, it's a business breakthrough as well, because it has been decreed that these discoveries can be privately owned. In his latest book, *The Biotechnology Century,* Rifkin says, "Already corporations are seeking patents on every one of these human genes as they're isolated. Within just a few years, a handful of companies will literally control the genetic blueprint of our species. They will have claimed all one hundred thousand genes as their private property in the marketplace, meaning that any human being that needs access to those genes for medical, screening, or therapeutic purposes will have to pay for that right. The genes of the human species will be controlled as intellectual property, as patents, by a few global companies."

Business corporations can now control these genes through the medium of patenting. But how and when was the patenting of life allowed? It's due almost entirely to a judicial decision made in the United States close to twenty years ago. Rifkin was in the courtroom and describes the event: "In 1980 the United States Supreme Court, by a ruling of 5 to 4, said that General Electric could claim a micro-organism that had been created in the laboratory as a patented invention. That set the precedent for companies all over the world to begin to control the entire genetic commons in the twenty-first century. Only seven years later, in 1987, the U.S. Patent and Trademark Office issued a chilling policy statement in which they said, 'Any organism on this planet, any gene, any cell-line, any organ, any tissue, is potentially patentable as a human invention.' Here, in one regulatory stroke, the U.S. patent office reduced the entire living kingdom, the genetic commons, to the possibility of private property owned and controlled by a handful of multinational corporations."

Rifkin and his organization appealed this narrowly won decision. He says, "Interestingly enough, the appeals court said this microorganism looked more like a chemical than it [did] a honeybee or a plant or a flower. In other words, they looked at the new construct, and it didn't look like an organism. Had General Electric brought a chimpanzee, a bird, [or] a pig, it would have never gotten the patent. It shows you the anthropocentric nature of this decision. What I'm saying is, this is a very thin reed upon which to base the enclosure of the genetic commons of this planet."

Rifkin tries to put this patenting practice into context: "It's comparable to saying, in the last century, if you discovered an element in the periodic table, then it's your invention. Obviously, we would find it rather amusing if someone said, 'Well, I discovered aluminum or oxygen or helium. I isolated it, I had to use my ingenuity to find a process to describe it, therefore I should be able to claim it as an invention for twenty years.' We would say to chemists, 'That's absurd.' Yet the analogy is exact."

The idea of patents was first conceived by Thomas Jefferson. The purpose was to stimulate innovation by rewarding inventors with exclusive rights to their creations for a limited time. When that period was up, the invention would revert to the public domain, where it would continue to benefit society. These days, there are also strong commercial reasons for a company to use patents — to recover its research investments, make a profit, and, of course, secure the new market for itself.

Genetic engineering involves a manipulation of DNA in a naturally occurring organism, and that change means something new has been created. That's how living creatures are rationalized as inventions. The control that patents confer on their holders is the exclusive legal ownership over what they may know, discover or invent. This concept of owning ideas, as well as things, is also called "intellectual property."

Dick Goddown, a former vice-president of the Biotechnology Industry Organization (BIO), which represents more than 700 companies worldwide, is a supporter of such patents. He says, "Patents are the lifeblood of biotechnology. Why? Because they are, in a very real sense, property. They demonstrate what is yours and not someone else's. And therefore they allow you to attract the venture capital, and to attract the stockholders, so that you have the investment, so that you can complete the work and get [a medical] product to the patients [for example]. From laboratory to bedside, the average time is seven years, and the cost is $500 million. . . . A patent, I dare say, is one of the best social compacts that we've ever arrived at. In exchange for the exclusive right to use and produce your invention for a period of years — and it has been seventeen in the United States and now it has changed to twenty — in exchange for that exclusive right, the inventor has to spread his invention on the public record for all others with an interest to be able to share his intellectual perspicacity, his advance, his spark, that magic that he's brought to light. And it has been a compact which has benefited mankind more than anything else that I can think of."

In terms of sheer research output, Craig Venter can be called one of the most productive biotechnologists in the world. He has developed new technologies that have accelerated the rate of decoding the genes for the Human Genome Project. He now runs his own genetic company, the Institute for Genomic Research, in Maryland. His name appeared on the first application to patent human DNA. Venter says, "Patents are very important in terms of developing new drugs. The genes for insulin were patented by Genentech and Eli Lilly, and that's why human insulin is now available around the world as a drug to treat diabetes. So millions of people have human insulin to use. . . . The only reason that it's available commercially . . . is because a pharmaceutical company got a patent on the process to produce it and make it. If it wasn't for intellectual property protection, there would be no human insulin now available as a drug. I mean, it's as simple as that. If people don't like gene patenting, they can send their drugs back to the pharmacy."

Most people in the developed world can afford to pay for expensive drugs like insulin. Adult-onset diabetes, which is tied to obesity, a lack of exercise and diets high in sugar, is a common disease in the industrialized world. Biotechnology is also heavily involved in developing *in vitro* fertilization and other means of making babies available to the infertile. Infertility, too, tends to be a problem that only the richer people of the world can pay to fix. But the diseases that destroy young lives by the millions, like schistosomiasis, malaria and dysentery, are largely ignored by science. Their victims are poor, so there's little money to be made in finding a cure.

Phil Bereano teaches engineering at the University of Washington and helped found the Council for Responsible Genetics. Over the past fifteen years, he's become an expert on the workings of this new industry. I asked him why biotech companies concentrate on First World problems like adult-onset diabetes and infertility. Bereano says the answer is obvious when you think about how these companies operate.

"Who in the corporations determines the design criteria for what form of genetic engineering they're going to have? It's the money-boys. . . . It's the guys who are dealing with the bottom line. The projects that are likely to make them the most money are the projects that are going to be developed, not the projects that correspond to some authentic ordering of human needs."

Not only do private companies decide which areas will be most profitable, they also take advantage of all the work done with public funds in universities and government agencies. With the advent of patenting, the companies can demand the profits without investing in all the research. Bereano says, "This technology of modern genetic engineering was largely created with public funds, with taxpayer funds. . . . And I think that because the purported benefits are for the public, and of course the risks are going to be borne by the public, the public ought to be much more involved in making these decisions. Why do we leave these kinds of decisions up to private entities? Why do we say that they ought to be able to do whatever they want to do? We have to remind ourselves that many important biomedical developments were not patented, like the Salk vaccine. The March of Dimes and Jonas Salk were both against patenting. They felt that it was completely inappropriate for something that was developed with public funds and that was in such public demand."

Eli Lilly and Genentech did not do all, or even most, of the work that led to the development of genetically engineered human insulin. Many years of government, university and other publicly funded studies painstakingly built up the knowledge base that eventually made gene manipulation possible. Yet private companies claim all the profits. Now that concerns have been raised in Britain about the negative effects experienced by thousands of diabetics using genetically engineered human insulin, the companies should be willing to investigate the reported side effects and accept liability for any damage that might be linked to their products. But that, as we shall see, is another story.

Patenting the Air

During colonization, we were told that our indigenous knowledge is unscientific and superstitious. Today the same

Western powers that rejected our systems are patenting and
privatizing our knowledge. Indigenous knowledge related to
the use of neem, basmati, karela, bringal, mustard, amla, jad
amla and many others have been patented. This biopiracy is a
theft of our knowledge, our biodiversity and our very survival.
— PRESS RELEASE OF THE RESEARCH FOUNDATION FOR SCIENCE,
TECHNOLOGY AND ECOLOGY, NEW DELHI

For thousands of years, the people of India revered a beautiful evergreen, the neem tree. They made extracts from it to use as an insect repellent, they isolated oils for soaps and skin cream, they cooked its leaves to make medicines. They even used its twigs as toothbrushes. The tree belonged to everybody, and was part of their culture. Not any more. Biotechnology companies have genetically modified the neem and components extracted from it. What was once free and available to everyone has become private property you have to pay to use.

There are now patents pending on almost anything you can imagine, including an ancient South American staple grain, quinoa; peasant-developed Indian chickpeas; and kava, a plant sacred to and much used by the New Zealand Maori. Patent applications have also been made for various Indian recipes, like a popular fried dumpling, the pakora. And of course, a patent is pending to give the "inventors" of Dolly cloning rights on all mammals, which includes us. Attempts have even been made by the United States government and private companies to patent cell-lines of indigenous peoples.

Andy Kimbrell, a lawyer who runs the International Center for Technology Assessment in Washington, D.C., tries to force U.S. regulatory bodies to face up to the implications of new technologies and regulate accordingly. Kimbrell is suing the EPA over biotechnology issues. He says, "It's quite a remarkable circumstance, and we really are talking about an ethical and legal free-fall, because there is no understanding right now of what is patentable and what is not patentable. It appears that we're seeing the corporate enclosure of literally the entire living kingdom, including the entire animal kingdom, with no real restraints at this point."

Things that have been owned communally for many generations are called a "commons" — like common land. In the eighteenth century, the English government caused enormous suffering when it confiscated lands that had been used communally by villagers for at least a thousand years and redistributed them among the aristocracy so they could farm sheep as a cash crop. This was called the enclosure of the commons. Now we are witnessing the enclosure of the very stuff of life — the enclosure of the gene commons by multinational corporations. All the corporations have to do is alter a single gene in a living organism; they can then say it's a new organism, patent it and claim it as theirs.

Jeremy Rifkin points out one of the ironies of the patenting regime. "None of these corporations [has] ever invented a gene *de novo*. All they are doing is tampering with and modifying genes that already exist. None of these organizations [has] ever created a new organism, either a simple organism or a multicellular organism. They're simply modifying existing organisms that have been the product of millions of years of evolution. I think that we need to understand that these are discoveries of nature. They shouldn't be private inventions. We've got to keep this gene commons open for future generations."

A key example of how closing the gene commons threatens the sharing of scientific information was reported by the *Los Angeles Times* early in 1999. There is now a strain of *Staphylococcus*, the most common infectious agent in hospitals, that is resistant to every antibiotic. Despite the danger this strain poses to public health, government and university scientists have been unable to prise information about the bacterium out of the private companies that are trying to decode its genome. The companies claim they've spent millions, and with a patentable product on the horizon they are not about to give up their information because of public needs.

The delay in making these data public "has slowed research by four or five years," according to Dr. Olaf Schneewind, a leading *Staphylococcus* specialist at UCLA. He says he understands the industry's position, but it doesn't have his sympathy. The resistance genes from this bacterium have the capacity to spread rapidly, and the disease has already killed a man in New York. Government and academic scientists argue forcefully that basic genetic information should be publicly available. Francis Collins, head of the government-funded Human Genome Project, says, "I believe science moves forward in unpredictable ways, and with something as basic as the instruction book of organisms, the more people who have a chance to look at it, the better the likelihood that a key insight will occur. The question we ought to be asking is, 'What is good for the public?' I'm not sure that all this gold rush is going to serve the public's needs very well in the long run."

Because of the Staph crisis and the industry's refusal to help, the U.S. government has had to commit more money to repeat what has already been done and decode the bacterium's DNA. No one thought that if it came down to a public health crisis, the industry would refuse to help. Since the information was available in the private sector, government agencies simply assumed they could get at it if they really needed to. They were wrong.

Global Pressures

> **Farmers' Group Storms Mahyco Office in Hyderabad**
> *Scores of activists belonging to Andra Pradesh Ryto Sangham*
> *stormed the regional office of Mahyco Company on Monday to*
> *protest against efforts to introduce genetically modified seed.*
> *Mahyco is the joint venture partner of Monsanto.*
> — *INDIAN EXPRESS,* BANGALORE EDITION, DECEMBER 2, 1998

The notion that you can patent life has now gone global. In 1995, the World Trade Organization (WTO) passed sweeping new rules under the General Agreement on Tariffs and Trade (GATT) that have changed lives around the world. Under these rules, countries cannot use national laws to prevent anyone from patenting living organisms within their territories. Chee Yok Ling, a lawyer and activist who operates out of Malaysia, says, "The whole fight in the eighties and into the early nineties under the GATT trade regime was to have an international agreement on intellectual property rights. Until then, countries had a national choice on whether they wanted to sign an international agreement or not. Whether a patent or a new invention would be protected in my country would depend upon a balance of national policy, public interest and corporate interest, with national laws being passed accordingly. For instance, in many countries, like India, pharmaceutical products were exempted from patent protection because [the people there] felt [that] for their national public health interest, drugs should be cheaply available. Food products [might also be exempted]. Because of food security, we would not want to have patent laws that protected one company's seeds over, say, locally developed varieties. But now all that has changed. Under the intellectual property rights agreement at the World Trade Organization at the international level, which all the countries have signed onto, . . . we are obliged now to change our national laws and honour all these patents."

Interestingly enough, most of the world's biodiversity — that is, the raw material of genetic resources that biotechnology requires — is in the southern hemisphere. But most of the biotech companies are in the industrialized nations of the North. This is why many in the Third World refer to the patenting of life as "biopiracy."

Vandana Shiva, a physicist and expert on food issues in the Third World, says biopiracy is nothing more than a modern version of the old colonial regimes. "Patents are a wonderful mechanism of collecting rentier incomes from things that nature does freely, that people do freely. [They force] people to make payments for what has been theirs, and their right: the public commons. In the 1920s, the British placed a tax on salt, salt-making, as a way of financing their armies. And Gandhi went out and said, 'No, this has been given freely to us by nature. We make it with our intelligence; we need it for our survival. We will not pay you the taxes you want, because you have not created the salt, and we must have it to live.' In a way, life patents are 5,000 times worse than the salt taxes of the British regime of those days. It's like patenting air! Because, after all, it's the biodiversity in life forms that makes all life possible. It's as vital to life as air itself. It's a condition of our life process. And when our life process and elements of our life process start to get patented, and someone can make money every time we try to use them, it is really the ultimate of organized greed. It has [not only] generated . . . an ethical crisis, but is really threatening to generate a crisis of survival."

In India, people may be more aware of this than anywhere else. Indians have staged huge demonstrations, burned test plots of genetically engineered crops and destroyed the offices and storage facilities of the major corporations involved, mostly Monsanto. And out in the countryside, the farmers of India are fighting back in a unique and preemptive way. Vandana Shiva runs an organization called the National Program for Conservation of Native Seed Varieties, which fights life patents. She says, "In every village where we work, every farmer we work with takes a pledge: 'This is a legacy I have received from my ancestors, and I make a promise to myself that I will ensure that this legacy passes onto future generations. I will protect it; I will defend it; and I will not allow it to be privatized.' Through this, we are setting up these regions, which we call patent-free zones, where the people basically recognize that these are laws that are so immoral and so unjust that they don't have to be obeyed."

This isn't just a Third World problem. It concerns everybody. And it creates ethical as well as economic and safety issues. Because of biotechnology, we have to ask questions we have never before had to face. Who owns trees or seeds or dogs or the secretions of your pancreas? Ferdinand Magellan and Christopher Columbus claimed ownership of the New World simply because they had sailed up to it. Is finding a medicinal plant in a Third World country and claiming ownership of it in order to charge royalties any different? That's what biotechnology companies do.

There is a startling lack of clarity in the patenting regime; as the lawyer and activist Andy Kimbrell says, "They've patented sheep and fish that have been genetically altered, [but] they've patented a number of animals that have not been genetically altered. Rabbits that are used for HIV testing, nematodes and various insects that have been taken from various parts of the world and brought to the United States have all been patented. The only interventive steps have been that they've been taken from one country, where they were indigenous, to another country, where they are not. That's supposed to be the inventive step. So you have what I like to call biocolonization; transport is now the only interventive step you need for the patenting of life." As a result, the U.S. government and a large number of private biotech companies are embroiled in international disputes. India, Ecuador, and Thailand are all fighting for their rights to hold onto their indigenous plants and breeds.

Rights and Responsibilities

Data from the Iowa State University department of entomology shows a relationship between the mortality of larvae of the monarch butterfly under field conditions with Bt corn.
— JOHN OBRYCKI, PROFESSOR OF ENTOMOLOGY, AND LAURA HANSEN, GRADUATE RESEARCH ASSISTANT

Water Companies Demand a Moratorium on the
Commercial Planting of Genetically Modified Crops
Amid Fears That Chemical Used on Them May Pollute
Rivers, Lakes and Reservoirs.
— *THE* LONDON *TIMES,* HEADLINE, MARCH 5, 1999

It's clear that holding patents offers substantial benefits to corporations:
enormous profits and an almost limitless field of material out of which to
create products. So what are their responsibilities? After all, genetically
engineered crops and animals could have negative effects, both on the
people who consume them and on the environment in general. In the
preceding chapter, we looked at a few of the potential hazards, like those
caused by the engineered *Klebsiella planticula* bacterium. There are
already indications of some negative effects of genetically engineered
foods and drugs on human health. For example, when a British scientist,
Arpad Pusztai, fed rats genetically engineered potatoes, he reported serious negative effects such as brain shrinkage and damage to the immune
system. A recent study in Sweden links exposure to glyphosate, which is
sold as a herbicide used to spray on genetically modified crops, to an
increased risk for non-Hodgkin's lymphoma, a serious cancer that affects
young people. And we haven't even mentioned biological warfare. As
long as biotech labs are so uncontrolled and unpoliced, there is nothing to
prevent some of them from experimenting with ebola and anthrax and all
the other potential biological weapons that ought to be very seriously
controlled.

If any of these frightening possibilities becomes widespread — and
some are already a reality — who is liable for the damages these new products cause? We all assume the inventors, those companies that hold the
patents and are demanding all the rewards of their research, will be held
responsible. In fact, under patent law they are not liable at all. Vandana
Shiva has made a study of the situation. "Patent law is a very interesting
form of property," she says. "With all other forms of property, you have
ownership rights; but along with them, you have responsibilities." If you
build a building that falls down or a car engine that blows up, you can be
sued by both the buyers and government agencies. This is not true in the
case of patent owners. "Patent law is a kind of ownership law in which

there is no liability," says Shiva. "There's no responsibility. There are only rights to exclude others from the use of whatever is your patent."

As things stand, the responsibility for any damage that biologically engineered products may cause falls upon the human victims or their governments. In fact, the current wording of the unfinished international Biosafety Protocol, which is being negotiated under the auspices of the UN's Biodiversity Convention, specifies that the importing country, not the patent holder or even the exporter, is liable for any problems that may arise. And if those problems affect nature or wild creatures — well, no one is responsible at all.

Some of the reasons for this situation are those familiar concerns: free trade and global competitiveness. Countries that have become signatories to GATT and the WTO are forced to reduce trade barriers and open themselves to new products in order to remain involved in international trade. One example of what can happen involves the hormones used widely in Canada and the United States to make beef cattle bulk up faster. A European panel on veterinary drugs says at least one of these hormones is carcinogenic. The European Union wants to keep the hormones out of its citizens' diets. The case was taken before the WTO, which found against the EU. In June of 1999 the EU said they would not accept the hormones, so they are subject to sanctions. The EU will lose about $128 million in trade concessions each and every year these hormones are kept out. If this cost proves too much, and the EU does allow the products in, and it then discovers that in fact they are dangerous after all, the manufacturer won't be liable. The regulatory agencies that tried to keep the products out in the first place will be held responsible for having allowed them in! It's bizarre. The biotech industry is totally off the hook.

Vandana Shiva points out another reason for the double-think surrounding the issue. "Governments are helping the companies get away with definitions that treat a genetically engineered crop the same as the parent for regulatory purposes. When it comes to getting a patent, you of course don't say a genetically engineered soybean is like conventional soy, but when it comes to safety regulations it's very commonly accepted that it is just the same. And that's the basis on which the U.S. FDA gives its clearances for safety. A genetically engineered potato with chicken genes in it will still be treated as a conventional potato, and therefore you will not look at the implications of the chicken gene in it. In fact, you're not allowed to look."

The story of how government regulations and industry interests became entangled is a long and delicate one. It's perhaps enough to say that in the United States alone, people have moved from very high-level positions in government regulatory agencies like the Food and Drug Administration, the EPA and the Department of Agriculture to biotech giants like Dupont and Monsanto. Opponents of the technology call this the revolving door; people whose careers were made in government regulatory agencies are recruited by Monsanto and vice versa. For example, Mickey Kantor, President Clinton's former secretary of commerce and U.S. trade representative, is now on the board of directors of Monsanto. Marcia Hale, Clinton's former assistant for intergovernmental relations, now holds the corresponding job, director of international government affairs, at Monsanto. Linda Fisher, who used to be assistant administrator of the EPA's department in charge of regulating pesticides and toxic substances, is now vice-president of government and public affairs at Monsanto.

So ubiquitous is the biotechnology industry's influence on government that there have been controversies and at least one scandal in other countries as well. In Canada, a Health Canada official claims that Monsanto offered the department $1 to $2 million with the condition that the company be given approval to market its controversial milk-production hormone, rBGH, without being required to submit further studies. CBC Radio recently reported that Agriculture Canada is permitting Monsanto to conduct its own research at government facilities. When asked by Tory Senator Mira Spivak to explain his ministry's relationship with a corporation it is supposed to be regulating, and to disclose how much money the ministry has accepted from the biotech giant, the minister of agriculture refused to divulge the information — on the grounds of commercial privacy.

Monsanto still indignantly insists that all its products are safe, even after Canada's ban and Europe's moratoriums. But it is instructive to remember that Monsanto Corporation was involved in the production and sales of DDT, Agent Orange and PCBs, which it also defended vigorously before they were banned. Monsanto also launched attacks against Rachel Carson and her seminal book *Silent Spring* back in the 1960s, taking out full-page ads that mocked and denigrated Carson.

The company continues to produce many substances banned in North America, like Alachlor and the extremely hazardous Butachlor, for export to countries whose laws are not as strict as ours. And Monsanto is a major producer of dioxins; the EPA has estimated that dioxins cause up to 3 percent of all cancers. Monsanto has been charged with manipulating data in studies it funded in the 1980s that exonerated dioxins of all danger. Despite a track record that includes four major convictions for various offences, such as neglect and widespread dissemination of misinformation, and including a $108 million liability finding in the case of the leukemia death of a Texas employee — despite ranking by the EPA as one of the largest corporate generators of toxic emissions into the U.S. environment — Monsanto obviously still has influence in high places.

As more and more products of Monsanto and other biotech companies are introduced into the food chain without rigorous government testing, it will become very difficult to trace any negative effects back to their cause. Vandana Shiva says that "not only . . . are we playing around with a very, very ecologically risky technology, we are playing with it in a context where [we are prevented from knowing] . . . what its risks might be. And we won't even know ten years down the line, because the early links in the chain of knowing are being wiped out. They're being erased."

Sterilize the World

Farmers who find that stray genetically modified seeds have blown onto their land from neighbours' fields could face massive fines if the agrochemical giant Monsanto wins a test case in a Canadian court. Percy Schmeiser, a farmer in Saskatchewan, is being pursued by Monsanto for damages and the profits from his fields because the company claims that the patent on its genetically modified (GM) seeds has been violated.
— MARIE WOOLF, *THE INDEPENDENT*, MARCH 14, 1999

Throughout human history, farmers have always selected and saved their seed for the next season, and shared and traded them with others. We have invoked gods, performed ceremonies and painstakingly developed seeds and techniques in order to increase the fertility of the life forms on which we depend for food. In late February 1998, a new development occurred in the biotechnology crop industry that should have set off alarm bells in the minds of every scientist, environmentalist and farmer. The U.S. Department of Agriculture and the American seed company Delta and Pine, an affiliate of Monsanto, were granted a patent on a genetic technique that sterilizes seeds for all time. Sterile seeds produce only one generation of plants. The new seeds are sterile because the patent holders want to be sure that farmers have to pay for new ones every year. This technique appears to have been created solely for the purpose of protecting and enhancing market share. Right now, companies like Monsanto pay a lot of money for their agents to police farmers' fields to make sure the farmers are not planting patented seeds without paying royalties. The Terminator gene, as it's called, will make policing unnecessary and also increase profits. As usual, the potential dangers of this gene have not been widely discussed or even explored, yet it is not far-fetched at all to imagine that these sterile plants may be able to transfer their traits to non-sterile varieties growing nearby.

The Terminator concept can be applied to animals as well as plants. A genetically engineered virus being researched in Australia could make all infected rabbits sterile. Bob Phelps, an environmentalist with an Australian group called Gene Ethics, says that one of Australia's national research organizations, the Commonwealth Scientific and Industrial Research Organisation (CSIRO), "is attempting to genetically engineer the myxamatosis virus in order to transfer the outside coat of the sperm or egg of rabbits into the virus. And the idea is that the virus would then be released to the environment, and would infect the rabbits. They would become vaccinated against their own eggs or sperm, and they would become incapable of being fertilized and could not produce young."

Obviously, Australians wish to eliminate rabbits, which have been terribly disruptive ecologically, but as Bob Phelps points out, "There are many downsides with such a strategy. First, they would need to be very certain that the viruses being used would not transfer to other species. And second, if a live virus for the sterilization of rabbits, for example, were released in Australia, then it's very reasonable to expect that it would go worldwide, as other viruses of rabbits have. . . . Do we really want these animals to disappear from the face of the Earth because we sterilized them? I don't think so."

Rabbits could be the least of our worries. Phelps says, "Perhaps the most dangerous is the work being done in India. Australian researchers are collaborating with Indian researchers and working on the sterilization of human beings using a similar strategy. They are not necessarily using live viruses, but [they are] using viruses nonetheless as a way of either temporarily or permanently sterilizing Indian women. And this, of course, raises tremendous ethical and social, as well as scientific, issues. In fact, this whole use of gene technology for so-called immuno-sterilization, the automatic sterilization of the organism, is fraught with some very real perils and dangers."

Liability and Insurance

> *European governments are drawing up contingency plans for a nuclear fallout–style emergency involving genetically modified organisms [GMOs]. A five-point Emergency Response Plan has been formulated by the European Commission, designed to cope if genetically modified plants result in widespread illness or the death of wildlife. The draft directive, set to be adopted by ministers across Europe, includes plans to "decontaminate" affected areas and destroy plants and animals exposed to GMOs. The plan is designed to prevent a human health disaster and stop genetically modified plants breeding wildly with native species.*
> — MARIE WOOLF, *THE INDEPENDENT*, APRIL 4, 1999

Who would be responsible if one of these sterilization methods got out of hand and threatened to wipe out an entire species? Could we control it? If one of the new engineered food crops ends up with unexpected side-effects, could we trace the source of the problem? Two points are very much at issue here: first, patent rights are not accompanied by social responsibilities; and second, the very nature of patenting involves industrial secrecy. As a result, getting detailed information about a product and its possible dangers would be as difficult as identifying and controlling the source of the problem.

We have been through similar situations already, and we should not forget what happened. The Union Carbide India Limited (UCIL) chemical leak at Bhopal, India, in 1984 was just such a disaster. Unlike the biotech companies, UCIL was insured, but the victims were never adequately compensated. India itself shouldered most of the burden of this catastrophe, for the simple reason that India was where the deadly leak took place. The factory was manufacturing a common pesticide, but the people trying to help the victims couldn't get full information about the chemicals involved because the poison was a patented, industrial secret. Chee Yok Ling, a lawyer with the Third World Network, is all too familiar with this kind of story. "We know from a whole history of consumer rights and environmental rights that if you don't attach liability to the release of a product, when things go wrong, companies say, 'Oh, we're sorry. We didn't know it would do that.' Or they just keep quiet. They go on to the next product; they go on to the next country. Who has to clean up the mess? National governments are usually stuck with it."

The doctors working with victims during the Bhopal disaster needed all the information they could get. If they'd had it right away, they might have saved more lives and saved more people from being blinded. But a corporation doesn't have to reveal patent information, even to a national government. Chee Yok Ling knows patent law, and she maintains that without strong regulatory controls companies left to police themselves will have the same response in a genetic emergency as Union Carbide India Limited had at Bhopal. "They will say, 'Oh, it's confidential business information. It's protected by a patent.' Crucial information that [is needed] . . . to make an assessment of whether a product is safe or not will not be there; most of the time, it will be blocked by the patent."

The biotechnology industry makes anybody who brings up such matters look hysterical. These things haven't happened yet, so even talking about them is said to be overly pessimistic in the face of the bright biotechnological future. Unfortunately, history shows us that all kinds of things — petrochemicals, CFCs, toxic dumps and nuclear power — that we thought, even insisted, were benign, turned out to be extremely dangerous. History informs us that caution is well warranted when it comes to buying into a powerful new technology. We must not forget why the regulation of such materials was created in the first place; we must not always wait until suffering begins before we legislate. Yok Ling says, "Strong consumer laws in countries like the United States or Canada . . . came because of disasters. . . . This history shows us that liability is absolutely crucial to balance the rights of different sectors of society. Strong liability laws are also a very [powerful] incentive for companies to have high standards of behaviour, because otherwise they will have to pay the price."

How do commercial interests usually protect themselves from liability claims? Through insurance. In fact, in our society, the litmus test for safety *is* insurance. You can be insured for almost anything if you pay enough for the premium, but if the insurance industry isn't willing to bet its money on the safety of a product or a technology, it means the risks are simply too high or too uncertain for them to take the gamble. What does this mean for biotechnology? Let's say a modified virus escapes into the environment and begins replicating. It wouldn't be like other forms of pollution because it couldn't be cleaned up like an oil spill. It wouldn't even degrade over time like nuclear waste. And its interaction with other organisms in the environment would be completely unpredictable.

Brian Goodwin is a theoretical biologist at Schumacher College in Devon, England, and an independent scientist — that is, he does not depend on private industry for grants or position. His independence and biological expertise have made him a major voice in the United Kingdom in discussions about how to regulate this new biological technology. He reports on the alarming fact that "insurance companies will not sell insurance to biotech companies, because they know that the results of using genetically engineered organisms cannot be predicted. There is no satisfactory risk-assessment procedure. And the fact that insurance companies won't undertake this shows that this is a very, very unreliable technology."

Jeremy Rifkin concurs. "The fact is, and I think that the public doesn't know this, there is no insurance against catastrophic loss from introducing these organisms anywhere in the world. The insurance industry has spoken on this. They're not willing to place insurance premiums on the potential for loss in introducing these organisms. The reason is that there is no predictive ecology. There is no risk-assessment science by which to judge what might happen when you place one of these organisms in the environment. The insurance industry understands that, and that's why they're not willing to insure this industry."

There are already problems with genetically engineered organisms around the world. There are problems with contamination in organic crops, for example. Two Saskatchewan farmers are being sued by Monsanto for growing genetically engineered seed without paying their royalties. But one farmer maintains that his crop was contaminated by wind or spillage, and is now countersuing. The other says he exchanged seed with a neighbour, as farmers have done for thousands of years, without knowing what he was getting. Neither Monsanto nor the farmers can be insured against these kinds of problems; but Monsanto, of course, can afford more lawyers.

In Canada, the National Farm Union (NFU) is demanding that Ottawa make agro-biotech firms liable for damages caused by genetic pollution; otherwise farmers believe they will have to shoulder the liability themselves. The NFU's Saskatchewan coordinator, Stewart Wells, says that he and other organic farmers could lose their certification and their livelihoods as a result of contamination from pollen drift. He points out, "Tax money helps their research, but the profits are always privatized." Ann Clark, an agronomist at the University of Guelph, says that Canada is typical in that $700 million of taxpayer money is going annually to further biotech research, while almost none is earmarked for risk assessment.

Jeremy Rifkin is so sure horrifying scenarios are coming that he thinks genetic engineering in agriculture will be forced out of business because of its extreme danger. "I suspect that we'll end up rejecting genetic engineering in agriculture," he predicts. "We'll end up rejecting the release of massive numbers of organisms into the environment, because we're going to learn in the next few years that the environmental risks of extending genetic pollution across this planet far exceed any short-term benefit we might get from placing any of these organisms into the environment in the first place."

We can only hope that none of these lessons will be as devastating as what could have happened if the *Klebsiella planticula* bacterium had been released — and that we won't see a man-made plague on the order of other horizontal-gene-transfer plagues of the past, like the 1918 flu pandemic.

What's in It?

> *Canadians generally remain confident in the safety of GMOs, but [Ray] Mowling [Monsanto chief in Canada] added that one cannot ignore potential problems, such as increasing calls for the labelling of GMOs and non-GMO products. He noted that while there is a hold in Canada on regulations to label products that have been changed in composition or ingredients relative to the traditional commodities, there is growing pressure to implement such rules.*
>
> — REPORT FROM A SPEECH GIVEN AT THE CANADA GRAINS COUNCIL'S 30TH ANNUAL CONFERENCE IN WINNIPEG, APRIL 14, 1999

Our health and well-being are directly related to the quality of our food. After all, when we take nourishment into our bodies, digest it, then incorporate it into our cells, food becomes us. Some of the main products of biotechnology are what the industry calls novel foods. Genes from a wide array of sources — viruses, bacteria, plants, mammals, reptiles, fish — are being put into our food crops. We've always assumed that regulatory bodies like the Food and Drug Administration (FDA) in the United States and the Food Inspection Agency in Canada exist to ensure the safety of our food. Furthermore, as citizens of a democratic society, we assume that we have the right to decide what to put into our bodies. But in order to do that, we have to know what's in the things we eat. That means they have to be labelled. Currently, genetically engineered foodstuffs are not labelled in either the United States or Canada, although increasingly they are being labelled all over Europe.

Andy Kimbrell has been pressuring the U.S. FDA to label genetically engineered food. He is angry about their response. "The FDA, in truly one of the major sell-outs to corporate interests that I've witnessed in my many years here in Washington, D.C., decided that the foods that have been genetically engineered should not be labelled, that they should not even have to go through what's generally regarded as safe certification, which is the basic requirement when you try to put a new element into the food chain." Kimbrell thinks it's very important, in terms of both health issues and ordinary democratic rights, that people know what's in the food they're eating. And as he says, "If the biotechnology industry thinks its food is safe or its food may be better than the food that is out there, well, [it] certainly [has] the money to advertise." But right now, in the western hemisphere, the fact is that there are dozens of novel engineered foods out there — engineered soy in our cereal, engineered canola in our mayonnaise, engineered potatoes in our fries — that are not labelled.

Andy Kimbrell tells a story that suggests that in Canada and the United States, we shouldn't assume our interests are being taken care of. "In perhaps one of the most shocking examples, we've recently discovered that the United States Department of Agriculture has, without telling the public, been allowing into slaughterhouses and into the food chain animals that have been involved in experiments making them transgenic. These are animals that have foreign genes in every one of their cells, and that have been part of experiments by major researchers and corporations. . . . These are animals with human genes; these are animals that have a variety of crippled viruses in them. They did this without consulting Congress. They did this without making it public. These animals have been in the food chain now since 1995. And this is really a shocking example of how an agency is doing nothing to protect the public interest, and absolutely everything to protect private interests."

Our new Canadian Food Inspection Agency has declined to label any of the genetically manipulated food we're eating. Public interest and environmental groups are pressuring for labels. Resistance to labelling is coming from the biotechnology industry. It has convinced the government that this material is safe, and it offers a large variety of reasons why labelling is just not necessary.

Russ Schneider works for Monsanto on regulatory issues. I asked him why industry doesn't want labels on food if their products are so good, but I felt his reply was evasive and didn't address the issue. He said, "Are we going to push . . . labelling of all biotech products? I can't say that we are. I don't know that, and I don't think that we would. I don't think that it is appropriate across all commodities. And for a number of reasons, whether they are just through segregation of all the commodities or handling of the commodities. . . . And where do you stop? I think that becomes one of the real difficulties. It's pretty easy to label a potato. It's pretty difficult to label soybeans that may be in tofu, or may not be. And that leads to the possibility that the labels may say something, that they may or may not be produced. I don't know how accepting that would be to the public either."

Schneider supports the industry's contention that it's technically impossible to segregate genetic from non-genetic varieties of, say, corn or soybean because they are so ubiquitous in prepared foods that it would be a bureaucratic nightmare. In North America, manipulated and normal crops are usually just mixed together. At first, the industry said that foods in which genetically altered crops were mixed could not later be identified, but that is simply untrue; if it were impossible, Monsanto wouldn't be able to keep track of who was growing its crops, and wouldn't be able to sue people growing unauthorized seed. Andy Kimbrell says, "The companies themselves have put markers into these foods . . . so they can test whether that food is consistent, whether that gene addition is there. . . . So it is knowable. It is not as if now that the genie is out of the bottle, we have no recourse but to eat these foods. No, we can test whether that food is genetically engineered or not."

Letting the genie out of the bottle seems to be what the industry was trying to do when it first introduced these foods into Europe about three years ago. They were simply slipped into the food chain unannounced. In 1996, 2 percent of U.S. soybean shipments to Europe were transgenic. The industry claimed that the food had passed government regulations, so there was nothing to announce. And since up to 70 percent of packaged foods contain soy, they had a pretty strong guarantee everyone would soon be eating it.

When Europeans realized there was a new factor in their food, there was a massive protest and blockade. Arnaud Apoteker is a biologist and the chargé d'affaires of Greenpeace International's campaign to protest transgenic crops. When ships full of Roundup Ready soy arrived from the United States, Greenpeace members put inflatable boats in front of them to prevent them from docking, or they chained themselves to mill doors so the shipment couldn't go in for processing. Apoteker says, "It was very symbolic, because obviously we cannot do that for years. . . . In Belgium, the industry asked the judge to put fines on us, which were really expensive. . . . It was like $15,000 an hour. So we had to stop blockading in some instances. In Portugal, when we tried to prevent a ship from unloading, police fired at our activists. In Spain, our activists have been beaten by the police. That means there must have been a very big pressure from the industry to make sure we could not prevent the unloading of this material. And in front of the headquarters of ISA, Nestlé, Danon, Unilever, or sometimes Monsanto, we blocked the entrance. . . . In Belgium, we dumped five tons of soybean just in front of the door of Monsanto to prevent employees getting in or out."

This is environmental-protection hardball, but it got people's attention. Today, only two years after the campaign began, Nestlé and Unilever, as well as virtually all the major supermarkets in the United Kingdom and several more in France and Spain, have pledged to become "gene-free." A full moratorium on growing genetically modified crops is in effect in Great Britain, and there is a *de facto* moratorium in the rest of the European Union. It's not just because of the protests, of course; recent research is confirming many of the fears of the opponents of genetic engineering. But the campaign alerted Europeans to the fact that they didn't know what was in their food.

Europeans have massively demanded labelling of genetically engineered foods, and they're finally getting it. In other words, the industry is now having to do what it once claimed was impossible — segregate genetically engineered crops — if it wants to keep the European market. This means that food giants like ADM and A.E. Staley are refusing to buy U.S. soy and corn unless it can be certified "gene-free." It also means that a country like Brazil, which did not yet have widespread plantings of genetically modified soy, is demanding extensive environmental-assessment procedures before it will begin planting transgenic crops, so it can continue to supply Europe. But it also means that the industry is redoubling its efforts to remove national laws that are barriers to commerce, and that it will challenge these laws more and more at the level of the WTO.

We have to remember that we have not always had food-labelling laws. Only a hundred years ago, manufacturers were still putting lead into children's sweets for colour, tapeworms into capsules as diet pills, and morphine and laudanum into medicinal tinctures without any indication. Every generation has to make sure that things do not slip back to the bad old days.

Brian Goodwin, the biologist who is involved in the British genetic engineering controversy, says, "You would never allow a new drug to be produced without a clear label, without knowing what company produced it, without knowing exactly where it was produced and even under what conditions, what batch it came from and so on. Genetically modified foods ought to be put in the same category as drugs because of their potential harm. They're actually even more dangerous than drugs, because after all, we eat a lot more food during the course of our lifetime than we take drugs. Even if there are small effects, they can accumulate over years. And therefore people should have the right to say, 'I'm not going to eat genetically modified food because I have no confidence that this is going to be safe for the whole of my lifetime.' Now that's a kind of baseline, it seems to me, for consumers."

Bioweapons

We have reached a point now where there is an obvious need for an international convention to control biological weapons.

— SPOKESMAN FOR PORTON DOWN,
BRITAIN'S BIOLOGICAL DEFENCE ESTABLISHMENT,
QUOTED IN *THE TIMES* (LONDON), NOVEMBER 1998

So far, we've been talking about the unpredictable behaviour of organisms that were designed to be benign. What about the other side of the coin — organisms deliberately designed to do harm? If important crop plants are sterilized to ensure a high price for them, couldn't they also be sterilized to starve a political or ethnic enemy? In 1967, a monkey virus escaped from a factory in Marburg, East Germany, and killed a number of workers. The virus, which was related to ebola, caused a horrible disease in which the victims drown in their own blood. A subsequent death a few years later in a Soviet-run research facility showed that the Soviets had seen the potential for using the Marburg virus as a bioweapon. They wanted to make it into a powder so it could be loaded into a missile aimed at the United States.

The Soviets were undoubtedly not the only ones with such ideas. There's a lot of money to be made in developing biological weapons for a wide variety of clients. Unlike nuclear technology, biological weapons are relatively simple, cheap and extraordinarily portable and easy to use. It's a combination that could prove irresistible to terrorists or renegade countries. Bob Phelps of the Gene Ethics Network says, "We have computer hackers. Why not gene hackers? It would only take, for example, somebody to genetically manipulate an existing pathogenic organism and release it to have a new and perhaps untreatable strain of some disease."

The whole spectre of bioweapons use is so horrible that most of us don't want to think about it. But it was a major impetus and funding source for biotechnology in its early days. Biological warfare was discredited in the 1970s, and most countries in the world signed a convention banning it on the grounds that it was useless weaponry: whatever you infected the enemy with could turn around and get you. But Andy Kimbrell says, "With the advent of biotechnology during the Reagan administration, . . . there was a whole renewal of interest in biological warfare. They realized that with genetic engineering, they could create designer weapons very specifically targeted at certain plants, animals and ethnic groups, through a greater understanding of the genetic makeup of those particular organisms. And they began a multi-billion-dollar program with over 120 university laboratories around the country, a program that was pretty much secret, to work and engineer the most dangerous pathogens known to man. We're talking about anthrax and botulism and venom. Every virus, bacterium and toxin you can think of that is quick-acting and deadly, they were working on it. . . . This use of biotechnology has been pretty much forgotten."

A recent scandal in Israel revealed that the Israelis were working on a disease weapon that would strike only ethnic Arabs. Most Israelis were horrified and demanded an investigation. But there is evidence that many countries are looking into similar weapons. And of course, like everything else in biotechnology, things may not end up working the way their creators hope.

Canada has a bioweapons laboratory in Suffield, just outside Calgary, Alberta. Like the Americans, we're told the laboratory is concerned only with defence against potential weapons that may end up in the hands of our enemies. However, to test antidotes and other defences, they first need the offensive bioweapons. So the distinction between offensive and defensive strikes me as pretty illusory.

What to Do

We, the undersigned scientists, call upon our Governments to:
Impose an immediate moratorium on further environmental
releases of transgenic crops, food and animal-feed products for
at least five years; Ban patents on living organisms, cell-lines
and genes; Support a comprehensive, independent public
enquiry into the future of agriculture and food security for all,
taking account of the full range of scientific findings, as well
as socioeconomic and ethical implications.
— WORLD SCIENTISTS' STATEMENT CALLING FOR A MORATORIUM
ON GM CROPS AND BAN ON PATENTS, APRIL 1999

The genetic engineering revolution has developed very quickly, but the
European rejection of this technology shows that it can still be controlled
if we act now. Vandana Shiva predicts, "There's going to be a contest
between coercive power, the manipulation of government systems, and
the public awareness and public consent to all this. The consumers and
citizens of the world are not nincompoops. The people of the Third
World are not imbeciles. Our voices need to be heard too."

At the moment, because of the untested, unregulated nature of these
new products, we can say for sure that only *one* group will benefit from
their introduction: the companies that make them. These products have
been put out on the market without public input and without labelling.
What recourse is left to an individual who doesn't want to eat new, genetically modified organisms, new viruses and bacteria, or new vegetables
containing genes from toads and frogs? Christine von Weizsaecker says,
"If people want to choose, they now have to organize. They have to . . .
defend a right that they always had, and that is to eat free-of-gene-tech
food. . . . Labelling is crucial. But patenting is also crucial. Because if there
is no patenting, the incentive to clog the market with thousands and
thousands of these types of products would disappear." We made a big
mistake when the patenting of life went unchallenged. But it's not too
late to correct it.

"We didn't get to vote on whether to take human genes and put
them in animals, which they're doing through genetic engineering," says
Andy Kimbrell. "It seems to me that we really can't call ourselves a

democracy until we have instituted ways in which we can vote on the technologies that are introduced into our society. . . . Do we really want unlimited genetic engineering of humans, of animals, of plants, and the cloning and patenting of life forms? Do we really want our generation and the generations coming after us to view the entire animal kingdom as so many machines to be reprogrammed, cloned and patented? Is that the image of animals that we want for successive generations? . . . I think [that] if the answer to these questions is no, we have to have the courage to say no to these genetic technologies, the way we said no to nuclear weapons proliferation."

Jeremy Rifkin is doing his part to resist this new technology. He's founded the Pure Food Campaign, which works with other non-governmental organizations around the world that are resisting unregulated biotechnology. He says, "This is the first global movement in modern history where non-governmental organizations are coming together across national boundaries to . . . say no to genetic foods for the twenty-first century. Health groups, environmental organizations, animal-rights organizations, organic and sustainable farmers, consumers, those involved in issues of social justice are [all] coming together in a new global network of resistance to the introduction of genetically engineered foods into the global marketplace. I think this is going to be one of the great social and cultural battles of the coming decade."

All around the world grass-roots, academic, human-rights and other groups are working on this issue. Canada has a number of such organizations, and some of them are listed at the end of this book. One of the most effective strategies worked for the British. Since government and industry weren't listening, citizens put pressure on food outlets and eventually got every major supermarket chain to divest itself of genetically engineered products. The lack of a market forced growers and the government to pay attention. Rifkin says, "We are asking every consumer on this planet to go to the grocery store, go to the supermarket, demand that the manager have a written policy that there are no genetically engineered foods in that store, and if there are those foods that they're clearly labelled. If that store manager cannot guarantee that they have labelled foods or that there are no genetic foods, then take your business elsewhere. I think the pressure has to be put on from the consumer end and from the farm end. If enough people do this in every country, this global boycott will triumph."

Once people's awareness is raised about food, we should be able to understand why we are hunting for gold in our pets and our houseplants and our own hearts and tissues. We should be able to get some kind of grip on what kind of world we want to live in, and whether the marketing of life should be part of it. But we have to understand that our underlying economic, trade and ownership systems are a fundamental part of this issue. Vandana Shiva thinks we are trading in our own cells because of a very severe crisis of capital. We are, in fact, running out of real wealth in the world. That's one of the reasons we're trying to make money out of anything we can think of. Patents enable us to charge money for formerly free goods. And as Shiva says, the current economic system, which drives the patenting of life, never recognizes the concept of having enough. "Capital," she claims, "like a cancer cell, needs to keep growing. If it stops growing, it must die. The need to keep growing is forcing capital to find new ways of accumulating [wealth]. . . . And it can stop only when this desperation destroys itself. My hope is that it'll destroy itself faster than it will destroy the world."

CHAPTER 6
FOLLOW THE MONEY

Economics is really politics in disguise. We need to unpack the whole thing and say, "Look, an economy is really nothing but a set of rules. Let's be up front about it. There's no actual science here."

— HAZEL HENDERSON,
FUTURIST

Over the past several years, I've noticed that when I discuss environmental issues, sooner or later someone says, "Listen, Suzuki, we can't afford a clean environment if we don't have a strong and growing economy." The economy — and the need to keep it strong and growing — has somehow become the most important aspect of modern life. Nothing else is allowed to rank higher. The economy is suffering; the economy is improving; the economy is stable or unstable — you'd think it was a patient on life support in an intensive-care unit from the way we anxiously await the next pronouncement on its health.

But what we call the economy is nothing more than people producing, consuming and exchanging things and services. Economists keep track of the money we exchange for goods and services, and then make judgements about how well we're doing. Hazel Henderson is a futurist and economic analyst who has been writing books about what's wrong with economics for the past thirty years. "An economy really is a fiction," she says. "You can't separate production, consumption and exchange and all of that from the rest of human life. It was always a mistake of the economic textbooks to say that the economy is some kind of separate thing."

As a biologist, I've always felt that economics was flawed in another way: it pays no attention to the goods and services that are provided by nature — the air, water, soil and sunlight that produce everything we need for survival and all the riches we are able to accumulate. In a paper for the National Academy of Sciences U.S.A., the renowned biodiversity expert Norman Myers offered some conservative estimates of what nature does for us for free. These services — the economic benefits of which are enormous, though they are never included in our economic calculations — include our climate; the earth's biogeochemical cycles, such as the carbon cycle; all hydrologic functions, including sewage disposal; soil protection and production; crop pollination; pest control; and miscellaneous services, such as potential insights into medical and pollution problems that are provided by resistant organisms. Altogether, such services provide annual benefits worth, if they could be duplicated by human-created services (which, of course, they can't), far more than the cash income of the entire Earth.

Robert Constanza is a leading scholar in an exciting field called ecological economics, which attempts to reconnect two disciplines whose profound interlinkages and interdependencies have been ignored. He led a group that refined Myers's efforts to put an actual dollar value on seventeen ecosystem services in sixteen different biomes. Astonishingly, they calculated that the services' annual worth was somewhere in the range of $16 trillion to $54 trillion (U.S.), with an average of $33 trillion! That compares with a total annual GDP for all nations on Earth of $18 trillion. And yet none of these services appears in the supply-and-demand handbook of mainstream economics!

Hazel Henderson points to another important part of our lives that isn't counted in the economic equation. She calls it the love economy, and it includes all the productive work that humans do that does not involve an exchange of money — things like raising families, doing community work, taking care of the elderly, being active in a club or charity. It may be impossible to put a price tag on these activities, but they are the very glue that holds societies together. In the Third World, with its traditional economies in which money does not play an overwhelming role, whole families are supported on home labour that is not part of any cash exchange: people raise vegetables and chickens; they barter and exchange with neighbours; they gather medicines and foods out in nature; they pool resources and labour. But none of this appears in the country's estimates of per capita annual income.

To illustrate her point, Henderson likes to imagine the economy as a three-layer cake with icing. She says, "The economists think only about what they call the private sector, which is the icing on the cake, and the public sector, the government and tax-funding, which is the next layer down. But they forget these two other layers at the bottom — the love economy and nature — which are holding the whole thing up."

Henderson isn't the only one who has noticed what economists don't include in their figures. Marilyn Waring, the youngest Cabinet member in New Zealand history, is known internationally for her book *As if Women Counted* and the National Film Board of Canada documentary called *Who's Counting?* She recalls an experience she had when she was a representative from a rural conservative seat and served as chair of the parliamentary public expenditure committee of the New Zealand federal government. A corporation had applied for a mining licence in Mount Pironia, the largest forest park in her constituency. In its cost-benefit analysis, the corporation included all the benefits that would accrue to the area in terms of exports, infrastructure development, employment and taxes. But there were no costs listed. "This was the largest mountain in our constituency," Waring says. "It completely controlled the microclimate, giving us the rainfall that had made us the richest area of the country. It controlled the water table and our expectations of a temperate, agriculturally stable climate. It provided the habitat for all the pollinating species on which we were completely dependent for our year-round agricultural economy. And of course, it provided lots of leisure and recreation."

The cost-benefit analysis never talked about the pollution that gold mining would bring to the watercourse. It never mentioned the seepage of arsenic and other toxins from the waste tailings. It didn't indicate what the toxins, the forest and water destruction, and the bulldozers and infrastructures would do to the habitat and the recreational desirability of the mountain. Waring found that there was "no way to express in the unidimensional formula of classical economics what the mine would *cost* our community."

Counting Money: The GDP

One of the main problems with the GDP is that it averages out income. If you average out income per capita, you could have a society with one or two billionaires and everybody else is homeless, and it would still look like it was great. This is how insane the GDP is.

— HAZEL HENDERSON

Economists must learn to subtract.

— SLOGAN FROM THE MEDIA FOUNDATION
AND *ADBUSTERS* MAGAZINE

Virtually all of the extremely important services that nature provides are completely ignored by conventional economics. The ozone layer, for example, shields all life from DNA-damaging ultraviolet radiation. But that crucial service, on which all agriculture, forest and marine industries depend, is not added to the balance sheet when economists figure out the profit margins for the industries that affect the atmosphere. The environment is also ignored when economists calculate the gross domestic product (GDP). This measure is accepted around the world as an indication of how well a country is doing. But is that what it really measures? The GDP totes up exchanges of money. Ralph Nader has pointed out that every time there's a car accident and people are hurt, the GDP goes up. They need ambulances, doctors and nurses, hospital beds, car repairs, even funeral services, all of it involving an actual dollar expense and therefore increasing the GDP. After the *Exxon Valdez* oil spill, to cite another example, the U.S. GDP rose by $2 billion; presumably, if we look only at the GDP, it's good for us to spill as much oil as possible, so we have greater clean-up services. But surely the GDP is no indicator of an improvement in the quality of our lives.

We take the love economy for granted too. Marilyn Waring is particularly concerned with the fact that most economists do not see women's work as valuable. She says that in her rural riding, "male farmers know more than anybody the complete dependence of the family farming operation on women's work, both in the fields and [in] balancing the books. And of course, anybody who knows farming knows that as soon as children are mobile and competent, they're engaged in the farming operation for at least some part of the day."

Waring gives an example of a wife on a sheep station who broke her leg just before shearing was to begin. New Zealand's Accident Compensation scheme didn't cover her because she wasn't considered "a part of the market." But for the farm to continue its operations, she had to be replaced by three "real, recognized workers": a shepherd; a rowsee, or clipper; and a housekeeper. The system ultimately recognized the shepherd and the rowsee and paid their wages, but it refused to pay any compensation to the housekeeper, since she was the woman's mother. The system recognized the love economy so far as to say that it was an "altruistic and community expectation" that the mother would help out. In some cases, then, the love economy *is* recognized and expected by economists — but not when they might have to allocate funding or subtract it from their totals. It's not only gender that's at issue here; it's cash. Economists don't recognize household labour because basically no cash is exchanged. There's even a famous economist's joke, which says, "When a man marries his housekeeper, the GDP goes down."

Hazel Henderson is involved with an investment fund called the Calvert Group, which is trying to come up with new criteria for measuring true economic and social well-being. She says, "We have twelve aspects for measuring the quality of life based on what voters all over the world, in democracies, say is important to them — education, health, recreation, environment, culture and some other things, like the poverty gap. People don't like it when the poverty gap gets too wide; it's very uncomfortable for us. And of course it creates a lot of crime."

In San Francisco, a group called the Redefining Progress Institute has developed a new economic indicator, the Genuine Progress Indicator (GPI), which *subtracts* those activities that negatively affect the quality of our lives through social disruption or environmental degradation. These activities consist of resource depletion, including loss of wetlands, farmland and minerals such as oil; asymmetric distribution of income so that when the poor benefit more, it is added, and when the rich receive a disproportionate increase, it is subtracted; unemployment and underemployment; pollution; long-term environmental degradation; and disposable consumer goods.

At the same time, the GPI *adds* such elements as housework, non-market transactions and increased leisure time. The Redefining Progress

Institute has found that while the per capita GDP in the United States rose steadily from an average of $7,865 in 1950 to $16,414 in 1992, the GPI was a far different story. The GPI rose from $5,663 in 1950 to a peak of $7,441 in 1969; then it *declined* to $4,426 by 1992. The GPI reveals that in striving to keep the GDP growing, we have seen a decline in the quality of our lives.

The GDP was invented for very good reasons. At the end of the Great Depression, politicians in the United States realized that they had poor statistics on factors like employment and average annual income. In order to measure rates of recovery, they had to have an instant snapshot of how bad things really were, and whether various economic policies were working. Then, during the Second World War, governments needed to be able to measure every aspect of our economies so they could figure out how much could be produced for the war effort. After the war, it was found that because he lacked such tools, Hitler had greatly underestimated his own economy's ability to produce. For all these purposes, an economic indicator was very useful. The GDP measures the actual cash transactions that take place during the course of a given year, an important statistic for a country to know.

There was never any suggestion then, however, that the GDP should be used for measuring the state of general prosperity of a country. It can't reflect pockets of misery, education levels, health and pollution problems. It can't gauge prosperity and well-being. Hazel Henderson says we need other forms of measurement that are multi-factorial and reflect more clearly the fact that we lead very complex lives. We can't reduce the joy our children bring us, our hobbies, our job satisfaction, the health of our environment and our neighbourhood safety down to a single number, especially a number that keeps track only of cash transactions. Robert Kennedy Jr. once said, "The GDP counts air pollution and cigarette advertising and ambulances to clear our highways of carnage. . . . Yet [it] does not allow for the health of our children, the quality of their education, or the joy of their play. . . . It measures neither our wit, nor our courage; neither our wisdom, nor our learning; neither our compassion, nor our devotion to our country; it measures everything, in short, except that which makes life worthwhile."

Many different organizations, including the United Nations, have been developing alternatives to the GDP. Even a former president of the

World Bank, Barber Conable, admits, "Current calculations ignore the degradation of the natural resource base and view the sales of non-renewable resources entirely as income. A better way must be found to measure the prosperity and progress of mankind."

Musings like Conable's appear to fall on deaf ears. Despite the efforts of Hazel Henderson and people like her, conventional economics continues to dominate our political thinking. Again and again, politicians point to the GDP as a measure of the success of their policies. And economics has all the trappings of a sophisticated, quantitative science. Articles in the field are filled with arcane terms, complex formulae and computer analyses, all of which give the appearance of mathematical precision. But Henderson says, "It's all complete rubbish. Economists use mathematics to cover up very, very simple propositions, which would be much better addressed in the mother tongue."

I once sat in on a university course in economics and was appalled when the professor said, early in the first lecture, "Sharing, co-operating and caring are emotional and irrational acts." He told the class that economists begin with the understanding that only acting in pure self-interest is rational; that's why modern economics rests on this principle. When I mentioned this to Henderson, she responded, "It's terrible. If the textbooks say the only kind of rational behaviour is maximizing self-interest in competition with all other comers, then that's a recipe for a society that is going to end up as a behavioural sink."

We Can't Grow That Fast

We seem to be moving towards the idea that rates of growth of money in the bank are autonomous, and [that] the natural world can accommodate this. Or if it can't, we can adjust it. That seems to me the wrong way to go.
— HERMAN DALY, ECONOMIST

Hazel Henderson could be thought of as an outsider, but there are respected scholars even within the economic mainstream who are critical of their own discipline. Herman Daly was a senior economist at the World Bank for six years and now teaches at the University of Maryland's School of Public Affairs. When I asked him what an economy is, he replied, "I would say that it's a community of people who, through division of labour and exchange, live a life in some mutuality or interdependence. And they depend not only on each other, but [also] on the natural world, the natural community, from which they extract materials and services and to which they have to return wastes. There are two levels of community: the natural community, which must be respected for the economy to be sustainable, and the human community, in its mutual interdependence and division of labour, where relations of justice and dependence have to be respected as well."

Daly is one of a growing number of economists who point out that nature sustains the economy, not vice versa. Everything we make comes from the Earth — plastic, paper, cars, computer disks — everything. As Daly says, "You sacrifice some of the natural system when you convert it into man-made things. And you have to balance those costs and benefits. In the past, we haven't focused on that. We've thought that if the economy grows, we'll be fine, and, oh well, yes, resources might become a little bit scarce relative to other things, but no problem, technology will solve that."

Not only is endless growth seen as possible, it's believed to be necessary. But growth in the economy and growth in nature are not the same. Money grows fast — so fast, in fact, that nothing in nature can keep up with it. For example, trees in British Columbia increase in size by about 2 to 3 percent a year. That means that if a volume of wood equivalent to 2 to 3 percent of a forest is logged annually, the equivalent of an entire forest can be cut over a period of twenty-five to thirty-five years and still leave an intact forest standing! In other words, trees could be harvested that way forever. Unfortunately, that would make no economic sense. It makes better economic sense to clearcut all the trees at once and invest the money. Returns would yield 10 to 30 percent a year! What CEO would keep his or her job with only a 2 to 3 percent return on investment?

Since money grows faster than trees, economic thinking demands that we trash the forest. "I once saw a very nice cartoon," Herman Daly says. "A fisherman is standing with a puzzled look on his face. On the one side, the fish in the sea and in his net are saying, 'Slow down! We can't grow that fast.' And on the other side, the banker is saying, 'Speed up! We have to grow faster!' And so, there you are. The fisherman is caught between the rate of growth of money and the natural, biological growth rates of species."

One doesn't have to be a forester or a scientist to know that our present rates and methods of forest extraction are unsustainable because they are driven by a corporate mandate to maximize profits. If we want "forests forever," as an ad for the forest company MacMillan-Bloedel once boasted, we should be working to match technology with the capacities of the planet. Instead, we stubbornly refuse to acknowledge that there are any limits to natural growth; we're trying to put nature on steroids. "We're striving to do the opposite of what we should be doing," explains Daly. "We're taking as given, or autonomous, the rate of growth of money in the bank and, by golly, we'll just redesign the genetic structure of everything we depend upon so that it grows as fast as money in the bank. So we increase agricultural growth rates and design new animal husbandry, using techniques of cloning and everything else, in order to get that growth rate up. And that strikes me as a rather dangerous thing."

In the past, local experiments with speeding up natural growth rates sometimes worked — such as when we learned to cultivate prairie land for grain — and sometimes didn't — such as when we desertified northern Africa, Spain and Greece by intensive agricultural practices. This saga continues to take place across much of the world; one recent example we found that illustrates the complexity of the natural world's limits to growth in the face of our constant expansion is North Carolina.

Eaten Alive

We have a new thing that's come up in our rivers, Pfiesteria — *single-celled animals that have lain for thousands of years at the bottom of our rivers. But our rivers are becoming what they're calling nutrient-rich — I love that [phrase] — full of hog and chicken manure. We've woken up these animals, the* Pfiesteria, *and they are actually eating the fish alive. And feeding on the fishermen.*
— HOWARD LYMAN, HUMANE SOCIETY OF THE UNITED STATES

It sounds like science fiction, but it actually happened. Beginning in the early 1990s, fishermen in North Carolina, along Chesapeake Bay, started to notice some terrible things. Fish had begun to die by the millions, and the dead and dying fish were covered with gaping, bleeding wounds. In 1991, North Carolina alone lost a billion fish. The piles of carcasses had to be bulldozed off the beaches. To add to their worries, some fishermen began to find open sores on their own bodies. They were told to wear gloves to avoid infection. Then water skiers in the bay found their legs were being attacked by a microscopic creature and eaten away. In 1995, after another 15 million fish died, researchers discovered that about 40 percent of the people who'd been exposed to the fish — the fishermen or those living nearby — reported memory loss and nervous-system problems. All these problems are now known to be associated with an estuary microorganism called *Pfiesteria*.

Where did this horrible bug come from? *Pfiesteria* is a dinoflagellate, an animal-like protozoan so small that thousands would fit on the head of a pin. It is found in nature all over the world. Normally, it's benign, sitting in the mud of estuaries like thousands of other tiny creatures we know little about, eating bacteria and algae. But under certain conditions, it can become toxic. At the moment, researchers like Dr. Joanne Burkholder, a professor of aquatic sciences at North Carolina State, believe that *Pfiesteria* use their toxins to immobilize fish. Then they transform themselves into amoeba-like creatures that attach to the fish and feast on the remains. We don't know what triggers this action.

"We have a very short-term database," explains Burkholder. "But some of the information, [which] we regard as provocative and somewhat disturbing, about cousins of *Pfiesteria,* other toxic dinoflagellates and toxic algae, is that they seem to be increasing in the world's coastal areas. In fact, over the past ten or fifteen years, [massive microbial blooms involving] something like twenty-two species [have increased to ones involving] sixty or more species. So that's a sign to me of coastal water-quality degradation. Some of these species seem to be very highly correlated with nutrient over-enrichment and other pollution problems in coastal zones. *Pfiesteria* is one of those species. It has been highly associated in poorly flushed, quiet waters with nutrient over-enrichment from human sewage, swine wastes and other problems."

"Over-enrichment" and "nutrient-rich" are terms invented by various industries to describe water with too much nitrogen in it — in short, water that is full of feces. And that's just what the rivers and oceanfronts around Chesapeake Bay are loaded with, especially on the North Carolina side. North Carolina and the Netherlands share the somewhat dubious distinction of being the most intensive producers of hogs in the world. In one small county of North Carolina alone, there are 2.3 million pigs — all protected by state legislation that forbids any zoning against the industry. Relatively recent methods of intensive hog farming produce tens of thousands of pigs in every barn, where they are so tightly enclosed that they can barely turn around or lie down. And the extremely nitrogen-rich wastes they produce are disposed of in exactly the same way they were when the area was home to more normal-sized operations and produced only a few hundred piglets a year. The manure is put in lagoons, then sprayed on the surrounding farm land as "fertilizer." It's also dumped directly into watercourses. Since there's far too much for the land to absorb, the nitrogen and ammonia drain directly into the water table and out into the estuaries, where they trigger changes in *Pfiesteria*.

Hog farming has been an ecological disaster for Chesapeake Bay, the second-largest estuary on the U.S. mainland. It sits behind the Outer Banks, where the water is relatively quiet and poorly flushed. As Joanne Burkholder says, it is exactly these kinds of places that are the most productive in terms of natural systems. "It's an extremely important place as a fish nursery ground. According to a recent Sea Grant document, this bay provides 50 percent of the total surface area of nursery grounds used by fish from Maine to Florida. They come to our nursery to breed or get born, and then they disperse north and south." But because of the poor flushing, it's a bad place to dump wastes. "Pollution," Burkholder says, "stays in the estuary, where it has time to cause problems like major algal blooms, [which provide] material to feed the *Pfiesteria* when [the microorganisms are] not killing fish. *Pfiesteria* likes these conditions, likes a lot of algae and other things that are associated with nutrient pollution."

Human and other crop wastes are also at fault in this situation. But the hog fecal output is the worst pollutant, the trigger for plankton blooms. How dangerous to people is exposure to *Pfiesteria*? Burkholder says there isn't enough scientific, clinical evaluation in the field, but the effects researchers know about with certainty are open sores, serious cognitive impairment and short-term memory loss.

This completely unforeseen consequence of large-scale hog farming brings us back to the point made in the cartoon referred to by Herman Daly.

We're trying to increase profits in the meat industry, but on a scale that outstrips nature's capacity to deal with the wastes. This effort to produce cheaper pork has created problems so horrific that they seem hallucinatory: people with serious brain damage or flesh invaded by microorganisms; fish eaten alive by the millions in the waters where they've come to breed. Our drive for quick profits ignores any understanding of the interconnected natural systems on which the whole enterprise depends.

Joanne Burkholder says, "It's a subtle thing. These connections are difficult to make. In *Pfiesteria*'s case, who would have known that a little animal-like creature could be strongly stimulated by human and swine wastes? Who even knew that it was there, until eight years ago? Who would ever have considered that diseased fish could translate into serious learning disabilities and memory loss for people? These kinds of effects will come back to haunt us if we don't develop longer-range vision about what we're doing."

Corporate Morality

Their proposition is to exploit, as much as possible, both people and resources. That's what they do.
— HARRY GLAESBECK, RETIRED PROFESSOR OF CORPORATE LAW

The *Pfiesteria*–hog farm connection in Chesapeake Bay is being studied, especially on the Maryland side, where an enlightened governor is monitoring the situation and amassing data. But the practices that created the *Pfiesteria* outbreak have not been altered. The hog farms are still producing "nutrients" at full tilt. And governments are reluctant to limit anything that has been so good for business.

Governments are often not very good checks on business. Corporations not only support politicians financially but they also know how to put on pressure on both politicians and voters to get what they want. A Republican congresswoman in North Carolina, Cindy Watson, dared to attempt to place some controls on the hog industry that was destroying her constituents' land and air, as well as their water. She became the target of a media campaign. Farmers for Fairness, a group created and funded by the hog industry, spent $2.6 million on television and other ads to discredit her for her opposition to their use of nature as a dumping ground for experiments in pork supply and demand. And they won when she lost her bid for re-election.

How did business interests gain control over the political process? During the past century or so, corporations have gradually achieved increased influence over political policy and economic analysis. Harry Glaesbeck, who taught corporate law at Osgoode Hall Law School of York University for more than twenty years, says, "A corporation is really an amazing kind of creation of the legal imagination. . . . Any individual in Canada who is eighteen, sane, not bankrupt, can go to a registrar and register a corporation, just as you would register a dog licence. It doesn't have to have any objectives. There is not even a requirement that there should be any capital in it."

Once that corporation is formed, it becomes a legal entity with the rights of a person. As Glaesbeck says, this person "is instantly matured. There is no incubation period. It is immortal. It will not die unless it voluntarily dissolves itself, or if it's bankrupted and loses all its assets. It is completely unseeable. It's untouchable. . . . Individuals who manage the corporation and who actually own it are very hard to get at. It's not impossible, but it's very difficult. It creates a shield between people who take risks and the obligations that arise out of those risks."

Jane Ann Morris is a corporate anthropologist who works with a group called the Program on Corporations, Law and Democracy. She says that especially in the United States, but to some degree all over the world, "Corporations have written themselves into the democratic process in the place of human persons." She thinks it's important to remember that corporations are not people, yet we've accorded them virtually all the rights that people have. Add to those rights their wealth and immortality, and it's no wonder they can be pretty hard to deal with.

It wasn't always so. In the nineteenth century, laws in many American states limited corporations' powers, forced them to hire local workers or gave the state the right to review their behaviour annually and to terminate their existence. Early corporate charters did not relieve the stockholders of liability beyond the extent of their investment, as they do now. And corporations were often not allowed to hold stock in another corporation. (This stipulation alone would solve a lot of today's worries about mega-monopolies in banking or the media.) States also retained the power to terminate the existence of a corporation if it violated state laws. But in the late 1800s, corporations began to press for rights that would allow them to appeal state cases to the federal court, or to have the kind of protection and due process enjoyed by human citizens, even constitutionally guaranteed protection against "unreasonable" search and seizure. All these privileges were accorded, despite violent protests, and since then corporations have been building on them, and on a global scale.

Jane Ann Morris says, "Now, let's put all this together. Corporations have some of the rights of natural persons to equal protection and due process. The concept of property is expanded to include ideas and future earnings. You can see how the noose is tightening, as corporations are getting themselves more rights and reducing the rights of humans." But how does corporate acquisition of rights reduce those rights for humans? "One example of the way that humans' rights — living, breathing, flesh-and-blood humans' rights — are reduced is [that] corporations have been getting increasing rights to restrict what human beings can do on their property," she explains. "Think of things like malls and shopping centres and the workplace. In all those places, we're bombarded by corporate speech, yet the rights of humans to free speech are severely restricted." Think also of mandatory drug testing by companies. Think especially of commercial secrets, the kind of secrets that threatened the lives and vision of thousands at Bhopal, because Union Carbide could not be compelled to disclose the composition of its private property, the ingredients of the chemical fertilizers that had been leaked from its factory onto the surrounding population. It had the legal right to do that. And that corporate legal right superseded even the moral obligation to save human lives.

Harry Glaesbeck goes so far as to say, "Corporations are criminogenic institutions, as we academics like to say. That is, the pressure on them to make profits is enormous. So in order to make profits, especially within a competitive situation, they have to mould the environment. They try to mould the environment to their needs, rather than the other way around. Now, they do that in a variety of ways. They participate in politics so that they get laws which are very lax. Then it's even easier to mould the environment. If they don't succeed in that, they'll break the laws or they'll try to have them not enforced."

We tend to assume that corporate interests coincide with human interests, and that can be true. Corporations employ people and manufacture the goods and services that we want. But they have also become a threat to humans, because our needs and theirs simply do not always coincide, and we are finding it increasingly difficult to control these ever bigger and more powerful multinational corporate entities when *they* want things that are bad for *us*. "It is beyond doubt that of Fortune 500's major corporations, 40 percent do not commit a crime annually. Sixty percent do," Glaesbeck asserts. "Now, some of the crimes are nothing. They're just small regulatory offences, not filling in the paperwork, stalling — I don't want to exaggerate. But some of the crimes are monstrous. They're like Union Carbide [India Limited] at Bhopal. They're like the asbestos boys, . . . or the Dalkon Shield manufacturers, or the Ford Pinto. They made these things for money . . . hiding the fact [that they later learned they were dangerous] from the public and the consumers at all costs, and paying a paltry amount of damages afterwards."

Corporations easily bully us by threatening to deprive us of their wealth. If we try too hard to control them, they threaten to leave and take their jobs with them. And as Glaesbeck says, "They're aggressive people. They're expected to aggressively go out and compete and fight and smash their opposition. So they're naturally risk-takers, especially as the risk is not theirs. It's the risk of other people's money."

We do hear about "good" corporations, of course, ones that fund softball teams and women's shelters and progressive documentaries. But these activities usually provide tax write-offs, and generally are justified only if they improve the corporation's bottom line. As Glaesbeck says, "If they can show that altruism incurs better profit, then of course they're allowed to do it. It's defensible. But there is no such thing as genuine altruism in the corporate sector under our present system." The way we've set up corporations, even a majority vote of stockholders cannot demand that a corporation's policies reflect the public good or preserve the environment for future use. That's because profit is the one and only motive. It's up to government and it's up to people to protect the public interest. Corporations are simply not allowed to.

I remember an occasion years ago when I was battling the clearcutting practices of a major Canadian forest company and encountered the CEO. "Dave," he said to me, "my job is to maximize profit for my shareholders. And I'm good at it. If you disagree with the way we log, your quarrel is with government, because we do everything within the legal limits." He was honest and right. If performing to serve the public good — say, to log forests sustainably so that future generations will have them, or to refuse to dump wastes into a nearby river or lake — in any way infringes on a company's profits, and it probably will, then shareholders can complain. That particular CEO won't last. What is more, as Glaesbeck points out, "How do the managers know the public good? They're not elected. They're unaccountable."

We always have to remember how corporations, those bulwarks of the economy, work. "The reason that they exploit the environment, dump wastes in the air and water, is because [natural resources are] considered to be owned by nobody; so they can be taken [and exploited with impunity]," Glaesbeck says. "When we put out regulations to stop that, corporations try to soften the regulations, soften the monitoring. And if none of that works, they break the law. Or they go elsewhere, where they're allowed to do what they want. They're always threatening to go elsewhere, where they can exploit people and resources to a greater extent. The consequence of that is we all lower our standards continuously. A balance between sustainable ecology and sustainable human life, on the one hand, and the unfettered drive for profit, on the other, is just an oxymoron."

Humans need to have control not just over environmental and justice issues, but also over the economy. Jane Ann Morris says, "Right now, some corporations are starting to say that they're socially responsible. And I think there are some genuinely well-intentioned people both inside and outside those corporations who want to be better than average and do good. But that doesn't help much if it doesn't change the locus of control. Instead of a corporation, think [of a] king. I don't want a king who's in a good mood or who's nice today. We don't want to be subject to arbitrary authority. Our problem today is not about a particular corporate harm, a sweatshop or a toxic dump, it's about the fact that we're no longer in control of the show. We need to understand that corporate, economic power has discombobulated our democracy. And we need to repair it or make it new."

People *are* trying to do that. There's a growing movement looking into corporate charters, for example, and trying to see how corporations can be brought back under control through local laws. With the push towards globalization, this becomes all the more difficult, but it's still eminently worth trying, because the alternative is becoming very dangerous to us all.

Greed Lock

*Exponential growth ... won't work. It works to a point, and
you can [have] a big bash and a big binge, and you can spend
all your global capital, and then it's all over. A sophomore
dropout can figure this out. Why can't all the bright people in
global institutions figure it out?*

— DAVID BROWER, FOUNDER,
FRIENDS OF THE EARTH AND EARTH ISLAND INSTITUTE

The modern global economy, fuelled by the top 200 big corporations,
didn't always exist. We came through a huge depression in the 1930s.
What got the economy going again was a war — the Second World War.
By the end of that war, the American economy had become the dominant economy in the world. Fuelled by genuine altruism and a fair
amount of self-interest, the United States — both the government and
eager corporations like Coca-Cola, Boeing and General Motors —
exported its largesse and American ideas about progress and development around the world.

David Korten has a Ph.D. from the Stanford Business School. He
taught at Harvard, and spent most of his career in overseas-development
work. Like so many other young American professionals, he wanted to
go out and help the rest of the world. He says, "I graduated from
Stanford in 1959 and in that year made a decision that I would devote
my life to development work, to bringing American management methods and economic theory abroad, so all the rest of the world could live
properly — you know, like we do. At the time I was very conservative
and concerned about the spread of communism and revolution. There
was an underlying sense that if we didn't do something to end poverty, it
would be a threat to our American way of life. But working within the
system back then, through UN agencies and things like the Rockefeller
Foundation, there was a very strong sense that we were doing this out of
our altruism and our concern to help other people live better lives."

With youthful idealism and energy, Korten plunged into Third
World development work. But over and over again, in places like
Ethiopia, Central America and Southeast Asia, he kept noticing that the
kind of prosperity and progress he expected from U.S. aid and modern

business methods didn't seem to be materializing. He says, "As you participate in this process, you notice that a lot of things don't seem to work very well. But [you assume] it must be working better someplace else, because if it were working this badly everywhere, then somebody would surely notice it and do something about it."

What Korten began to notice was that the major beneficiaries of American aid were an elite minority within the developing countries. Large numbers of poor people remained mired in poverty. And just as alarmingly, the natural environment they depended on for their livelihoods was being rapidly destroyed by the industrial development that was enriching the tiny elite. He says, "Behind the facades of development, more and more people are being displaced. There's more and more deep misery. The forests are being stripped away. You go out snorkelling in the tropical coral reefs, and the coral reefs aren't there any more. It looks like a barren landscape under the water instead of rich gardens of coral and fish along the coast. And then it gradually begins to dawn on you that something is really more deeply wrong."

These are just impressions, of course, of travellers who leave the hotel districts to explore the slums or the countrysides. But there are ways to determine whether the impressions are true. Korten tells us how: "If you start looking at the statistics and the studies, you realize these problems are not just local. They're everyplace. What really became a shock for me ... in Southern countries was continual, deepening poverty and inequality, environmental devastation, and a breakdown of the social fabric. That's when I realized that something deeply systemic is wrong. It's not that we don't have just the right fine-tuning on our concept of development. Our whole concept of progress is wrong, in that most of our dominant institutions were creations of a mindset that focused purely on growth and production and the monetary value of the products produced by the economy."

Not only has this mindset failed in the Third World, but by the 1980s all the problems in the developing world were also present in the developed world. They were, however, masked by our greater overall wealth. The paradox is that while the economy has continued to grow, and we have in fact made great advances in global medical care, more and more people are becoming truly poor, and overall human suffering has not diminished.

How do we know this? Certainly not from the statistics presented by international agencies like the World Bank, the United Nations and the UN Development Program (UNDP). These agencies report encouraging trends. They claim, for example, that great progress has been made in reducing poverty over the course of the twentieth century, especially in the last decade or two, when the International Monetary Fund (IMF) and other international agencies have been advising poor countries on how to manage their finances. Their measuring stick, the Human Poverty Index (HPI), indicates that only around 11 percent of Mexico's population is now "poor." Yet a report in the *Washington Post* states that real income in Mexico fell drastically between 1982 and 1992, infant deaths due to malnutrition *tripled,* the real minimum wage lost more than half its value, and the percentage of the population living in poverty increased from just under half to two-thirds of Mexico's 87 million people. Figures compiled by UNESCO tell a similar story. When the world's population is ranked by wealth and subdivided into five groups of equal number, "in 1990, the richest group received 59 times more than the poorest. Despite growth of almost three percent per annum worldwide of per capita GNP over the past three decades, this is almost double the ratio of 30:1 in 1960. In that year, the richest 20 percent already controlled over 70 percent of global GNP. In 1990 this had climbed to 83 percent. In 1960 the poorest 20 percent had to get by with only 2.3 percent, which by 1990 had fallen to 1.4 percent." The report goes on to state that "these figures conceal the true scale of injustice, since they are based on comparisons of average per capita incomes of rich and poor countries, and do not take into account the wide disparities between rich and poor people in each of these countries. . . . The absolute difference in per capita income between the top 20 percent of world population, expressed in 1989 U.S. dollars, increased between 1960 and 1989 from $1,864 to $15,149."

Michel Chossudovsky, an economist teaching at Ottawa University, is a specialist on the macro, or world, economy. His latest book is entitled *The Globalisation of Poverty.* He maintains that David Korten wasn't imagining things when he noted a general grinding down of social and environmental conditions in developing nations. Chossudovsky has observed a global decline in living standards that is a direct result of classical "development" policies. He says the UN agencies that deal with development, as well as international economic entities like the IMF and the World Bank, are completely committed to vindicating the free-market system. That is, they fully support the idea of continuous economic growth and the belief that natural systems are secondary to purely "economic" concerns, like industrial development and free trade. Chossudovsky points out what everyone knows: that people in Russia and the countries of the former Soviet Union are far worse off than they were in the 1950s. He also points out that in very recent years, despite UNDP reports that fail to note such things, "local famines have erupted in sub-Saharan Africa, South Asia and parts of Latin America; millions of schools and health clinics have closed down; hundreds of millions of children have been denied the right to primary education; and all over the Third World, Eastern Europe and the Balkans, there has been a resurgence of infectious diseases, including tuberculosis, malaria and cholera."

In large part, the conditions leading to the degradation of human health and poverty are the undermining of local communities and their air, water and soil, which are the real basis of well-being. David Korten puts it all together. He says that government agencies contend that things are getting better for everyone because, since 1950, "there's been rough-ly a five and a half times increase in total global economic output. And our policies are still driven by the presumption that the solution to pover-ty is growth. The solution to the environmental problem is also growth, because then we generate the resources with which we can be rich enough to afford to clean up the environment. And of course, as we do that, what we do is we continue to increase the burden on the ecosystem. We break it down so that the very foundation of all wealth, of all of the total productive system, is being diminished. We're destroying the natu-ral capital. But the other thing that we do is intensify the competition for that resource base between the rich and the poor. And, of course, the rich win that competition."

Unfortunately, when the economic advisers to our governments and to global bodies like the UN see increased social deterioration, more poverty and greater insecurity, they seem to have only one way to respond. As Korten says, "The worse the crisis gets, the more the people who are making the decisions become determined to press ahead with exactly the policies that are creating the destruction."

Trickling Up

The doctrine [is] that if the horse is fed amply with oats, some
will pass through to the road for the sparrows.
— JOHN KENNETH GALBRAITH, ECONOMIST

It's interesting to ask ourselves what money and wealth really are.
Money is a construct, an agreement among people. Wealth is what we
can actually use: food; shelter; clothes; transport; access to clean air,
water and light — those last three increase the rent on an apartment,
because everyone knows their true value. "When the money system is
working properly, it's essentially a mechanism to facilitate transactions,"
David Korten says. "[But in] what some people refer to as finance capitalism, [people are] essentially creating money out of nothing. People
think of it as creating wealth, but actually what they're doing is captur-
ing wealth; they are creating claims on the wealth of the rest of society."

This gets us to the age-old question of whether wealth is created or
merely taken from one place to another. The answer is both. Sometimes
it's created, and sometimes it's just stolen. Korten says that the system
currently favours people who are taking wealth, rather than people, like
farmers or craftsmen, who create it. Of course, some say that it doesn't
matter if more than 450 billionaires in the world have sequestered almost
80 percent of the world's wealth for their own use. As they do use it, we
are told, it will "trickle down" and support us all. But Korten says, "It
doesn't 'trickle down.' It's totally a process of 'trickle-up.' It trickles
down to a few people, the rich guys' lawyers and accountants and pool
attendants. But in terms of trickling down to ordinary people, that's not
the name of the process, particularly since the reality is that we are dealing with a finite, natural wealth base. It is not a growing pie. It is a fixed
pie in that regard. And so to keep expanding the wealth of the very
wealthy, you basically have to push more and more people off the basic
source of sustenance. And that's pretty much the story of our times."

What Korten says about the developing world is equally true within
the richest country on the planet. The journalist John Cassidy wrote, in
a 1995 *New Yorker* magazine article, "Until recently, it was an empirical
law of American politics that the majority of citizens . . . received steadily
rising earnings." And for the post-war boom years this was true. From

1945 to 1973, "the rich got richer, but almost everybody else got richer with them and at roughly the same pace." Cassidy says that in those years "the annual growth rate of family income was between 2.4 and 3 percent regardless of where the family stood in the income distribution." If the distribution of incomes is divided into fifths, or quintiles, then the incomes (in constant, inflation-adjusted dollars) in each quintile doubled. But since 1973, says Cassidy, "The bottom two-fifths of American families saw their incomes fall." Even with more working mothers, the average incomes of the middle quintile barely rose, from $36,556 in 1973 to $37,056 in 1993.

In contrast, the top third increased by 7.9 percent over the same period. Incomes of the richest 5 percent grew from $137,482 in 1973 to $177,518 in 1993, an increase of 29.1 percent, and the top one percent skyrocketed from $323,942 to $576,553, a 78 percent rise! Twenty years ago, the average CEO of a large corporation earned forty times as much as the average employee. Now the differential is 190! Today the top 5 percent of American households receive 20 percent of the nation's income, while the top 20 percent receive almost half. Unless the figures are broken down this way, the extreme concentration of wealth among a diminishing minority of the world's population is hidden by simply averaging income.

It's a Mad, Mad World

There's this enormous irony that the so-called proponents of the free market ... support when it comes to reducing public welfare programs. We must have a free market, level-playing-field situation for young teenage mothers. But for the big industrial players, the arguments get turned on their head, and suddenly we absolutely have to have these government handouts and support payments and logging and agriculture and building subsidies.

— ALAN DURNING, HEAD OF NORTHWEST
ENVIRONMENT WATCH

Economic issues are constantly in the media and our consciousness. Governments are slashing social services, including medical care, welfare and education, to "reduce the debt and stimulate the economy." With the debt and deficit dealt with, we're told, the economy will grow and we will be able to afford things like social security, better health care and environmental protection. But even after the budgets are balanced, even after there are all kinds of surpluses, we still don't seem to have enough money to pay decent salaries to nurses, finance our children's educations or make hospitals run properly, to say nothing of protecting wildlife and controlling pollution.

Alan Durning thinks there's plenty of money to pay for all of this, but right now it's being misdirected because of our wrong-headed approach to economics. He wrote an important book for the Worldwatch Institute entitled *How Much Is Enough?* and now he's head of Northwest Environment Watch in Seattle. He's got a surprising list of ways we destroy our natural surroundings, and how we use our tax dollars to do it. He lives in the homeland of the Pacific salmon, as do I, and as Durning says, "You hear people in public life all the time saying that we may not be able to afford to save the salmon. It just costs too many billions of dollars to protect them. But in fact, exactly the opposite is true."

Salmon are almost mythical creatures in West Coast society. They're born far inland in clear forest streams; they travel to the ocean, mature and then somehow, after years, they find their way back to their natal river, and fight their way upstream to spawn and die back in the headwaters where they started. Because of the immense distances they travel and their competition with humans for forest, farmlands, estuaries, oceans, rivers and so on, it seems as if it's very difficult to protect them. But Durning says that protection wouldn't be so hard if, at every stage along the way, we weren't spending taxpayer dollars to harm them.

Here's the full picture as he paints it. "In the headwaters, hundreds of millions of tax dollars are paid to build roads so loggers can go into publicly owned forests and cut them down. From the roads, soil washes into the salmon streams and ruins salmon habitat. A little bit farther downstream, we find big public subsidies for ranchers to run cattle on land that is also publicly owned, and that also erodes into the salmon streams. A little farther downstream, we find hydro-electric dams and irrigation dams built with enormous public subsidies that run to billions of dollars just in the Northwest region alone. Then, a little farther downstream, we come to the aluminum smelters that are using the subsidized electricity from the dams and emitting pollution into the water, emitting global warming chemicals into the atmosphere. A little farther downstream, we find suburban developments along the sides of the rivers, all of which are subsidized with local tax dollars, because developers don't pay the full costs of providing roads and sewers and so on. So people's property-tax dollars are going to subsidize local development. A little farther downstream from that, we find the U.S. Army Corps of Engineers dredging out the channel of the rivers so that ocean-going ships can come in and out of the river and put into port. And again it's tax dollars, tens of millions of tax dollars, paying for the dredging of the river."

If that wasn't enough, Durning continues, "And then, finally, we come to where the fish hatcheries are — tens of millions of . . . tax dollars going to provide fish hatcheries which are supposed to mitigate the effects of the loss of salmon upstream, [where they are] affected by the logging, farming, development, damming and dredging. But in fact we now know that the fish hatcheries are weakening the genetic stock of the wild fish. Then, because of all of this upstream damage, all [wrought] at our expense, the federal government has to put in disaster-relief aid to fishing communities, welfare cheques for unemployed fishermen, and flood relief when the denuded shores can't contain the river and it overflows onto the subdivisions. And then we spend even more money to try to repair habitat or do research on how to help the fish survive or to stop flooding. So it's not that we can't afford to save the fish. It's probably that we can't afford to keep on killing them."

This story illustrates one of the many ironies of our current economic system: we give with one hand and take with the other, impoverishing ourselves as we go. A few developers and loggers get rich while rivers are dammed or forests are clearcut and lost to future generations. And the salmon, a resource that once returned annually by the tens of millions, also need ancient forests and pristine watersheds, all of which are being destroyed. We're losing the fish not because we can't afford to save them, but because we're actually paying private corporations to rub them out and to sequester that wealth and our taxes for themselves. "Billions and billions of dollars out of government treasuries or in tax write-offs go to stimulate and encourage the pollution and resource depletion and habitat destruction that we're all so concerned about," asserts Durning. "We're paying to have it all destroyed."

Taxing the Wrong Thing

*Automobiles' private benefits are enormous and well
understood, yet their abundance makes them the source of a
disturbing share of social problems. They are the cause of more
environmental harm than any other artifact of everyday life
on the continent.*

— ALAN DURNING

What we've done to the salmon is a classic example of the misdirection of
public money, but it's not the only one. All over the world, we are paying
billions of dollars in perverse subsidies to industries that cause social and
environmental breakdown. Alan Durning has many more examples.
"Most of the resource-extraction industries are fairly heavily subsidized,
[as are] the mining industry, the oil and natural-gas industries, the timber
industries and to some extent agriculture," he says. "But just as significant are subsidies to urban real-estate development and particularly to
suburban real-estate development. Subsidies to cars — to driving and
burning fossil fuels — [are] typically about a hundred dollars a month,
per car, in North America. Those subsidies range from the free parking
provided all over many cities to the price of gasoline, which doesn't
include the full medical costs of caring for all the people who are run over
by automobiles or the $20 to $40 billion that are spent by the American
military each year in order to project power to the Middle East to keep
the shipping lines open and the oil fields providing the gasoline."

As Durning points out, "The roads that you drive on are subsidized.
They're paid for not only out of gas taxes, but also out of local property
taxes and sometimes income and sales taxes. Just about everything that
you do in the car, you're paying part of the cost and somebody else is
paying another chunk of it."

Once upon a time, a great deal of freight — to say nothing of people
— was moved around this continent on trains. Most of that freight is
now being transported by trucks, which are far less efficient and hence
less environmentally friendly than trains. It's commonly assumed that
trains just cost too much, that they're not competitive because they
have to be subsidized. Yet trucks are heavily subsidized too, and somehow mainstream economists consider that perfectly all right. "The

huge subsidization of the highway infrastructure has resulted in a long shift away from rail and onto the roads for the movement of freight," explains Durning. "Now, in the United States at least, train companies own their own railbed. The truckers don't own the roadbed, right? It's paid for through tax dollars and subsidized. So the rail system has a real hard time competing. If we simply eliminated the subsidies to road transportation, that would shift some of the freight back onto the rails, and make that a much more viable venture economically."

So-called perverse subsidies are the tax dollars that support an activity that creates a social problem that we then have to pay tax dollars to correct. Durning says we could make everyone's life easier and happier if we stepped back from our current arcane and absurd economic rules and rewarded people for doing things that make society better. For instance, taxation of payrolls could be stopped to encourage employers to hire people and give them careers. Instead, taxes could be levied on polluting activities. The industries would not be any worse off, but society would fare far better. As Durning says, "We're taxed for working, for saving, for investing. And we're subsidized to pollute, to deplete natural resources and [to] consume natural habitats. If we actually eliminated all of these subsidies, then we would find incredible improvements in environmental quality, and in economic performance as well, because all of these subsidies are big drains on the true economic vitality of our continent."

We have to look at history to see how we got ourselves through this particular looking-glass. Back when these subsidies were enacted, we saw forests as impediments to farming and rivers as roads to fill with ships. We didn't yet understand how they provided us with our most basic needs: fresh water, the millions of fish we scooped up and used for fertilizer, our very climate. We paid people to set up industrial infrastructures because we thought that was where the public good lay. But now it's time to say that if goods like timber, upscale housing and metals are really worth having, then the activities that exploit them shouldn't have to be subsidized. As Durning says, "These subsidies reflect political power. They reflect organized constituencies that, over many decades, have sufficiently ingratiated themselves with the lawmakers that they got subsidies written into the books. The public has yet to be sufficiently informed and organized to get the subsidies out of the books. That's all it is."

Capitalism Equals Democracy

We're in a particularly weak position to look at economics,
capitalism, the business sector or plain old money-making in a
cool way, because we feel that everything that is socially
successful is dependent on the success of the marketplace. We feel
that to in any way analyze the marketplace, change the shape
or direction of it, is in some way to endanger democracy, by
endangering prosperity. So it's a whole logic that we've
accepted without any critical debate.

— JOHN RALSTON SAUL, HISTORIAN

Human cultures use words to define themselves. So we say we live under a
"capitalist" system within a "free-market economy" that fosters "democracy." These terms all have positive connotations at the moment. But
sometimes, as when we look at the expense of saving salmon, we find our
basic assumptions and definitions are what should be questioned first.

John Ralston Saul is an historian. Two of his best-selling books,
Voltaire's Bastards and *The Unconscious Civilization,* examine the current
state of Western culture. Saul says one of our biggest problems is equat-
ing our current economic system, capitalism, with our current political
system, democracy. He says, "We're victims of an idea of how democracy
works, and how our society works in its relationship to economics and to
capitalism. And essentially what you hear all the time from perfectly well-
meaning people who automatically accept what we would call the nineteenth-century liberal, or *laissez-faire,* approach is that in order to get
democracy, you have to have a middle class; in order to get a middle class,
you have to have prosperity; in order to get prosperity, you have to have
economics leading the way."

Saul claims that these assumptions do not have any historical basis.
"You end up by mistake with this definition of democracy: capitalism
leads to a middle class, which leads to democracy. And that idea is not
only common, it absolutely dominates throughout the West today — in
all age groups, most political groups, most political parties. And it's just
garbage. It doesn't stand up to a historical analysis in any way, shape or
form. That's what I was trying to show in *The Unconscious Civilization*
in particular — the extent to which individualism, real individualism, and

the concepts of responsibility, the public good and democracy didn't come out of the Industrial Revolution and the formation of the middle class. They, in fact, came out of a very long process that you can take back to Athens."

The reason that history is important is that unless we can look back and analyze how we've painted ourselves into a particular corner, it's hard to even see the corner. Saul points out that democracy had its roots in ancient Greece, long before capitalism made its appearance. Although capitalism didn't arise in Europe until the Middle Ages, nineteenth-century historical analysis led us to believe that democracy grew directly out of capitalism. We therefore believe that democracy can exist only in a capitalist system. Saul also says that because of this positive bias towards the model of business, our society has become fragmented into interest groups based on competition and elitism, as groups are in a corporation. His reaction to our modern economy's rejection of the public good in favour of self-interest is similar to Hazel Henderson's and mine. He says, "In a corporatist society — which is essentially a society where people exist through belonging to self-interest groups, and are rewarded and promoted if they break down their relationship to society into smaller and smaller interest groups and specializations — it becomes increasingly difficult to come up with any sensible, inclusive economics. The whole structure of the [corporatist] society moves towards breaking things down to smaller and smaller interest groups, not bigger and more socially inclusive ones." Self-interest is exalted as the defining motive of such a society. As each individual or group makes a case for the overriding importance of a vested interest, we lay waste to the notion that there may be other levels of needs and relationships that ought to have greater weight and importance.

Our economic system has muddied our real needs. The idea of self-interest being normal and desirable has taken hold so strongly that we've almost come to believe that there's no other way of doing things. "Every day you hear words, sentences, phrases, approaches which reveal this assumption that society is interest-based," Saul says. "The environmental movement is filled with people who actually talk and act as if society were interest-based. Even in winning their victories, they're undermining the idea that real society is driven by something completely different, which is the common good. The public interest, historically and in actual fact, not capitalism, is what is tied to the rise of democracy. Public interest is tied to the rise of the idea of citizenship, and to the whole idea of responsible individualism. Self-interest was what democracy was trying to *combat*."

Sharing the Pie

An economy is a little like a human child. When it's born, it has a tremendous appetite for raw materials, and it clamours for them. The more raw materials it consumes, the more waste and pollution it creates and the more its appetite grows. This persists, but only until the child matures. Then, all of a sudden, the phase of physical growth levels out for good. That doesn't mean the growth of that person has come to an end. On the contrary. The richest and most protracted phase of growth is just beginning — mental, intellectual, emotional, spiritual growth. Somehow, we have to get our economies out of this adolescent phase into a more mature adult phase. It won't be easy, but we can do it. We have to do it, because the growth economy we've had over the last few decades simply cannot continue.

— NORMAN MYERS

Herman Daly, a highly respected mainstream economist, is one of a growing number of thinkers who believe we have to reassess the entire purpose of economics. He says, "I think that economics should be about sufficiency as much as it's about efficiency. But it's not." Daly and others are beginning to challenge the idea of limitless growth, for the very good reason that nothing else on this planet is able to grow without limits — except cancers, and even cancer has limits set by the death of its host. That there are limits to growth is a simple law of hard sciences, like math and physics, but it hasn't penetrated soft ones, like economics. Where did this idea, which has no echo in the natural world or in human experience, come from? Daly says, "We built the modern economy around the idea of growth, I believe at least partly, in order to avoid facing up to the problem of sharing. If you don't continue to grow and you still have poverty, then you have to redistribute. You have to share in order to cure poverty. How do you cure poverty without sharing? Well, the only way we've been able to come up with is by growing."

How does growing avoid sharing? Well, it involves that old assumption that the rising wealth of the elite will somehow lift up everyone else. There will be that famous "trickle-down" to the poor. "Number one," says Daly, "that generally doesn't happen. But even if it did, it's still a substitution of growth for sharing, to avoid the moral problem of sharing. We find moral problems too difficult. So we convert them into technical problems of just growing faster. Then we won't have to deal with them."

The problem with continuous growth is that, as the science of physics tells us, we live in a closed system with respect to matter. We can't have a systematic deterioration of the productivity of nature — of species diversity, for example — and still maintain the ecosphere's abundance. And in order to have a chance of acting sustainably, we need a society that is just, equitable and distributes resources fairly. Without such a society, some people will take far too much while others become so desperate that they will chop down the last trees or use up the last drop of water.

Paul Hawken, a businessman and author of the best-seller *The Ecology of Commerce*, developed a concept he calls natural capitalism. This notion maintains that we need to see nature as the true capital on which our lives and economy depend. And if we learn to value nature, our real wealth, we'll take better care of it. He says that our economic system "works for practically no one, except maybe the one percent at the very top. Our system wastes the environment. It wastes people. And it's very, very expensive. We need a radical change in how we relate to resources and people and the environment."

It's plain that if we are to survive on Earth, we have to make some fundamental changes in our economic value system. Growing forever and not sharing hasn't worked, and we're now stretching the limits of the natural envelope that sustains us all. As Herman Daly says, "We got away with that approach, growing and not sharing, for a long time [because] we were living in a relatively empty world with abundant resources and plenty of space. Now that we're in a full world with much tighter limits, I don't think we can get away with that strategy any longer. And maybe, in some way, that'll force us to face up to the moral issue at long last."

Conventional economics suggests that with steady growth, life will get better and better. But even in industrialized countries, rising GDP and more material consumption have been accompanied by family and community breakdown, pollution, atmosphere change, depleted resources, violence, alienation and drug abuse. It is time to look for different goals and other ways to assess progress. As an example of how we can change, Hazel Henderson points to Jacksonville, Florida, which has had its own indicators of quality of life and progress since the 1980s. "The citizens get together, and if they're doing well on their school and education indicators, for example, they'll say, 'Okay. Let's move the goalpost now. We're ready to achieve higher standards here.' Then they do the same with water quality. They have a feedback component from the citizens, a huge kind of forum, and the media picks this up. This is a living, breathing process. It's part of a new system of collective decision making."

If Jacksonville can do these things, so can many other cities. Henderson says, "For 98 percent of our experience, we have lived in nomadic tribes of twenty-five or so, as gatherers and occasional hunters. We got quite good at living in villages. We had to develop these kinds of feedback systems to run our affairs. And then we moved into towns and cities, and we now are living in mega-cities, and they're new to us. We have absolutely no experience of how to manage our affairs in these big arenas. These well-being indicators are a rudimentary form of social intelligence. I see them as real social learning and cultural evolution, which is really what has to happen right now."

We have made changes before. In fact, that's what humans are best at — adapting to new conditions and change. And we've had the paradigm of growth economics and corporate power for only about a hundred years, which is a brief moment of our evolutionary past. As Hazel Henderson says, "We're talking about cultural development and full development of the human being, not just economic development. Basically, haven't we all been talking about the evolution of the human species?"

I once flew into a village of 200 people in a remote part of British Columbia. I was met at the dock by most of the villagers, and that night went to the community centre for a feast. Everyone was there, and the tables were overflowing with delicacies from the sea, aromatic fruits and wild vegetables. After dinner, the tribal leader began his speech to me by saying, "We are poor. We need development." He then went on to explain why it was necessary to allow forest companies to log. When it was my turn to speak, I began by saying, "I live in a city called Vancouver, which is highly developed. In the one block where I live, there are probably three times as many people as there are in this village, yet I know only ten or fifteen of my neighbours. At night, I lock the car and my house because we've been broken into several times. My children can't play in a nearby park at night for fear of deviants or drug users. We buy our water in bottles for more than the price of a similar amount of gasoline. We have to stay inside when there's a smog alert because the air is so bad it harms our health. I could never put on a feast like the one I've just eaten here. To me, you are far richer in community and resources than anyone is in Vancouver."

On my way out of that place, I realized that it is our idea of economics and progress that actually impoverishes people. Those village folk had a rich, productive ocean and forest and a vibrant community. Yet they believed they were poor, and people like me seemed rich in comparison. Our current use of economics forces us all to destroy the very things that sustain us. Of course, those people in the villages want many of the things that we take for granted in cities: books, doctors, even TV and running shoes. But must they come at the cost of vibrant societies and rich ecosystems? We need new ways to measure wealth, ones that put value back onto community, air, water and the richness of life around us. Some people have already started finding out how to do this. They are shifting their priorities and setting up institutions and agencies to pursue that kind of wealth. We've done that before, when we founded democracies to strive for the common, not the particular, good. We can do it again.

CHAPTER 7
GLOBALIZATION BLUES

Economic globalization involves arguably the most
fundamental redesign of the planet's political and economic
arrangements since at least the Industrial Revolution. Yet the
profound implications of these fundamental changes have
barely been exposed to serious public scrutiny or debate.

— JERRY MANDER, HEAD OF THE INTERNATIONAL
FORUM ON GLOBALIZATION

The global village anticipated by Marshall McLuhan is reality. We are
plugged in electronically to the remotest parts of the planet. Through
that network, consumer goods, information, culture, politics, even sports
and children's entertainment, are being transported around the world.
But the force driving this takeover of the world is not military might, as it
was for the great political empires of the past. Today, power is no longer
the exclusive prerogative of the nation-state. Now it is increasingly exer-
cised by private corporations; and the change has been revolutionary.

John Cavanaugh is the author of a book entitled *Global Dreams* and
the co-director of the Institute for Policy Studies in Washington, D.C.
The institute is a think-tank that examines the way national and international political and social policies affect people's lives around the world.
Cavanaugh says that of the one hundred biggest economies in the world
right now, fifty-one are private companies; the number of countries in
this group is steadily declining. "That means that the big companies like
Mitsubishi, Mitsui, the giant Japanese trading companies, for example,
are bigger than Denmark, Thailand or Indonesia," says Cavanaugh.
"That means that Toyota or Royal Dutch Shell is bigger than Norway.

Exxon is bigger than Finland. Wal-Mart is bigger than Poland." Not only are these corporations bigger and more powerful than countries that have hundreds of years of independent history, they are also "economic entities of a size and power that are unequalled in the history of the world."

This is an entirely new development in the history of humankind. There have been big companies in the past, mostly beginning in the nineteenth century. But the fact that now there are so many and they are so big reflects the current demand for constant growth. Since individual countries and their consumer markets are finite, the only way for these corporations to keep growing is to go beyond national borders. Take a look in bars in Australia, South Africa or Thailand, and you'll find Heineken, Guinness or Tuborg, all originally coming from the small European countries of the Netherlands, Ireland and Denmark. As Cavanaugh says, "They all, over twenty-five years ago, saturated their local market and, by nature of the corporate need to expand or die, went overseas. . . . In the past twenty-five years, most large companies have gone global. The extreme case would be a company like Coca-Cola. It's over one hundred years old. Americans are saturated with Coke; you'd be hard pressed to get them to drink any more of the stuff. But the Chinese market isn't saturated with Coke. Nor is the Indonesian market." Today, whether you make cars, software or running shoes, you'll eventually have to go global to stay competitive and profitable.

These companies amassed their enormous wealth so quickly by expanding into new territories just as aggressively as Alexander the Great and the British did when they claimed their empires. This corporate empire-building went largely unnoticed, however, because their power was measured in terms of wealth, not military might. Cavanaugh says, "For much of the Cold War period, 1945 to 1990, the growing power of these global corporations was obscured by the Cold War itself, and by the dominant military and economic force of the United States in global markets and in world politics. With the end of the Cold War and with the shift from what we might call the age of national security to the age of globalization, more and more people started to become aware of the fact that the true economic power in the world is no longer the United States, per se, but a phalanx of 200 large companies whose sales are the equivalent of over one-quarter of global economic activity. It is these entities that more and more determine the working conditions, the health conditions and the environmental conditions of people around the world; in this regard, they have more power than the military might of the United States by itself."

The 200 largest companies in the world employ less than one-third of one percent of the global workforce, but they control more than a quarter of the world's wealth. How did so much power and wealth become corporate instead of national? The idea of a global economy is usually portrayed as a natural outgrowth of modern progress. Globalization is seen as not only positive, but also inevitable. Jerry Mander, head of both the International Forum on Globalization and the Foundation for Deep Ecology in San Francisco, says, "Globalization tends to be described as something that evolved, as though it were some sort of force of nature. But ... [it's] not an accident, and it's not just a natural evolutionary process. It is a designed system, set up for the specific purpose of enabling corporations to make the rules of economic activity globally. The underlying belief in that designed system is that they, and not any kind of government, are the logical, rational system to do that."

Globalization was deliberately designed by a particular group of men quite a while ago, according to Mander. "This global economic design was in the minds of economists in the 1920s and 1930s, but it came to fruition ... at the end of the Second World War in the United States [during meetings at Bretton Woods], where the leading economists, corporate CEOs and government leaders got together to make new rules. They were coming out of the Great Depression and the Second World War. There had been tremendous devastation, and they were trying to figure out how to design a world economy in the wake of all this horror and devastation."

These people weren't trying to seize power from democratically elected governments, and in many cases weren't trying to amass wealth for themselves. "I think they thought of themselves as 'do-gooders,'" Mander says. "They were trying to think of what kind of system would prevent such terrible things from happening again; what kind of system would provide the things people needed; and how they could help spread the wealth, so to speak. So they designed a system. The best one that they could come up with was one that accelerated economic development everywhere in the world. They believed that economic development was the final answer to people's problems, so they actively tried to accelerate free trade. They broke all the rules that countries used to control economic activity, and they put real power in the hands of large corporations via such institutions as the General Agreement on Tariffs and Trade, the World Bank and the International Monetary Fund."

When news of these new global institutions first hit the media, I think most people were confused and maybe a little bored. They seemed like arcane entities that had little to do with people's daily lives. But their impact on ordinary lives has been immense. As Mander says, "Since then, the GATT, NAFTA, APEC, the European Union and all these mega-institutions have essentially integrated all economic activity and put all countries under the same economic system. Now they create rules that all countries must follow. The purpose of these rules is to free up corporate and financial activity so that [industry] can be completely unfettered, so it can find and use up more resources, locate the cheapest labour and operate globally without any interference. The theory is that this has general benefit for us all."

Winners and Losers

> *Under a system of global free trade, the losers will, of course, be those people who become unemployed as a result of production being moved to low-cost areas.... The winners will be the companies [that] move their production offshore, ... [that] benefit from paying lower salaries at home, ... [that] invest where labour is cheapest and [that], as a result, receive larger dividends. But they will be like the winners of a poker game on the* Titanic. *The wounds inflicted on their societies will be too deep, and brutal consequences will follow.*
> — JAMES GOLDSMITH, PARLIAMENTARY REPRESENTATIVE
> FOR BRITAIN AT THE EU

In the aftermath of the Second World War, the new monetary twins, the World Bank and the IMF, were impressively successful in aiding the recovery of the economies of war-ravaged countries. With Europe and Japan back on their economic feet, these financial institutions turned to the Third World, whose poverty, it was believed, could also be conquered by greater trade and economic growth. The wealth created would trickle down to the benefit of all sectors of society and the global community. The Organization for Economic Co-operation and Development (OECD), which is made up of twenty-nine of the world's richest industrialized countries, is a kind of club, an economic think-tank of people who consider themselves to be in the best position to give financial advice to others. The OECD was founded after the Second World War to monitor and encourage trade in the interests of peace and stability. Today it's one of the leading voices supporting economic globalization. As the secretary-general of the OECD, Canada's Donald Johnston has a very clear idea of what a global economy is. He says that in its ultimate form, "a global economy would be the same as a national economy. In other words, it would be an extension essentially of a national domestic marketplace and, through it, obviously through a process of evolution, of a global marketplace. There would be a free flow of goods, capital and, perhaps some day in the far future, labour."

Canada's first foray into the new global economy was the Free Trade Agreement (FTA) with the United States. Following that, we signed the North American Free Trade Agreement (NAFTA), which brought Mexico into our economic circle. Then the Chrétien government proposed extending NAFTA to include Chile (which pulled out of the negotiations in August 1999) and even possibly adopting a common currency. But opinions are mixed about how beneficial free trade itself has been. Johnston thinks it's been a resounding success. "The numbers are certainly very impressive," he asserts. "The trade in North America has increased dramatically from 1993 to 1996, an increase of something like 43 percent. Mexico has now replaced Japan as the third-largest trading partner with the United States. Unemployment in all of the countries has actually decreased, and direct investment has increased. So I would say that NAFTA has been a great success. And in fact, one could say, looking at it from a regional point of view, that this is hopefully what this so-called globalization would bring to an ever-increasing universe."

To flourish, the globalization movement, like the rest of the economy, needs to grow. So whenever there's a new union, such as the European Union, NAFTA or the Asia-Pacific Economic Community (APEC), the OECD applauds and calls for even bigger economic organizations. As Johnston says, "In other words, these regional agreements should be looked at as stepping stones to a more global arrangement — so that there will not be excluded countries, so that there won't be anyone on the margin."

Proponents of globalization envisage one world so closely linked by economics that there would never be a reason to go to war. Why would there be ethnic or religious hatreds when we have so much in common? A global economic vision even foresees a future in which humanity would have ways to unite, to combine our labour and aspirations, to work for global goals. For anyone who wants global sanctions against dumping toxins into the air or the seas and endangering species, globalization could be a very good thing. In fact, for a number of reasons, consolidating into larger entities is not necessarily bad. But the first problem is to judge whether the current method of economic union is working, and if humanity in general is benefiting. If the answer is yes, it's a lot easier to jump on board.

Despite the glowing report card that Donald Johnston and many others give NAFTA, however, numerous critics believe that it's been a disaster, and that further economic unions have to be very carefully assessed. Maude Barlow is one of the critics. She's the chairperson of the Council of Canadians, a grass-roots organization that led the battle against NAFTA and its predecessor, the FTA. She claims globalization has had very different results. "What free trade did was improve the health of about 200 corporations that work across the North American border. And it improved the investment opportunities for some of the people who are able to invest in those companies. So yes, there's no question — some people did just fine. But it was not fine for the 58 percent increase in child poverty, the children who are caught in that statistic since the Canada-U.S. Free Trade Agreement was signed. It is not good for all the people who had their hospitals closed down and their schools underfunded because we suddenly have no more public funding for social programs in this country. It's not good for the seniors who've seen $8 billion come out of the pensions in the past five years."

Jerry Mander says that the theory that free trade benefits the general population has had twenty-five years to prove itself. Initially, during the particular conditions of post-war recovery, it looked good. But he says it is not living up to that early promise. "It's already clear that it doesn't promote the general welfare; that poor countries are getting, relatively speaking, poorer as compared to rich countries. The poverty gap is widening within the rich countries, too. The people who have really benefited by this expanded trade are the corporate heads and very few others. They talked about it being a rising tide that will lift all boats, but as it turns out it really lifts only yachts. Worse than that, this accelerated trade, this freeing-up of all resources, the 'no controls' on development (which means no environmental controls, no labour standards, no social programs) have brought us to the brink of an environmental breakdown faster than anything before has. We're seeing global warming. We're seeing ozone holes. We're seeing the loss of species and habitat. We're seeing pollution and terrible over-exploitation of the oceans. And all of this because of the theoretical benefits that will come to the general human population from this free-trade system of unlimited, global industrial development."

At least as far as environmental issues go, anyone who has looked at the statistics since the start of globalization will be inclined to agree with Mander. Maude Barlow says, "Globalization is not good for the environment. We have seen cuts of two-thirds support for natural-resource protection at the federal level, and between a half and two-thirds in most of the provinces across the country. It's not good for the animals. It's not good for the forest. It's not good for our water protection. It's good for the mining companies. It's good for some of the forestry companies. It's good for American transnationals and their subsidiaries here. Yes, it's good for them."

Barlow and the other critics contend that there's no money to pay nurses or radiologists or to maintain art, music and sports programs in our schools, despite all our newly balanced budgets, because of the naked grab for public money by the private sector. Wealth that once went into public coffers is now being rerouted to corporations. So when it comes to assessing globalization, she says, "If you're on the winning end, it looks grand. If you're sick in hospital, if you've been cut off welfare, if you're an unemployed, pregnant, eighteen-year-old who's just been told there are no jobs, no programs, no help, you realize that in this system, you don't count. This system has created winners and losers. And the analysis that says that free trade has worked is an analysis coming from the winners."

What's Good for General Motors Is Good for Us All

Corporations, by their nature, do not function as democratic organizations, yet it is they who have stepped into the vacuum created by failed political institutions and taken up the daily work of politics. Their tremendous financial resources, the diversity of their interests, their squads of talented professionals — all these assets and [more] are now relentlessly focused on the politics of governing.
— WILLIAM GREIDER, POLITICAL JOURNALIST

When Canada signed NAFTA, many people were worried about its effect on political sovereignty, national culture and our ability to protect the environment. But we were assured that a separate environmental department, the North American Commission on Environmental Cooperation (NACEC), would harmonize the environmental laws of the three signatories, Canada, the United States and Mexico. The assumption was that Mexico's laws would be brought up to our level. But that's not what has happened. After environmentalists struggled for decades to get better standards, trade agreements like NAFTA pushed these standards down. Maude Barlow says governments no longer have the power to establish independent regulations, and "a lot of us don't have problems with that, if we're talking about higher regulatory standards. But what happens is that these trade agreements take precedence over the international environmental agreements. Multilateral Environmental Agreements, or MEAs, are overwhelmed by trade agreements like NAFTA, because trade agreements have enforcement measures that the environmental agreements do not. The untold story to date about the Canada-U.S. Free Trade Agreement, the GATT, . . . NAFTA, the World Trade Organization, which is the body that came out of the GATT, and now the Multilateral Agreement on Investment, called the MAI or the MIA, is that they all try to lock in environmental standards where they are now, and they actively try to roll them back in some of the countries where they have attained 'too high' a standard to suit the activities of the transnational corporations. They do try to establish international environmental arenas where global standards are set, like the Biodiversity Convention or the Codex Alimentarius of the UN, but these are increasingly influenced — and even staffed — [by] the corporations. And therefore, when they talk about 'standards,' they're not standards that many of us would consider acceptable. In fact, they're never what most of us would consider acceptable."

Barlow thinks this situation threatens not just environmental standards, but also our right to have a say in how countries and corporations are allowed to behave. She says, "We're basically entering a period that some of us are calling 'corporate rule,' where transnational corporations have replaced nation-states in setting the dominant standards around everything from social programs to health-and-safety standards to the environment. And they are using international agreements to cement these new rights in international law, so they are able to supersede those of nation-states."

Barlow's statements sound a little exaggerated. After all, surely Canada and the United States and Australia and the United Kingdom — the wealthy democracies — would never give up the right to decide what kind of laws and regulations their citizens will live under. But what we take for granted — sovereignty over the basic rules that govern a nation — is experiencing profound attack. How do companies acquire the ability to nullify the regulations of nation-states? John Cavanaugh says it's been a gradual process:

"A hundred years ago, companies were local and served primarily local markets. They employed local people, were the pillars of the local tax base and cared, necessarily, about the health of the community, because that's where they got their sustenance. In most countries, those companies created national markets by the 1930s or 1940s. In 1952, the chairman of General Motors, which has long been the largest U.S. industrial company, testified before the U.S. Congress and uttered the now-famous words 'What is good for General Motors is good for the United States. And vice versa.'"

Cavanaugh says that back in the 1950s, you could legitimately make that argument. General Motors, like many other companies — think of Sony in Japan or Volvo in Sweden — was still perceived as rooted in a national place and was a major local employer. It was also a leading force for racial integration in the United States and brought many black Americans into the unionized workforce. GM paid millions of dollars in taxes back when corporate earnings were still taxed significantly. So it made sense for U.S. policy to make life easier for the company. Today, however, what's good for U.S.-founded corporations like General Motors or Monsanto or Coca-Cola is not necessarily good for the United States or its citizens. "General Motors thinks globally," Cavanaugh explains. "It doesn't care about unemployment in the United States or the trade deficit. It cares about making cars cheaply and profitably using a global production base. I think fifty years ago you could say the interests of large Canadian corporations were linked to the Canadian economy, and the interests of large U.S. or British companies were linked to the U.S. or British economy. They now no longer are, and that's creating enormous turmoil, social tensions, environmental problems. It's creating a mess."

Jerry Mander concurs. He says all these corporations went global partly because "the high economic growth rate that became the norm throughout the rapid development of the 1960s was not sustainable. Corporations began to run into shortages of resources; they began to max out their markets, so they couldn't keep selling at high profits to masses of people. This combination of declining resources and used-up markets meant that in order to keep growing so wildly, corporations had to be able to get at the resources that were still supposedly 'locked up' in countries that were protecting them from serious exploitation through trade or environmental or labour barriers. And the corporations also needed to get at the cheap labour markets, which in theory would produce goods less expensively, give them bigger profits and enable them to sell to people they hadn't been able to get at before. This corporate desire for expansion was building up, and then when the Soviet Union broke down, [there was] no opposition to any of the prerogatives that the corporations wanted to establish. There was no resistance to this process at all. And so, since then, it's been a free-for-all."

The role of government has always been to regulate and balance the various sectors of society in order to protect citizens from the excesses of, say, the military or other specific interests. One of the most common questions people ask is, If Macmillan-Bloedel's or Monsanto's or Shell's interests aren't really linked any more to Canada, the United States or Holland, why do politicians in these countries still bend over backwards to make policies that favour them? Why would national politicians give up their own powers and responsibilities to private corporations? John Cavanaugh has an answer: "There's a certain amount of corporate blackmail that goes on. . . . For instance, corporations can say to governments, 'Look, we still provide some jobs here. We still pay some taxes here. If you don't continue to give us the sort of rules that we want, the sort of corporate favours that we ask for, we can pick up our production and move it overseas.' And so, to a certain extent, governments are in a horrible bind, trying to create the incentives that keep corporations at least partially loyal to their national roots. It's a horrible game that governments play. And ultimately I think it's a game that they lose."

A big part of our problem is that politicians are elected for only a few years at a time. In that time, they have to provide benefits that can be seen quickly, like construction jobs, new factories and shopping malls. Since social and environmental problems take years to be revealed and just as long to be averted, different politicians will be around to take the credit or the blame when they become critical. So people elected to office find themselves naturally concentrating on short-term quick fixes, like helping a pulp-and-paper company open a new mill. They know they'll be long gone by the time the effects of deforestation or dioxin contamination from that mill are felt by the public.

Most democratic governments have another built-in problem that explains why national politicians and transnational corporations have grown so cosy. "Politicians in most of the world are elected into office in increasingly expensive campaigns with corporate money," says Cavanaugh. "It's not in the interests of government leaders — be they Clinton or Chrétien or Zedillo or whoever, as well as the members of the congresses and parliaments of those countries — to make it clear to the public that the interests of large corporations are now diverging substantially from the interests of countries."

Globalization means opening up markets, lowering trade barriers, becoming more competitive. Transnational corporations want the same rules to apply wherever they go, so that they can operate globally the way they did in their countries of origin. They demand what's called a level playing field. But getting that level playing field involves a lot of multi-level dealings. It means jobs from northern hemisphere industrialized countries going to the South. It also means that people in the South will never acquire unions, minimum wage and workers' compensation. As

Cavanaugh says, "We live in a world of very unequal nations. Rich nations, poor nations. Countries like Canada with very strong union structures versus countries with no independent unions, like China. Countries that have strong social welfare states and programs, again like Canada, versus much of the world, where that doesn't exist. This creates a beautiful atmosphere for large companies based in Canada or the United States or Western Europe to move production into poorer countries ... like Mexico or Indonesia or China, where they can exploit workers. They can ignore environmental standards. They can press production costs way, way down, yet still get very high levels of quality, very high levels of productivity."

Cavanaugh continues, "When northern workers try to get better wages or hours or working conditions, the corporations have enormous bargaining power to say, 'Look, we, the Ford Motor Company, or we, General Electric, can make these products at a tenth the cost somewhere else and still get the same levels of productivity and quality. Why should we be paying you this much? Why should we be paying you these lavish health-care benefits?' That dynamic is one that in the United States, for example, has led to a stagnation or decline in real wages for 60 to 70 percent of the workforce over the last generation. In other words, there's been an enormous shift in power from workers to corporations with this advent of a global economy."

Under Our Thumb

> *As a result of GATT, Third World countries are under*
> *obligation to accept all investments from abroad; give*
> *"national treatment" to any foreign corporation that*
> *establishes itself within its borders; ... eliminate tariffs and*
> *import quotas on all goods, including agricultural produce;*
> *and abolish ... [any] regulations to protect labour, health or*
> *the environment that might conceivably increase corporate*
> *costs. Conditions more favourable to the immediate interests of*
> *transnational corporations can scarcely be imagined.*
>
> — EDWARD GOLDSMITH,
> PUBLISHER OF *THE ECOLOGIST*

The global economy is managed by at least a dozen organizations that administer, fund, regulate and police economic activity worldwide. You may have heard of many of them, but others are more obscure or have been in existence for only a few years. The big one today is the World Trade Organization (WTO), which is the final arbiter in trade disputes between nations and corporations. Another is the World Bank. Then there are regional trade organizations, like NAFTA, APEC and the European Union. Together, they add up to a new form of global government, with the power to enforce their rules. One of the oldest of these organizations is the International Monetary Fund (IMF), founded in 1944. In a pattern that would be repeated again and again, the good intentions it started out with were transformed into something quite different.

Michel Chossudovsky, an economist who teaches at the University of Ottawa, says the IMF, like all the other global institutions, was founded for the best of all reasons. It was set up with a pooled fund from several nations to stabilize the rate of exchange for member countries so they wouldn't be subject to the disastrous inflation and currency devaluations that were experienced during the Depression and contributed to the start of the Second World War. But over the years its role shifted almost 180 degrees. "In the late seventies," Chossudovsky says, "the IMF started to police country-level economic reforms of debtor nations, imposing very harsh conditions on . . . Third World countries [that had become] indebted both to governments and to private banks. They were unable to service these debts. Then the IMF came in, more or less representing the interests of creditors, and said, 'We will help you to reschedule your debt. We will give you certain facilities. We will give you money. But you have to accept and implement a certain number of reforms.' Essentially what happened is that the creditors of the state, using the IMF as their bureaucracy, started to impose a whole series of economic policy measures. And in many regards, these were very drastic reforms."

We have to remember that Third World countries got into such terrible debt in the first place largely because organizations like the IMF and private banks and corporations urged them to. It was like being encouraged to use a new credit card to buy expensive goods before you have a steady job. A line of credit was offered to these poor countries so they could build infrastructures like roads, modernize and accommodate the factories of all the corporations that wanted to locate in the new markets. They were urged to grab this opportunity to take part in the same measures that had lifted Italy, Japan and Germany out of post-war poverty. And most countries did. Throughout the 1960s, in Africa, South America and Asia, governments were encouraged to make their resources available to transnational exploitation and grow cash crops like coffee and shrimp in order to "participate in world markets." These new industries were funded with generous loans from the World Bank and private corporations. But by the 1970s, the debt load of most developing countries had become so enormous that they were struggling just to meet interest payments. The profits generated by the economic activity went directly into the coffers of the multinational corporations, or into the pockets of a tiny cadre of their local friends, while the general economies of these countries stagnated.

At this point, the IMF came in to help. Their solution was called "structural adjustment," or "economic rationalization," and involved massive cutbacks in public health, education, environmental protection and social services, as well as the dismantling of food and farm subsidies. With missionary-like zeal, the IMF imposed a kind of *laissez-faire* capitalism on countries that had neither basic development nor a long history of citizen involvement, and where riches were already concentrated in private hands and thus unavailable to most people. Michel Chossudovsky thinks several of the most horrible human catastrophes of recent years were the direct result of this *laissez-faire* attitude. He has lived and worked in many parts of the world and continues to work for the Third World Network, a highly effective group of academics and activists that tries to protect the poor of the world.

He says that if we look at apparently political or ethnic tragedies around the world, we often find that they have been triggered by an economic crisis, and that the IMF was frequently there first. In Yugoslavia, for example, internal quarrels and schisms led to tremendous instability and culminated in the ethnic cleansing in Kosovo. Chossudovsky says, "In 1990, the IMF ... intervened in Yugoslavia and implemented a very drastic austerity program, which was based on cutting transfer payments from the Belgrade government. It was a federal system, so there were transfers to the separate republics or provinces, just as there are here. It's as if in Canada the federal government said,

'From now on, the provinces are left entirely to their own devices.' Well, obviously, under those conditions, the federal system collapses. And that is exactly what happened in Yugoslavia." The IMF actions were meant to redirect payments to the creditors of the Yugoslavian state — that is, to rich North American and European banks — but the result was that the federal fiscal structure was destroyed, and within eighteen months Croatia and Slovenia had seceded.

Chossudovsky adds, "Another very important policy was implemented in 1989 and 1990 in Yugoslavia. Called a bankruptcy program, it was run under the jurisdiction of the World Bank. Similar types of bankruptcy programs have been adopted in virtually all these debtor countries." The World Bank would come in and pinpoint various sectors of the national economy, regardless of whether the industries within those sectors were state enterprises or were managed by the workers. And, Chossudovsky says, the World Bank would decide "this one, this one and this one have to close down. . . . Ultimately what happened is that virtually the entire industrial sector in Yugoslavia was closed down. This was not a spontaneous, market-driven process of bankruptcy; it was a bankruptcy program imposed by Western creditors so they could get their money back."

The same kinds of bankruptcy programs have been implemented in Indonesia, Thailand, Korea, many African countries and Russia. Chossudovsky says that after most enterprises were declared bankrupt, Western companies came in and bought them for a song. General Electric, for instance, purchased for $330,000 a company that equipped the entire civilian aircraft industry in the Soviet Union. "This wholesale privatization of an entire industrial system is dramatic because in fact it's a whole economy that has been sold. In other words, it's a process of recolonization. There's no justification for these programs. They are destructive. And ultimately they lead national economies down the drain."

And as we have known for at least 300 years, when a population is impoverished and desperate, it often turns on its neighbours. When people don't really understand what these international agencies have done, why an industry has collapsed and jobs and a future have disappeared, it's easy to believe that old enemies — Serbs, ethnic Albanians, Tutsis, Catholics or Jews — are responsible.

The Global Diner

Trade liberalization was imposed on Mexico [by NAFTA], and specifically, Mexico had to import corn surpluses from the United States. That destabilized grain producers throughout Mexico, especially in the southern region of Chiapas, where small farmers were literally destroyed. [The IMF and the World Bank] say these are political problems; but in fact, if you follow through these reforms, you see how an insurgency in southern Mexico was triggered [by] an economic process which impoverished people.

— MICHEL CHOSSUDOVSKY

Of course, even the IMF and the World Bank can't impose their will without a country's political co-operation or obeisance. How do they get it? Michel Chossudovsky thinks it's a combination of co-option of the powerful through both money and ideology and plain old arm-twisting. He says it goes something like this: "If you don't do as we say, you'll be left out of the global trade club. You'll be isolated and have no access to modern markets and the riches that we have." And then, of course, there's the biggest threat of all: "You'll starve."

Proponents of globalization point to increased trade figures to prove that countries that co-operate with their reforms are better off now in terms of food trade than they were before. But there are many critics who take issue with that. Vandana Shiva, the physicist and activist for the Third World Network, says, "As [for] the myth that through trade there will be more food security, . . . you just have to look at the Indian experience over the last year [1998]. We've had more trade in food, but we've had a declining consumption of food domestically. Let me illustrate this with concrete facts. In June, we were told by the World Bank, 'Your food stocks are high. You're spending too much money holding your stocks. Sell your wheat.' So India obeyed and sold 2 million tons of wheat. In December, obviously we were short of wheat because we had sold the wheat that we were holding in stock for our own use, and India had to import wheat at a much higher price. As far as trade figures are concerned, there's been a tremendous growth. After all, 4 million tons of increased trade in wheat took place. And the pundits of free trade say,

'This is 4 million tons more of wheat!' But it's the same wheat going out and the same wheat coming in. And in the meantime, more people, more peasants, have become poorer and are eating less food. So if you look at the economy of food, people are worse off. But if you look at the economy of trade, you say, 'Four million tons of more wheat!' Finally, if you look at the discussions at the WTO and the discussions undertaken by global agribusiness, every single one of them says, 'More trade means more food.' No. More trade can mean *less* food."

Shiva adds, "Trade liberalization is in fact creating a situation where more and more people are moving out of food production, more and more peasants are being made unviable. Agriculture is being pushed into growing shrimps and flowers for exports, not food. Add all that up together, you don't have more food. You have more food traded, but you don't have more food grown. You have less food grown and less food security overall."

Chossudovsky concurs. "I would say it's the most serious economic crisis in modern history. What has happened in Southeast Asia, for instance — Indonesia, Korea, Thailand — is abrupt and rapid impoverishment of large sectors of the population. . . . What we are now seeing is that all the achievements of the post-war period in the developing countries — in other words, the post-colonial economic- and social-development process — are being dismantled by this new system of globalization."

The IMF and the World Bank are still giving out advice based on policies that have already proven to be failures. In Mozambique, the minimum wage was set by the IMF at seventeen dollars a month, after a series of devaluations. "You can imagine what kind of standard of living you have at seventeen dollars a month," says Chossudovsky. "But the IMF said to the Mozambique government, which wanted to increase wages, 'No. That would be unsustainable. You won't be competitive on the world market with wages of twenty-three dollars or twenty-five dollars a month.' In other words, they intervened, blocking the government's desire to raise these wages."

Somalia followed World Bank reforms for an entire decade. The reforms started in the early 1980s, and before the end of the decade public-sector wages had fallen to three dollars a month. The country collapsed and civil war ensued. Says Chossudovsky, "The World Bank said, 'Well, perhaps we've gone too far. We will now negotiate a program with the government which is intended to raise the levels of wages in the public sector. However, this program will have to be financed by firing 25 percent of the Somalian civil service.' The whole exercise was absurd, because by this time the whole civilian administration had collapsed and the country was at war. But the IMF was still talking about austerity and budgetary restraint."

The austere measures imposed by the IMF and the World Bank on developing countries are familiar to those of us in richer countries like Canada. The civil service has been stripped down, hospitals closed, entire research departments terminated and schools underfunded. In fact, our social problems, which have been made worse by severe economic policies, are the same as the Third World's. It's just that our greater wealth has helped mask the destructiveness of these policies — so far.

Save the Dolphins

Under the new system, many decisions that affect billions of people are no longer to be made by local and national governments but instead, if challenged by any WTO member nation, would be deferred to a group of unelected bureaucrats sitting behind closed doors in Geneva. [They] can decide whether or not people in California can prevent the destruction of their last virgin forests or determine if carcinogenic pesticides can be banned from their food.... Moreover, once these secret tribunals issue their edicts, no external appeals are possible.... A country must make its laws conform or else face perpetual trade sanctions.
— RALPH NADER AND LORI WALLACH OF PUBLIC CITIZEN

A uniquely Canadian story illustrates how globalization, as currently practised, not only impoverishes and undermines developing nations, but also endangers the most comfortable and complacent countries in the industrialized world as well. Ethyl Corporation is an American company that introduced lead into gasoline decades ago as a means of increasing octane to get better combustion. But lead proved to be a toxic neurological pollutant, particularly in growing children, and was eventually banned from use in gasoline. Ethyl Corporation then switched to a manganese-based compound called MMT, even though studies have shown manganese to be a neurotoxin that can attack the brain and induce tremors similar to those in Parkinson's disease. Car manufacturers complain that MMT gums up engines, and many refineries have refused to work with it. Several American states have banned it, and it is generally not in use south of the border. In Canada, however, MMT has been allowed in gasoline for the past twenty years. Eventually, objections to its use mounted, and in June 1997, after a parliamentary debate, the Canadian government banned the compound.

Ethyl Corporation saw the ban as restraint of trade and invoked Chapter 11 of NAFTA, claiming that Canada, as a signatory to this trade agreement, could not ban its product. Ethyl sued the Canadian government for $350 million for restraint of trade and for daring to discuss the subject in Parliament, thereby damaging the reputation of the corporation. Instead of fighting the claim, the Canadian government settled out of court in June of 1998. Canada paid Ethyl a penalty of 19.2 million of our tax dollars, rescinded its ban on MMT and issued a formal statement that there was no evidence after all that MMT was hazardous.

Analysts believe there were two reasons for the government's about-face: first, they were afraid they'd lose if the matter went to the trade tribunal, because NAFTA does indeed have the power to override national health laws; and second, Canada, as a committed partner of the United States and other global powers in the trade revolution, did not want to appear uncooperative. So Canadian children will continue to be exposed to an unwanted additive that is largely banned or unused in its producer's home country.

For Canadians, this is a vivid example of how the rules of free trade can override the sovereignty of national governments. And the Ethyl case has even greater implications for our future. Maude Barlow, whose Council of Canadians fought NAFTA and supported the now-rescinded ban on MMT, says, "What we are so fearful about, and the terrible precedent that the Ethyl case has set, is that governments are going to negotiate with these corporations before they get to the trade tribunals, so that nothing becomes public. We call it the chill effect. And what will happen is that . . . governments will no longer even contemplate certain legislation because they will be told by the industry sector, 'Well, we've had our auditors and our accountants do an assessment, and we think it'll cost you a billion dollars to stop us. You'll have to pay us off if you try to legislate against us.' Many governments, rather than face that kind of payment or the humiliation of the public knowing about it, will either back off legislation or, if there's sufficient pressure in the community, pay off the corporation when no one's looking. So you'll find taxpayers in Canada and other countries *paying* transnational corporations for their governments to have the right to implement legislation that the [people] voted them in for."

The MMT case demonstrates the vast implications of global trade for the environment. Environmental regulations have been enacted in a helter-skelter way, from country to country. Some populations demand strict controls on pesticides and toxic-waste dumping, for example, while others allow corporations to do whatever they want. When trade is liberalized, corporate demands often come into conflict with the more stringent local regulations.

The World Trade Organization (WTO) is our brand-new arbiter of all trade disputes and will make the important decisions about global environmental standards. Maude Barlow predicts that the laws in individual countries will have to fall in line with whatever the WTO says. "Under the WTO, some very important American environmental laws have already been knocked down — for example, the law that banned the sale of tuna caught in drift nets that kill dolphins, the famous 'dolphin-free tuna.' Mexico challenged that ruling at the WTO successfully, although few people know it. So you can't protect dolphins that way any more. There was a more recent case of [a challenge to] a law to protect rare sea turtles from drift-net fishing that catches shrimp in Southeast Asia. Again, that's been knocked down through the World Trade Organization."

Why would the WTO say that Americans or Canadians, for example, no longer have the right to ban ecologically destructive practices? Barlow says, "The way it works is that they use what's called the principle of the product as you see it. In other words, a tomato is a tomato is a tomato. Tuna is tuna is tuna. It doesn't matter how it was grown or caught, or by what humane or inhumane practices, including labour practices." That means that it doesn't matter what terrible things were used — slavery, inhumane animal trapping, banned toxins — in the production or the sale or the growing of the product. "What happens is that if it's still a piece of tuna or a tomato in the end," says Barlow, "that's all you're allowed to look at."

The proponents of free trade argue that the environment is protected in the global economy. The case for dolphin-free tuna might have been lost, but they point out that the WTO considers the individual merits of each case brought to it. In principle, this is supposed to protect the interests of local regions and countries on a case-by-case basis. So what is the WTO's track record on environmental issues? Elizabeth May, of the Sierra Club of Canada, says, "When you look at the incredibly powerful forces of global trade agreements like the GATT and its enforcing organization, the World Trade Organization, you realize that it's not just now and then that they strike down an environmental provision. There has never been a domestic environmental protection regulation that's gone before the World Trade Organization panel on a challenge and survived. Every single time an environmental regulation has been challenged in a trade dispute before the WTO, the environmental regulation has been struck down."

Who are these people who decide whether anyone on Earth has a right to protect dolphins, avoid dioxins or hire more research scientists? May says that when you look at the composition of the trade panels, you realize why environmental regulations are not high on their priority list. "None of the people who sit as judge and jury at the WTO has any knowledge of environmental or health issues. All they know is the doctrine of trade liberalization. It's a very effective cadre of people who have a very complete and reassuring ideology that trade liberalization will lead us to a better world. For example, I heard them speaking at the WTO First Ministerial Conference, and one of the delegates said, 'You know, someday, if we go on down this road of trade liberalization, telecommunications and globalization, someday every single village in Africa will have its own telephone. And that will mean survival!' I was thinking, 'What are they going to do with a telephone? Order out for *water*?' What is this priority that every single village [must have] a telephone before every single village has drinkable water? They're certifiably nuts! But that's the governing ideology. Honestly, I've met some of these people. They're not evil. They really believe in the mantra that trade liberalization will lead us to a better world. It could. But not the way they're doing it."

Some people will argue that the globalization juggernaut must be stopped in its tracks. But May believes that there is a way to bring a global world economy into balance with the environment and with human rights. "I think the best way to redress this imbalance between the rights of economic entities and the unspoken rights of all living beings, like forests and the creatures of the oceans, is to have real global clout for all those rights that have been abandoned at the nation-state level," she says. "We need a global institution that is as powerful as the WTO, but that's a world environment organization. We need global standards that can be enforced at least as powerfully as the WTO enforces its pronouncements. This is the irony of globalization and free trade. People like me — environmentalists — are not necessarily against either globalization or free trade. But we're desperately against the way it's being forced upon us now. There's no logical reason why you couldn't construct a system where expanding trade and expanding globalization mean that every country has to meet the highest standards of anyone else within that trading system. And then we'd all really be better off."

We're All Brown Now

> *Chrétien wanted to look good in front of the military dictators of China and Indonesia. There they don't see or hear protests, and he promised them the same when they came here. It's ironic, because people always say, "Oh, if you trade with them, then they'll get our human-rights standards." But it appears that if we trade with them, we'll get theirs.*
>
> — DENIS PORTER, STUDENT AND APEC
> DEMONSTRATION PEPPER-SPRAY VICTIM

I was sitting in a United Nations meeting, talking about the extraordinary powers that corporations now have to restrict the freedom of everyone, not just the poor, and not just those in countries of the southern hemisphere. The three women I was talking with were from the Philippines, Malaysia and India. One of them smiled at my outrage and said, "Yes, we're all brown now." She meant that these new global rules give corporations the right to take away due process, discourage dissent and even provoke violence on the coddled elite of the northern countries. We're finally beginning to understand, first-hand, what it means to be colonized.

The recent Canadian boycott of Daishowa, a giant Japanese timber company, illustrates the extent to which transnational companies can override our sovereignty. Back in 1989, this multinational was given logging rights to a huge area of Alberta at bargain-basement prices. The area included the traditional territory of the Lubicon Cree, and the Lubicon have been fighting to save their forest ever since. To show their support, three students in Toronto, Kevin Thomas, Ed Bionchi and Steven Kenda, got together and organized a boycott of Daishowa products. Among other things, Daishowa made paper bags that were bought by big chains like Roots, Club Monaco, A&W and Kentucky Fried Chicken. The students were pretty successful in persuading a growing number of companies, as well as individual customers, to support the boycott. Daishowa stayed away from the Lubicon lands for several years. When they eventually went to the courts, however, they targeted the so-called Friends of the Lubicon. They accused the three students of "political guerrilla warfare and economic terrorism," for, as Kevin Thomas puts it, "leafleting in front of stores where Daishowa sold [its] bags. We handed out flyers letting people know who Daishowa was, whether the company they were patronizing bought from Daishowa and what the situation was with the clearcut. That was the extent of it."

For these acts of "terrorism," the three students were sued by Daishowa for $12 million in damages; the company also obtained a blanket injunction outlawing any boycotts against Daishowa products across Canada. For several years, the three activists lived with the suit hanging over their heads. When other groups heard about the case, they also began to back away from boycotts. It was astonishing. A foreign corporation was given huge amounts of Canadian territory and multi-million-dollar incentives to extract the most valuable and irreplaceable resources. They were given our tax dollars to build themselves a huge, subsidized pulp mill to make the clearcuts even more profitable. And now they were using Canadian courts to sue Canadian citizens and deprive them of their right to complain about it all. The company was even able to forbid the defendants from talking publicly about their lawsuit, on the grounds that it might cost Daishowa more business.

Karen Wristen was the staff lawyer with the Sierra Club Legal Defence fund, which defended the three students. She says, "The issue was freedom of speech versus corporate profit. There's just no other way to look at it. The significance for the Canadian public at large is enormous. The effect of thinking that if you go out and advocate for change in any way, and if you make statements about corporations and their activities in the world, you could be subject to a lawsuit where you're going to have to pay damages of $12 million — that's going to have an incredibly chilling effect on people. They're not going to step forward to advocate. And we see it happening right across Canada. [These cases] don't make sense as commercial lawsuits. None of these people can ever pay the millions of dollars they're being sued for. So you have to look beyond that and wonder what is the real reason. Well, the real reason may very well be to shut down this kind of legitimate public debate."

Fortunately, this story has a happy ending: the Ontario court found in favour of the defendants and their right to boycott. But the process took more than two years, and not everyone can find a lawyer willing to work *pro bono*. The headaches and constant pressure were enormous for the defendants, but not for a corporation like Daishowa, for whom the costs were only a drop in the bucket. And activists could have lost one of the only tools they have available to defend themselves from corporate excess — the right to know who makes what and the right not to buy it!

The courts aren't always so reasonable. In Quebec, a similar advocacy group tried to help people in Guyana who alleged they were poisoned when effluent from Cambior, a Canadian gold-mining company, contaminated their river and estuary. The allegation was that the spill killed thousands of fish and made many people sick. When the Guyanese couldn't get legal standing to pursue their claim to hold the company liable for damages in their own country, a Canadian advocacy group headed by Dermot Travis tried to get it in Canada. They were immediately hit with a Strategic Lawsuit Against Public Protest (SLAPP) suit, which prevented them from discussing the situation with the press; they were also sued for millions. Once again, the defendants were accused of terrorism. But a Quebec court ruled the company could not be sued in Canada in the circumstances of this case, even when Cambior's Guyanese lawyer admitted there was no way for people to address the situation legally in their homeland. Cambior was never sued or made to defend its actions on the merits of what occurred in Guyana. The effect of the courts' decisions was to grant the company what amounts to complete immunity from liability, both in the country where it was founded and in the country where it practises its activities. The implications are pretty obvious.

Monoculturing the Planet

Ideas, knowledge, art, hospitality, travel — these are the things which should of their nature be international. But let goods be homespun whenever it is reasonably and conveniently possible; and above all, let finance be primarily national.

— JOHN MAYNARD KEYNES, ECONOMIST

Globalization as it is now practised erodes the ability of governments and citizens to freely make decisions about their countries' welfare. It's destroying the public sector itself, the social glue that has kept our societies together. In 1997 alone, $167 billion worth of public assets around the world were transferred to the private sector — prisons, hospitals, roads and schools. And that's not all. Maude Barlow says, "The essence of globalization is the assault on everything left standing in the public sector, everywhere in the world — from social programs to public education to the protection of the environment. That includes the notion that this river belongs to the people who live on it and fish it; the notion that the air that we breathe is common property; the notion that knowledge is our common heritage, that the genetic inheritance of the developing world belongs to the people who cultivate it. All these fundamental beliefs are under profound assault."

Barlow backs up statements like this with examples that should strike a chord of recognition among Canadians. The notion that global trade organizations can scuttle popular democratic reforms explains, in many cases, why politicians like Lucien Bouchard and Bob Rae, who were elected to protect social services and clean air and water, seemed to switch priorities once in office. Barlow says, "Bob Rae promised to bring in public automobile insurance when he was elected in Ontario. And within two years of being elected, he reneged on that promise under the threat of a billion-dollar lawsuit from the American private automobile-insurance industry. They said, 'If you do that, we've got rights in your country now because of NAFTA. We'll sue if you don't run things the way we want.'"

So if our own democratically elected governments can't, or won't, look after our interests, who will? David Korten's Ph.D. in business from Stanford University and years of teaching at the Harvard Business School made him an enthusiastic believer in the benefits of international aid programs that promote unfettered trade and unlimited economic growth. But when he saw first-hand that such programs were making things worse in many poor countries, he started to rethink the entire paradigm. As a result, he wrote *When Corporations Rule the World.* Korten believes that the very nature of the corporate system, which not only encourages greed but actually demands it, is affecting our ability both to govern ourselves and to control private interests. Corporations are compelled by the drive for profit to squeeze out even the small percentage they'd lose if a national government put limits on their activities. That's why they expend so much energy trying to control both governments and people — to make sure they don't miss out on a single dime.

"These corporations . . . are under enormous pressure to maximize their profits," Korten asserts. "The kind of contemporary experience with profits that we're experiencing creates an expectation that if you have money invested, you should rightfully be getting a return of 20, 25, 30 percent, and that if you're not, then somebody's ripping you off. Now, there's no way that you can get that kind of return from a real, productive, long-term investment if, in fact, it's a responsible investment that's producing useful goods and services, and you're paying a decent wage, and paying your share of taxes, and being responsible about the environment, and so forth. It would probably be closer to historical returns of somewhere between 5 to 7 percent."

The inflated investment profits we've come to expect are based on taking public resources — labour, state subsidies or a clean environment, for example — and turning them into private profits. CEOs are under staggering pressure to increase the returns they're giving the shareholder every single quarter; in other words, every three months they have to show not just the profit they had the previous quarter or year, but an even bigger one. This has become the norm, and in the last few years the biggest corporations have been increasing their profits at a rate of 20 percent each and every year. Korten asks us to put ourselves in the place of one of these CEOs: "Now, you're running a multi-billion-dollar corporation. How do you get that kind of increase in profits every year? Well, you'd better find a lot of people to fire. You'd better contract out more of your production to sweatshops. You'd better find places to dump your environmental waste more cheaply. You've got to press the government and buy some politicians to get tax breaks and public subsidies and so forth." Obviously, you'd also better make sure you can control any protests from the citizens by using public relations, lawsuits or government back-up.

History reveals what went wrong with our faith in corporate rule. When the Soviet Union fell, proponents of free enterprise were ebullient because the Russians could join our way of life; it seemed that capitalism had conquered communism. But as Korten explains, "The system that defeated communism was not a pure capitalist system. It was more what you'd call democratic pluralism, or what is often called in Europe democratic socialism. This was a system in which you had a balance of corporate power, state power and union power, to represent worker interests. That system was enormously productive, enormously successful. It had very, very little in common with the system that emerged, triumphant, from the fall of communism. In the new system, government was being discarded and the labour unions were being destroyed, so there are no checks and balances within it."

Korten continues, "As long as our minds are trapped in the idea that the only choices are the communist system or the capitalist system, we're dead, because they're both failed systems." The advocates of capitalism would have us believe that there is no alternative, but that's not true. We do have other choices. "One of the things that we might actually try would be a market economy, because again we're told that we have a market economy, but that's like being told that we have democracy," says Korten. "We do truly have a capitalist system in the sense of rule by big capital. But that's very different from a market system." Korten says that if we look at what the patron saint of the free-market economy, Adam Smith, actually wrote about it, we'd see that one of its most critical tenets is "the assumption that the costs of production are *internalized* by the producing firm and reflected by the prices of its products. Now that, of course, is one of the most egregious areas in which market theory is violated by our present system."

Perverse Subsidies

Why should companies receive tax credits for their research and development when they are simultaneously shrinking their

> *[local] employment? Why should governments pick up the tab*
> *for cleaning up social [and environmental] problems that*
> *were generated by private employers who failed to observe*
> *minimal ... obligations to their workers and communities? ...*
> *As it stands now, in the name of fostering prosperity, workers*
> *and taxpayers are helping to finance enterprises that do not*
> *reciprocate the loyalty.*
>
> — WILLIAM GREIDER

Environmentalists and social critics say the problem with corporate power as it exists today is that it keeps *externalizing* its costs by making society pay for its wastes and getting its resources for free or at the expense of the state. If industry really had to pay the true market rate for resources, labour and waste disposal, things would change rapidly. In a recent book, *The Tyranny of the Bottom Line,* Ralph Estes estimates that in the United States alone, the externalized costs of industry to society — that is, costs that should be borne by the private sector but that are borne by the public — amount to $2.6 trillion every year. As Korten says, "That is one incredible corporate subsidy! If you begin to look at the extent of externalization of costs, ... it becomes very clear that these mammoth institutions could not survive without [their] massive subsidies. So if we began to apply just a single principle of a true market economy — that the producer must internalize costs — that in itself would result in a massive break-up of these enormous mega-corporations. And it would very quickly move us in the direction that an awful lot of the alternative-development thinkers are committed to: namely, economies in which markets and capital are more localized. You might call it real people's capitalism. And the more we localize markets, the closer we move to the more traditional village concept, where people begin to learn to live within the limits of their own ecosystem."

The mechanics with which we could gain control of the situation are not beyond our grasp, even now. What is needed are real regulations and controls at the global level. That's not impossible. Indeed, we've been doing it in North America since the 1930s. And today, the same lightning computer accounting and information networks that have made business global could obviously be used to control it. What if profits above 7 percent could trigger a worldwide legislative body to investigate a given company to see how, if it were really paying its taxes and paying decent wages and internalizing its pollution, it could generate such profits? If it was found to be profiting through tax evasion or dumping wastes, the company could be fined to such a degree that continuing to behave like a buccaneer would cost it more than it could make. This should be at least as easy as our current methods of pursuing individual taxpayers who appear to have too much money for their stated incomes.

The global bodies are already set up; the OECD or even the World Trade Organization could do it. But the proponents of a "free market" argue that global economic transactions by multinational corporations must be completely unregulated so that their capital can "flow freely." They also insist that, to get debts under control, national economies must be regulated and controlled by austerity programs imposed by these global authorities. It's this idea of debt that puts countries at the mercy of global institutions like the World Bank in the first place. Third World countries got into debt in an effort to catch up with us. But First World countries like Canada and the United States, which were fully industrialized and economically robust after the Second World War, ended up borrowing heavily too. That's because they not only gave away public resources to private industries, but stopped taxing them as well.

We are constantly told the reason countries like ours got in debt is that we "overspent" on social programs. We allowed ourselves the luxury of health-care systems, good schools and community centres. Michel Chossudovsky has an opposing theory. "How do we get indebted?" he asks. "First of all, we get indebted through the handouts we give to corporations. That's been ongoing since the Reagan-Thatcher era. We give out generous tax write-offs and state subsidies and grants. But there's another phenomenon, which is not always understood. Since the early 1980s, we've seen the development, on a massive scale, of offshore banking — the development of tax havens. All the Canadian chartered banks have offices in the tax havens. All the major Western banks have branch offices in the Cayman Islands, in Switzerland, in Luxembourg. And the amount of wealth held in these offshore havens is staggering. It's equivalent to something like 25 percent of world income."

A lot of us wouldn't mind paying taxes in exchange for what we used to get: dependable research and regulatory agencies; schools and health care; protected ecosystems; and laws that respond to local needs and desires. But now most of us feel that we're not getting much for our money, and that we pay far more than we ever did before. Governments in the United States and Canada are striving to balance their budgets; some even boast of surpluses. But budgets are balanced at the cost of hospitals and schools, animals and trees, water and soil. And the sacrifice was unnecessary, claims Michel Chossudovsky. "What has happened is that corporations and rich individuals have transferred large amounts of money to these tax havens. And this money, of course, has escaped tax. It's been estimated that in the United States, the capital flight to the offshore havens, in terms of undeclared profits, is equivalent to the U.S. budget deficit; so if we were able to appropriate even a fraction of this capital flight, we wouldn't have had these budget deficits in the 1990s."

One suggestion to redress the imbalance is to impose a small tax — a fraction of one percent — on every single international financial transaction. The tax would help keep track of these exchanges and could fund useful reforms. The Sierra Club is one of the many citizens' and environmental groups around the world that support this idea, which is known as the Tobin Tax, after James Tobin, the Nobel Prize–winning economist who proposed it. Elizabeth May says the tax would provide a way of tracing the "hot" money that has no nationality, that pays no taxes and accepts no internalization of costs. The only major criticism of such transaction taxes comes from supporters of globalization, who claim they would be too difficult to collect. However, it's not difficult to trace computer transactions. Supporters say all that's needed is the political will. And that's where citizens of all countries can get involved. "People can understand what it's about, how it could work," says May. "Maybe it's not the best tax, maybe there's another way of organizing it. But the notion that the global economy should be wholly unregulated is just bogus."

In recent years, investors making what amount to bets on the stability of currencies have pushed societies into economic chaos in countries like Mexico, Korea and Brazil. In Canada, the dollar has dropped to close to half its previous value because currency speculators decided to bet against it in order to make some money. "It took the stock-market crash of the 1920s in the U.S. to bring about the kind of constraints and regulation of the stock market that were necessary to protect all of society and to keep the whole system from collapsing," asserts May. "Yet at the global level, [the globalization cheerleaders] seem to be living in some sort of dream world. They don't see that [having] unregulated currency transactions at the level of over a trillion dollars (U.S.) a day whizzing around the world is inherently unstable and dangerous."

We're Not Powerless, We're Just Lazy

Little by little, we have lost our sense of mutual aid and cooperation. Two-thirds of us give no time to community activities. Fewer than half of all adult Americans...regard the idea of sacrifice for others as a positive virtue. Over 70 percent of us do not even know the people next door.
— DAVID MORRIS, COMMUNITY ACTIVIST

So what can the average person do? Elizabeth May says, "It may sound too goody-two shoes for words, but write Paul Martin. Say, 'Come on. We know what's going on. We think this is an important issue. We want to see Canada in the lead at the G-7, discussing and promoting the need to do this. We want to see our representative at the IMF change our tune.' I mean, changing the positions Canada takes globally will happen only when they realize that votes might be lost or won over these issues." We have to remember that, at the moment, governments think we're more concerned with the economy than the environment, even though the latter completely supports the former. "This government has decided that the environment doesn't lose them votes, doesn't win them votes, so it's safe to lift the ban on a neurotoxic gas additive and issue a bogus statement written in advance by the lawyers for the manufacturer of the chemical," asserts May. "It's outrageous. But if the public didn't just put the newspaper down and think, 'Well, isn't that awful,' but actually started organizing, started contacting their newspapers, writing their MPs, contacting the ministers, they might change their tune."

Even our representative at the OECD, Donald Johnston, makes it clear that politicians and civil servants alike wait for input from us. When they don't get it, they feel they can go ahead and make all the decisions themselves. Johnston says, "Once I [called] a town hall meeting [in Montreal] because there were so many important issues on the constitution and health care and so on, . . . and three people showed up. . . . Having been active in the political process as an elected representative, as a member of government and also as a party official, I can tell you that people in Canada, and I think elsewhere as well, really should spend a lot more time involving themselves in the fundamental political process. And they don't do it. They should be there at the conventions of the NDP and the Tories, Reform, Liberals, adopting resolutions which deal with these issues. Then they can deal with [global institutions and agreements like] the MAI. They can deal with health care. The fact of the matter is that there are very few Canadians involved in that process."

Citizens have to get involved because the corporations and the people who believe so fervently in globalized free trade are organized. They're coming up with new international bodies, new ways of making sure their agendas are not disturbed by diverse laws, national traditions or citizens' movements. The MAI (currently being called the Multilateral Investment Agreement, or MIA) is intended to cover the globe. And it has very big teeth. Elizabeth May says, "The MIA extends the definition of investment dramatically. It includes culture. It includes natural resources. It includes every kind of so-called financial transaction you can imagine. So from the day that the MIA would be signed — and eventually they want most countries in the world to sign it — any government could be sued by any corporation that felt that any piece of legislation they were implementing or even starting to enforce in a more organized way than they [had] done in the past [would] . . . cost the corporation money. They could sue for financial compensation."

The earlier incarnation of this agreement, the MAI, was leaked onto the Internet, where its provisions were seen to be so sweeping and so destructive to national sovereignty and democracy in general that a worldwide protest forced its withdrawal. But the proponents of open markets are still pursuing their agenda. May is less alarmed than some, but even she says, "The Multilateral Agreement on Investment was just one form of a concept that's already established in Chapter 11 of NAFTA. That [concept] is that transnational corporations are considered equal to nation-states in international law, which then supersedes the constitution of individual nation-states. Then they are given tools with which to sue if their interests are in any way hurt. . . . In other words, no one can sue corporations back, and that includes environmental groups. The MAI is not only not dead, it's here. It's living. It's already present." And it's expanding. Michel Chossudovsky says that under the provisions of the MIA, day cares, Boy Scouts, everything you can think of, could be privatized for profit. People who wanted to keep them as non-profit entities could be sued for restraint of trade. Assets like water or timber would no longer be maintained as national resources. Instead, they would be opened up to all bidders. Mining companies could lay claim to copper or silver under your front lawn. It's so far-fetched that it seems absurd and hard to believe. But the MIA's provisions can be read on the Internet. For all who are alarmed, the underlying thrust of NAFTA and the WTO can also be examined.

This brave new world was fashioned with the best of intentions. It was based on the idea that a single world built on co-operation is a good thing, and that trade is the unifying principle that will promote both peace and prosperity. But since the fall of the Soviet Union, which used to provide an alternative to runaway capitalism, everything has been turned upside down. In a world now led by fervent apostles of a magical entity called the Market, governments that attempt to protect basic social programs are depicted as disruptive to free trade. In this new world, it is believed, the rich will care for the poor voluntarily, not because some government makes them. And because the rich will have so much wealth, they will inevitably spread it around.

Maude Barlow believes that Canada is not just another place where getting rich is all that matters. She doesn't believe Canadians think that the rich will help others voluntarily. She doesn't want "Survival of the Fittest" to be our national slogan. She says, "This is not the Canadian way. We built a fundamentally different society here, [one] based on the concept of universality, not the notion of deserving poor — you know, the widows' and orphans' fund. Instead, we built a system that said 'We are a family.' Any of us can lose a job or lose our health or lose a child or a spouse. Any of us, and all of us, at one time will need our family. And we'll need the safety net our family provides. Because we live next to the largest superpower in the world, we know that we have to share for survival. And that, in my opinion, is the Canadian narrative. That's the soul of our history. And when we share, we do it by establishing systems of interdependence — I call them ribbons of interdependence — like our child payments, our social and cultural programs, our universal health care, our pensions."

The new economic ethos that encourages the amassing of wealth at great speed and all costs is being supported by the impulse to give corporations legal rights that are not even held by countries or people. "I can't find words strong enough to say how this betrays one hundred years of jurisprudence in our country," says Barlow. "This removes the rule of law. We're dealing with international agreements that have given transnational corporations — that is, private capital — fundamental rights in international law for the very first time. There's never been anything like it anywhere in the history of jurisprudence."

Imagine

> *The real voyage of discovery lies not in seeking new lands but in seeing with new eyes.*
>
> — MARCEL PROUST

It's a frightening situation, but David Korten has some reassuring thoughts. "To me, the fundamental principle that we as citizens, as ordinary people, have to bear in mind is that these seemingly overwhelmingly powerful institutions have only one source of power. It's the power that we as people yield to them. They're all human institutions. And in a sense, they exist only in our mind, and they draw power only from the extent to which we accept them as legitimate and yield to them as legitimate institutions. If we withdraw that legitimacy and withdraw that power, they almost literally no longer exist. It's like the fall of the Soviet Union. When people finally got their act together and said, 'This institution is not serving us. It's not legitimate,' it collapsed in an instant."

The first efforts to pass the MAI were stopped in their tracks by groups of citizens that circulated its provisions, wrote governments, organized teach-ins and fought back all over the world. As a result, a lot more people are aware of what's at stake in the global casino these days. "There's no question in my mind," says Korten, "that we're seeing a massive shift in consciousness among people all around the world. The system has really overstepped itself with this press towards globalization. The consequences are breaking out in ways that people can see, and they can see the connections between the trade agreements and [the fact that] more and more people are losing their jobs, and [that] the labour unions are having a harder time maintaining wages, and [there are] egregious environmental abuses, and so forth." Korten jokes about something we've all noticed. "If you went back, say, four years ago, and you tried to get together a group of people to talk about the GATT and trade policy, you'd have a very small meeting. People's eyes would glaze over. But now . . . you can get a pretty good turnout and people don't fall asleep. In fact, they're on the edges of their chairs. And the more they learn about it, the more incensed they become."

John Cavanaugh, of the Institute for Policy Studies, believes the time is ripe for the kind of public pressure Korten says has to be mounted. "The key here is that governments have been getting all of the pressure from the corporations. Corporations have been giving them the money to get elected, and they've been saying, 'In return, we want new rules. We want a World Trade Organization. We want a NAFTA. We now want NAFTA expansion to the rest of the world.' Governments have not been getting enough of a backlash from citizens' groups saying, 'Absolutely not. You can't give this away.' Governments, after all, respond to pressure, and they've been responding overwhelmingly to corporate pressure and corporate money. And again, here's a piece of good news. There is a growing citizen backlash in Canada, in the United States and in many parts of the world. People are standing up and saying, 'This incredibly accelerated push towards corporate globalization is not in our interests, and we're not going to let you get away with it.' "

Even Donald Johnston, who as secretary-general of the OECD believes in the benefits of globalization, says, "Here at the OECD, I brought with me the concept I had of government, which is that what one has to do is maximize economic growth . . . because without that you cannot have social progress. But you also have to have social cohesion and social stability. So the benefits of economic growth have to be transferred, in an equitable way, to populations at large. And the agency for doing that . . . is good governance. And it's these three together, essentially, which make societies progress. And when any one of them breaks down, countries and societies come to a halt. That domestic triangle . . . is now international. We have to ensure that the benefits of the ... liberalization-of-investment agenda, the benefits it's clearly providing, are equitably distributed on a global basis. And that has not happened yet."

Maude Barlow argues that not only do the current global institutions *not* ensure the balance Johnston hopes for, they actively work against it. She says, "We have to stop these international agreements, and we have to build international systems and codes and processes that will create truly international standards. I'm not a nationalist in that sense. I would easily give away a great deal of sovereignty in this country for higher economic, social, environmental standards around the world for everyone. That's got to be the goal. There's a great deal of work being done now on ways that could happen — how governments could work to cut off tax havens for corporations; how they could work together to establish higher standards in terms of these global agreements; how you could build a Multilateral Agreement on Investment that gave citizens, governments and NGOs [non-governmental organizations], and not just corporations, fundamental rights."

We have to imagine the kind of world we want and then work to create it. That's what we did in the past, and that's how we got universal suffrage, free public schooling and national health care. If we could do it nationally, we should be able to do it globally. Barlow is trying. She says, "What if we said that we would revoke the licences of corporations [that] pollute or [that] use child labour? There are a thousand ways that we, as citizens of the world, can start to talk about how we are going to bring the rule of law to global capital."

What suffers most violently in the drive to acquire riches as quickly as possible is nature: the trees we chop down and the soil and oceans we mine for quick returns. The unsustainable loss of the natural systems that are so vital to our lives is all related to economics and globalization. "If we don't bring the rule of law to global capital," says Barlow, "we cannot save the environment. We cannot save the Earth. We know the environmental realities of global warming, for example. But unless we address the systemic undermining of our democratic ability to do anything about that through these international trade agreements, through globalization, through privatization, through deregulation — unless we address that, we're sitting in a leaking boat, taking water out with a little thimble. And we're going to drown."

I travel a lot. Whether I deplane in Shanghai, Moscow or Buenos Aires, the airport is immediately familiar to me because it has all the same shops, computers and consumer products. That's what a global economy does. On trips to Papua New Guinea, the Amazon and the Serengeti, I have encountered children running around in Nikes, dancing to Madonna or Michael Jackson, or watching *Baywatch* on TV, once again a reflection of globalization. But what makes travel to exotic places and meeting people with different customs so fascinating is the *differences*. The world is being homogenized through a single notion of progress and development. But this process runs counter to one of the great biological insights of this century — namely, the importance of diversity for long-term survival. By maintaining a tremendous variety of genes, species and ecosystems, life has always been able to adapt to the unexpected changes that keep occurring on this planet. Diverse cultures have given our species the same kind of resilience in different and changing environments.

It is the differences that maximize the chance that there will be survivors under new conditions or different circumstances. Homogeneity and monoculture run counter to this basic principle, making us vulnerable to sudden changes. We are performing a huge experiment on humankind and all life on Earth by pushing one kind of economics around the world. As it is currently set up, our global economy has no balance and no input from varied sectors of society; it's all run for one sector — business — and for one goal — profit. What if that's a mistake?

CHAPTER 8
THE OTHER WORLD

Shell has waged an ecological war in Ogoni since 1958.
An ecological war is . . . omnicidal in its effect. Human life,
flora, fauna, the air and finally the land itself die. . . .
Generally it is supported by all the traditional instruments
ancillary to warfare — propaganda, money and deceit.
Victory is assessed by profits, and in this sense Shell's victory
in Ogoni has been total.

— KEN SARO-WIWA, NOBEL PRIZE–WINNING AUTHOR,
EXECUTED BY THE NIGERIAN GOVERNMENT IN 1995

Despite the sophistication of the twentieth century, we still perceive the world through our sense organs and our personal experiences in our local surroundings. It is natural, therefore, for us to focus on our own local problems. It's difficult to identify with people who live far away and quite differently from us. We worry about our taxes, the decline in the quality of our schools or health care, and local problems like air pollution, urban sprawl or computer breakdowns. But people in many other countries of the world are worried too — about us. They have to be, because our demands, and especially those of the companies that are responsible for providing us with the goods that are part of our comfortable, modern lives, are ravaging their countries and their futures.

The enormous wealth of resource- and expertise-rich nations enables us to live very well while mitigating the extra costs of worsening air, water, soil and social conditions that are a direct result of our lifestyles. But increasing numbers of people in the industrialized countries are questioning the value of a quantity-driven, rather than quality-driven, lifestyle. And they are finding that some of the societies in the Third World that we think of as poor still cling to values and customs from which we could benefit.

The Niger River Delta in Nigeria is a typical area of the "undeveloped" tropics that is affected by the lifestyle of people in industrialized countries. The delta is incredibly rich in biodiversity, one of the largest and most productive wetlands in the world. Its mangroves and lowland rain forests are nurseries for thousands of species of tropical animals and plants. Around 7 million people from twelve different tribes live there, making their livings through subsistence farming and fishing. But there's another presence in the area. One of the largest and richest multinational corporations in the world, Royal Dutch Shell, the international parent of Shell Oil, has been drilling in the Niger Delta for the past forty years. The company has extracted an enormous quantity of oil and gas to feed the fuel demands of countries in Europe and North America that make up what is called the First World. It has made vast profits, much of which has been externalized (that is, hardly any of that money has gone towards land rights, taxes, equitable wages, compensation or waste management). Shell has been able to keep such costs largely non-existent by allying itself with successive governments and forming a mutually beneficial relationship.

Danny Kennedy works for Project Underground, a small but highly effective California-based human-rights organization that works with communities threatened by mining and oil operations. He says, "As long as Shell Oil has been in Nigeria, they've had this revolving-door arrangement with Nigerian dictatorships, one after another. It's a constant transfer of power from the upper echelons of Shell's staff to the upper echelons of government — and vice versa. Shell has extracted huge wealth from the nation — in terms of dollars, something like 30 billion. And they have done [very little] in terms of basic, compassionate, human welfare considerations, community relations practices, let alone environmental management, which a normal resource company might engage in."

But how is this a problem for the rest of the world? At first glance, it seems to be a problem only between Nigeria and Shell. Oronto Douglas is an environmental human-rights lawyer who works with the Environmental Rights Action (ERA) group of Nigeria. He says, of Shell, "They control government and control our very lives, our very existence. So I wonder, how did this come to be? . . . Why have we Nigerians sold our conscience, our humanity, to multinational corporations? Why can't we take back what rightfully belongs to us? Part of the answer, I think, is [that] the governments in the North are allowing the multinationals to do what they are doing."

Douglas is a member of the Ijaw tribal group from the Niger River Delta. Four years ago, Ken Saro-Wiwa, the Nobel Prize–winning author, was executed by the Nigerian military dictatorship for protesting Shell Oil's activities. Douglas was Saro-Wiwa's lawyer. Just for showing up to defend his client, he was arrested, flogged with a six-millimetre electric cable and tortured. He still bears the scars. He says that behind the torture and deaths of more than 2,000 of his countrymen and -women stands an unregulated global corporation that provides the rest of the world with fuel. Largely because of Saro-Wiwa's death, Shell Oil has become a symbol of what has been termed multinational corporate recolonization.

Ken Saro-Wiwa was a member of the Ogoni, one of the smaller tribal groups in the area. He was also an internationally known author. Beginning in the early 1990s, Saro-Wiwa found himself speaking out against, and then rallying his people to protest, the presence of the big oil companies. In 1993, he organized one of the largest peaceful protests ever seen on Earth. Three hundred thousand Ogoni (out of a population of only 500,000) turned out to tell Shell Oil to get out. Using non-violent tactics, they blocked access to the oil-flow stations and pipelines, as well as the few roads and airports entering the delta. Shell backed off and let the Nigerian military in.

At least 2,000 Ogoni have been killed since 1993, yet as Danny Kennedy says, "The Ogoni still haven't broken. They still haven't let Shell come back in, and as a result their land is actually healing in some small measure. We were able to conduct the first scientific analysis of the background pollution in the Niger Delta in February of 1997.... We took samples, the first in Ogoni. We found that in an apparently normal stream, the levels of background hydrocarbon contamination were over 300 times what the European Union considers a safe public health standard! Elsewhere in the delta outside Ogoni, where Shell has continued to operate, ... we found background hydrocarbon levels *over 700 times* what the European Union considers healthy."

What does this mean to the health of the people and the ecosystems of the area? Environmentalists keep repeating a simple fact: gas, oil and their derivatives — our fossil fuels — are highly toxic substances. That's why they're so dangerous in car exhaust. In Alberta, about 4 percent of the gas released by oil drilling is flared (i.e., burned), a level that's considered dangerous and unacceptable by many countries and is illegal in the United States. In Nigeria, more than 70 percent is flared. As a result, toxins are released directly into the air and rain down onto vegetation, the soil and bodies of water. Danny Kennedy reports that partially burnt hydrocarbons permeate the soils and the waters of the whole region. "The yam yield has [been] reduced. Everyone from the delta talks about how the gardens are less productive. Obviously, they would be. People's skin gets covered with blemishes because their bodies are reacting to these toxins." Still, this situation can be remedied. Standard industry practice is to reinject the gas down the drill hole instead of burning it. But of course that costs a little more money and has to be monitored.

Shell is not the only offending corporation in Nigeria. There are many others, including Chevron, and to some degree, they're as culpable. But Shell is getting most of the heat because it was the first to drill in the region, it has a documented involvement with the Nigerian military and it produces more than 50 percent of the highly repressive Nigerian government's revenues. One would assume Shell has a lot of influence with the government, but what has the company got to say about the ecological problems associated with oil development? Basically, that it's an internal problem for the country, and the company wouldn't dream of interfering.

Others don't agree with Shell's assessment of the situation. There are judicial proceedings against Shell, a worldwide boycott and general bad press. When we were preparing our radio series, we invited the company to discuss the issues at length, corresponding with them for weeks. But in the end, Shell refused the opportunity to present its position. The company did send us some glossy public-relations brochures on how ecologically damaging practices are slated to be "phased out" in another decade. In earlier brochures, the date for the phasing-out was supposed to be 1998. Shell also claims that there's no proof that its activities cause environmental damage. However, until a recent and superficial World Bank study, Shell itself had done all of the environmental assessments of its own activities.

Death and the Bottom Line

*Shell [has] paid field allowances to the operatives of a squad
called Kill and Go, the mobile police squad of River States,
which comes into villages and does what its name says. They
bought ammunition and other munitions for the military
actions in the River State. All of this is on record. They've
acknowledged all of it.*
                    — DANNY KENNEDY, PROJECT UNDERGROUND

Shell's behaviour, although particularly well known, does not stand
alone and, in general, merely points out a basic truth about global
business: when an unregulated company can accumulate wealth without internalizing any of the costs, it will do so. In countries that either
cannot or will not protect their citizens, corporations will be tempted
to ignore every precept of morality. Unregulated business driven to
maximize profit may simply not take responsibility for protecting
people or nature.

We operate under a system that talks about spreading wealth and
helping the poor, and that urges one model of development to do so.
But that same system is encouraged, even forced, to find every possible
loophole, every imaginable shortcut, every devious way to save money in
order to return larger profits. In countries that for whatever reasons do
not protect labour or the environment and do not impose stringent
health standards, corporate logic encourages private enterprises to take
advantage of the situation, and to fight any upgrading of standards that
will hurt that lush and unfettered bottom line. Shell Oil is one of the
most flagrant examples of this behaviour, and it's been richly rewarded by
this system; it is the single most profitable company on the planet,
according to *Forbes* magazine.

Danny Kennedy says that even when its own shareholders voted
in unprecedented numbers — 12 percent of all the stockholders —
for more adherence to Shell's own stated but unenforced human-
rights policies, the company's response was merely to increase its
public-relations efforts. Meanwhile, Shell has admitted that it has
purchased weapons for the notoriously violent Nigerian military, and
has maintained a private "security force" of its own. This is a chilling

view of how the future will look if corporate powers are allowed to operate without restrictions and without outside controls.

I interviewed Oronto Douglas at a teach-in on corporate rule at the University of Toronto. He had to be smuggled out of Nigeria for the event because he cannot travel to and fro at will. His life is in constant danger simply because he tries to tell outsiders what is happening in his country. But he takes these chances because he's trying to get us to help, even a little.

Douglas has shown great courage in his fight for his people. Indeed, it is remarkable that Ogoni strategies remain staunchly non-violent, especially when one considers the violence and brutality of their opponents. But immense forces are arrayed against them. "What we are saying is that the West, the North, should join hands with us by fighting for these ideals — for us primarily, perhaps, but also for the world generally," says Douglas. "How can you do that? You can exercise your freedom that you hold so dear, that you fought for, and say, 'Look, Shell, you can't do that any more.' People should boycott Shell. Cities should boycott Shell. . . . Governments should impose sanctions. And people should boycott any other multinational that is implicated in the ugly situation in the Niger Delta."

To the development model argument that says Nigeria can support its people only by mining its resources, Douglas responds, in a way that should make us all pause to reflect, "What we have is not just oil wealth. There are more riches in the delta. A lot of people don't know that we have wonderful forests, mangroves, tropical rain forests. There are other minerals, wonderful foods, crops, a lot of birds flying everywhere, fish. This is our wealth. . . . We should not be thinking of fifty years from now. We should be thinking of 2,000 years from now. That is an African philosophy; that is our perspective. If you come to my village today, people will tell you about past ancestors who fought to protect the community, ancestors who link us to the past in terms of religion and so on. . . . You go to a typical African community, they think both retrospectively and prospectively. They do not think only of themselves."

A friend of mine who has lived in Africa once remarked that the reason famines there are so devastating is that no one starves until all the food is gone; then everyone starves, because they share. They have values and a way of life we would do well to heed. Oronto Douglas tried to express it when he said, "We do not own this planet. You will live and you will die, and some other person will come. Why should you make life difficult for those coming after us? Why? We think about what the planet has given us, and what we give the planet in return. . . . This struggle is not an oil struggle alone. It is a struggle that is all-embracing. It is holistic. The utilization of oil or any other wealth must be done with the consent of the people, with equality. As a people, we have mobilized to be [the guardian] of our environment and our resources so that the resources will be used for the benefit of all and not by a greedy elite, . . . whether they are locally based, or nationally or internationally based. We will never accept that. We will not."

Recolonizing the World

> *We must find new lands from which we can easily obtain raw materials, and at the same time exploit the cheap slave labour that is available from the natives of the colonies. The colonies would also provide a dumping ground for the surplus goods produced in our factories.*
>
> — CECIL RHODES, NINETEENTH-CENTURY
> INDUSTRIALIST AND POLITICIAN

The people of the Niger Delta are fighting for their very existence, and the struggle has brought out a heroism that's dramatic and overwhelming and far from anything most of us have ever faced. And yet it's not atypical. I've encountered many similar situations in poor countries of the Third World. On the one hand, there are terrible tragedies — violence, environmental despoliation, injustice and greed — that are both endemic and external. On the other, there are large groups of citizens, and sometimes even their governments, who have a very clear vision of a better world, who are tirelessly fighting injustice, environmental destruction, commercialization and corruption.

As a member of a rich, industrialized country, I brought to these countries my preconceptions about their societies. The first of these is based on our notion of "development," and holds that all people who do not have telephones, shopping malls, cars or VCRs are "poor." We've come to believe not only that everyone *should* be like us, but also that they *want* to be like us. So we take it as our responsibility to help them achieve what we think is a universal human aspiration: to acquire what we have. And it isn't just clothes and food and shelter any more; our lifestyle is presented as a kind of heaven, a pinnacle of desire that everyone must achieve for true happiness.

Today's drive to push Western development onto Third World countries is very much like our previous forays into new lands. Many centuries ago, Europeans brought Christianity and Western medicine, as well as disease, to other countries. The devastation unleashed on these viable, balanced and healthy cultures and economies was incalculable. Yet in general, the colonizers really thought they were helping. They thought that European life, worship, dress, thinking and farming were all supremely desirable, and that any other way of life was barbaric, primitive, heathen, dirty and sinful.

Now we're back — with a largely North American vision of economic progress and global development that looks at any other kind of society as underprivileged, inefficient, outmoded, dirty and poor. This time the conquerors are armed with a new religion: material gain and salvation for all through global trade. The first wave of colonialism forced everyone to become Christians, farmers or producers of wealth. Now we want everyone to watch TV, drink Coke, wear Nikes and consume the goods we offer. But a lot of the people we're trying to convince remember what happened the first time. The inducements we offer are not instantly seized upon by people in the Third World. Indeed, just as in the First World, billions of dollars are spent annually on advertising to convince people that they really want and need products.

It has been said that television softens up Third World cultures for consumerism the same way Christianity softened them up for colonization. Images of *Baywatch*, *Miami Vice* and *Star Trek* are dispatched as harmless fun.

Jerry Mander, the ex-adman who runs the International Forum on Corporate Rule, says, "About 70 percent of the world population now has television. Very little [programming] is produced locally; in most cases, it's from the U.S. and a few other developed, northern countries. So you have people in the tundra up in the Arctic and people living in grass houses in the South Pacific and people living in slums in Asia and

South America seeing a bunch of white people in Dallas standing around swimming pools drinking martinis and aspiring to nothing more than killing each other to take over each other's corporate activities and make more money. Or they're watching cartoons or MTV or the Nike ads. And what you [have] is a set of images that are homogenizing consciousness in the world." The incalculable cost of this is erosion of local, diverse values, cultures and communities.

Mander points out that the reason advertising is so successful is that it works — images have power. Our brains have evolved to take visual stimuli very seriously. Once we see images, we can't forget them, and their contextual emotions of happiness, fun, contentment and triumph become associated with the commodities they sell. "It's a tremendous invasion of cultural and economic values, . . ." says Mander. "Since these images are so believable, all that goes with them [appears to be] attainable, achievable, easy, nice and good. It's got such a gloss and an attractiveness to it that everybody kind of wants to go for it. And it's presented to them as a real alternative to the way that they live. . . . There's no corresponding counter-force that tells people that this stuff that they're watching, this lifestyle, is producing alienation — drug abuse, violence, suicide, family violence and disempowerment — on a level they've never imagined. And it's also bringing a tremendous breakdown of the environment. The level of consumption that's presented in this kind of imagery is directly connected to the overuse of the resources of the planet and the terrible waste problems that cause global warming, ozone depletion and our current destruction of habitat. All of the tremendous problems that are bringing us to the brink of evolutionary breakdown — forever — are hooked directly to this set of images that look so attractive [and harmless] in the first place."

There are not enough resources on the planet to provide everyone with the lifestyle of *Dallas* or *Knot's Landing*. This is not only an impossible goal to achieve, however; by aspiring to it, we accelerate social and environmental degradation. As Mander says, "The sets of values that are really survivable and sustainable are being driven under completely, because these consumer values are replacing them. To have sustainability on this planet, we need cultural values that are consistent with less consumption, the development of local economies, less transport of goods, a more diverse economic base within regions and more equitable distribution. These are the things that will lead to a future."

For some, it may be reassuring to get off the plane in Manila and hear the same joke you saw last week on *The Simpsons*, to exchange hip talk with an Asian teenager about the latest supergroup and to meet people who have a picture of your country based on television images. It *is* easier to understand people when you share some of the same culture. But as the people of the Third World realize that although a global economy may make a pair of Nikes accessible, an education or decent drinking water is not an option, their enthusiasm will be replaced by frustration and anger. In fact, in many parts of the Third World, people have already recognized the new colonization for what it is.

Jocelyn Dow is a businesswoman from Guyana, a poor South American country of only 6 million people, mostly ex-slaves from Africa and the rest of East Indian, Chinese and Native origin. She says, "The mysticism and the romancing of the idea of commodification should not fool a single Caribbean person; you have to remember that except for the indigenous people, we're all here because we were the actual commodity. We were the energy, the slaves and indentured labour." Buying and selling to send riches around the world looks better if you're not one of the things being bought and sold. "Caribbean society was designed for a world that wanted sugar," says Dow. "It was designed to produce sugar. There was a whole philosophical system, a whole religious system, to support the reason why this commodity and this system of production were not only justifiable, but [also] desirable. And I always say that what you have to remember about this whole cult of the market is that for 400 years *we* were the market. We were the items. So we should not in any way be caught up in any world-view that talks about how wonderful the market is."

Fighting Back

There simply aren't enough policemen in India to deal with 600 million farmers. And that's something that's difficult [for companies] to understand. Our quarter of a million farmers in Canada can't conceive of that kind of direct action. But there are people who can.

— BREWSTER KNEEN, FOOD SYSTEM EXPERT

John Cavanaugh says one of the countries where citizen opposition to corporate globalization is the strongest is India. He says, "There is a strong history [in India] of people rising up and fighting for their rights. In that country, half a million people took to the streets to protest Cargill, a giant agribusiness conglomerate that is trying to take over their seed banks [in an effort to gain further market share]. Thousands went out into the streets against Kentucky Fried Chicken, who they saw as trying to homogenize consumer food tastes." In fact, at UN meetings, on the Internet or on television news, if you're watching for it, you'll see that the countries our culture is trying to colonize are fighting back. Cavanaugh mentions the Philippines, Thailand and Ecuador, all of which have made efforts to protect their markets and their crops from global homogenization and piracy.

But one of the most volatile battles is going on closer to home, and it's being fought by one of Canada's key trading partners. "More and more organized resistance against corporate globalization [is] coming from indigenous communities," says Cavanaugh. "In Chile, for example, 10 percent of the population are Mapuche Indians, and they have joined in an alliance to keep NAFTA from expanding to Chile. But by far the most impressive indigenous opposition has come from the Mexican state of Chiapas. [In] the southernmost state, where Mexico's most heavily concentrated indigenous population exists, . . . there has been a massive resistance to NAFTA, and to the entire Mexican economic model that has come with NAFTA, which is disenfranchising people from their land."

As they did with Rwanda or Yugoslavia, members of the media portray the rebellion in Chiapas as an internal or ethnic conflict when, in fact, it reflects a global economic and trade crisis. In Chiapas, it has a lot to do with First World corporate and government desires to make money at the expense of the poor. "Much of the issue in Chiapas is land," says Cavanaugh. "With NAFTA came new Mexican laws [that] permitted what were formerly state lands, communal lands, to be sold; and the selling of land in indigenous Mexico is really the end of life and the end of culture. So there's been a massive resistance. It's been an armed resistance as well as an organized, citizens', non-armed resistance."

Not only was the traditional land base sold to agribusiness, as also happened in other developing nations, but both the World Bank and

NAFTA tied agricultural reform to their loan and trade deals. That meant that there are no more subsidies to or protections for the indigenous corn growers, and that at the same time the market has been flooded with cheap U.S. grain — in this case, corn. These people — whose agricultural base, not to mention their entire culture and history, is centred around the growing of corn — were instantaneously deprived of a market, as well as the land. They were also left with no homes. One assumes the proponents of these economic measures expect the displaced peasants to migrate to the cities and find computer jobs, or else just disappear. What was not expected was that they would arm themselves and go on the Internet to publicize the situation.

What is most remarkable about this rebellion is the outpouring of sympathy and support it inspired from middle-class people not only in the United States and Canada, but also in Mexico itself. In the fall of 1998, 1,001 Zapatistas, some of the Maya of Chiapas, started to retrace the famous entrance into Mexico City of Emiliano Zapata, a hero of the Mexican Revolution. They set off to walk barefoot hundreds of kilometres to the capital in order to publicize the plight of the Indians of Chiapas.

By the time they reached Mexico City, they had been joined by thousands of other indigenous people, as well as by ordinary Mexicans of every social class. Together, they entered the city's central square, directly in front of the main cathedral and the president's mansion — the equivalent of massing in front of the White House. Hundreds of thousands of residents of Mexico City had turned out to greet them, waiting more than seven hours in an incredible crowd estimated at half a million. They were all there, as John Cavanaugh says, "to announce, very vocally, their opposition to NAFTA and to the entire free-trade model. It was an enormous statement in a country where the racism towards indigenous people is even greater than in the United States or Canada. It was an enormous statement of solidarity amongst the various segments of Mexican society that are adversely affected by these economic policies."

Eyewitnesses reported that thousands of middle-class Mexicans, most of whom had also been disenfranchised by the collapse of the peso, NAFTA policies and IMF austerity programs, burst into tears when the bleeding, exhausted Indians finally appeared. The crowd began to chant, "You are not alone! We are with you!" One can imagine how this was received — hundreds of thousands of people chanting and crying together.

Cavanaugh says, "Among other things, Mexico City had recently elected a mayor who came out of the anti-free-trade camp, Gauatemo Cardinas. So you had this wonderful symbol of an indigenous movement against the dominant model of recolonization, marching into a Mexico City that was now ruled by a leading opposition figure. It was a sign that Mexican history has been changed forever."

The people who feel the effects most directly are showing the rest of us how to have a say in this new, globalized, monocultured world. "Mexico, I think, is perhaps two or three years ahead of most of the rest of the developing world in terms of the crises and the contradictions and the pain and the struggle of corporate globalization, partly because it was so singled out as the model of free trade," states Cavanaugh. "So much attention was put on it, so many financial resources were lavished on it. So the growth was faster, the inequalities were greater. And now the divisions and the pain are greater. But in Mexico, you can feel history being turned."

When the Student Is Ready, the Teacher Appears

> *We really would like to continue to exist in this world, but in a manner that we ourselves define. A manner in which all the others can respect our diversity. And maybe some . . . others would also like to learn from us, and adapt our values to their communities.*
>
> — VICTORIA TAULI-CORPUS, IGAROT TRIBE MEMBER,
> THE PHILIPPINES

Mexico? India? These are not countries many of us think of as having answers that could benefit *us*. The fact of the matter is that we think of the Third World as a place full of people we have to save. We never even think of them as being able to take good care of themselves without our help, our money and our technological expertise. We've felt this way for a long time. Way back in the sixteenth century, we were going to save their heathen souls and now we're bent on saving their economies, their businesses, their farms, their lives.

In the Third World, food and crops are always key issues of discussion. We're always talking about developing new technologies to save the poor of the world from starvation. Vandana Shiva has spent much of her life investigating the politics of modern economic development, especially in terms of food. She likes to quote Alfred Howard, a British agronomist who's been called the father of modern agriculture. He was sent to India at the beginning of this century as the imperial agriculturalist, and was supposed to teach the Indians how to farm in the modern European way. In his book *The Agricultural Testament,* he says, "I came equipped with sprays, because I was, of course, a modern agriculturalist. And very soon, I threw my spray cans away, because in the fields where I was working, there were no pests. At that point I decided that I had to learn from the peasants and the pests about what system keeps pests under control; because quite clearly, pesticide sprays do not."

Shiva says that methods for keeping pests under control are known and practised by many Third World farmers. "The first strategy is nutrition. If your crops are getting organic food, they are much more resistant to pest attacks. If they are fed with chemical fertilizers, the vulnerability to pests is much higher; there's data, endless data of comparisons available now, both from field and university studies. The second most reliable alternative is to have polycultures, or mixtures of crops, in the same field, so that your pests never literally have a field day; the entire field is not food for them. Somewhere along the way there are other insects, which are also their predators. In any case, the variation and diversity of the crops keeps the pests within a limited population. Even if some pests still occur, there are all kinds of ecological ways to control them."

We are told that high-yield modern farming methods developed by northern countries necessitate heavy use of petrochemicals (i.e., fertilizers and pesticides), and that's true — if you insist on growing huge fields of monocultures. The small land-holdings of the Third World have always been planted in a bewildering variety so that the farmer could feed his family, his cattle or his goats, and put some back into the soil. These farmers are consistently told by outside experts, and their own modernizing governments, that their methods are outdated and inefficient; that without monocultures and petrochemicals, their crops will fail. Yet as Shiva points out, "The very same companies that sell pesticides also pirate our knowledge of plant-based pesticides, without admitting that the fact that they are patenting this knowledge is proof that it works. Otherwise, they wouldn't be trying to commercialize it and trying to monopolize the market of ecological pest control. Every field on every farm in India that has not been destroyed by the Green Revolution is a biodiversity system of pest-control agents. Whether you're using the oil or leaves of the neem tree or the pungamia, they're right there. They've been replanted by the farmers over centuries because society had experimented and had already figured out that these species control pests."

There are pest repellents as well, as any good gardener knows — marigolds, niger, amaranth, pepper, even marijuana. They can be planted near susceptible plants like beans, and they will protect them from infestation. Growing monocultures in huge fields obviates such methods, and makes necessary the use of dangerous chemicals, heavy machinery and certain forms of land ownership. It results in the poor being thrown off their ancestral lands to make room for rich landowners or agribusiness, as happened in Chiapas. Shiva calls modern farming a "substitute for intelligence." She says, "I don't see why we should adopt a very distorted system of agriculture, which must be based upon pushing 98 percent of the farmers off the land. It has been disastrous for the North in many ways, and would be totally explosive for the Third World. It's a system in which the only way you can farm is by literally being in constant war with all the other species that grow or live around you, by being at war with your own soil, by being at war with nature's diversity itself."

Shiva is not alone in her assessment of the efficiency of traditional agriculture. In 1997, the World Bank carried out productivity studies on variously sized farms, as did the international Food and Agriculture Organization (FAO). "It turns out that the highest productivity is [on farms of] up to three acres," explains Shiva. "After that, there's a decline. After only three acres, you cannot increase productivity. You can manufacture data that seem to prove you're producing more, but you can't actually do so."

A recent study reported in *Scientific American* corroborates what Shiva has already told us. A chemical-industrial farm requires 300 units of energy — fertilizers, fuels and so on — to produce only 100 units of food. An organic polyculture farm requires only 5 units of energy to produce the same 100 units of food. It's only when looking at the "harvestable material" data so popular with industrialists that a chemical farm looks good. Those data do not include the costs of fertilizers and pesticides or the non-specific biomass, such as edible weeds, fodder, medicinal plants and green manure, all of which are eliminated in an herbicided monoculture. It's only when we start to look at the Earth as a finite system, and we try to figure out how many units of the sun's energy we have to expend to get our food, that we realize that it is close to insane to farm the way we do now, essentially converting petroleum, very inefficiently, into food.

Shiva has used modern methods to point up the failure of modern agriculture, and so have researchers from the North, especially over the past ten years. Marty Crouch was a well-known plant geneticist working on crop modification at Indiana University. She had gone far and fast in the field of molecular biology. Because of her prestige and expertise, Crouch had the opportunity to travel and teach others how to farm the modern way. She says, "I taught molecular genetics in China and New Zealand, and I worked in Pakistan. I got to see a lot of the other ways that agriculture is done around the world." The situation changed for Crouch when she toured a Pakistani fertilizer plant, where, she says, "The guide said, 'We make our nitrogen fertilizer out of natural gas and this is what has allowed yields of rice and wheat in the region you're visiting to triple in the last decade.' So someone asked him how long the natural gas was going to last. He said, 'About ten more years.' They said, 'Can you afford to buy it from somewhere else?' He said, 'No.'"

While she was thinking that over, the same tour went by a valley where they'd been growing rice continuously for more than 2,000 years in a traditional way. Yields weren't as high as they were with the fertilizers, but production could continue forever. Crouch says she suddenly thought, "'Hey! We're putting our lives, billions of peoples' lives, on the line with a technology that is destined to fail, and to fail utterly, on a grand scale. We're using ten times the energy to produce one calorie of food.' In the old methods, I realized, you'd take calories from the sun and you'd turn them into food calories, and you'd get a net increase. Now we have an actual decrease. Our agriculture is at war with nature and we're eating fossils. How long can we eat fossils?"

Having had this revelation, she gave up her career and began to work to revitalize traditional methods and to restore an energy balance that could be sustained indefinitely. She says many people in northern countries resist this approach because they think it's a return to the past, "and it scares them, deep in their bones. Because we've all heard these horror stories of the past: how life was brutish, hard and short; that the past was ignorance and disease and starvation. But I didn't have that memory."

Marty Crouch grew up with her grandmother, who was a traditional subsistence farmer in the Midwest. Neither of them thought that life was so bad. She has also lived in the Third World, and knows the disadvantages and the advantages first-hand. She says we in the North have an unconscious cultural mindset based on a desire to conquer, colonize and dominate. It's not only part of our culture, it's part of our food-getting process. She says, "In the West, we think of agriculture as a punishment. In the Judeo-Christian tradition of religion, we were kicked out of the Garden of Eden, and as punishment, forever more, we have to do this terrible, hard toil. We have to wrest poor little tubers and things out of the ground. Our entire relationship with our food is one [of] hard work and punishment. Crops are something we have to force the Earth to give us."

Crouch was especially impressed by what she saw on a recent trip to Peru. She says, "They have no such tradition. They go into their fields with a feeling of ritual; it's where they go to listen and to converse with the soil, . . . with the weather and the plants and the animals. There isn't a big separation between the cultivated things and the wild things either. And they think of that as a very centre of diversity. And I sure would like to integrate more of that kind of thinking into the North American idea of agriculture."

Vandana Shiva says that when she talked to an eighty-three-year-old peasant farmer in India who has developed twenty varieties of rice, she asked him if he would try to patent them in order to control them and make money. "How could I own them?" he replied. "They are my friends. They are my partners. I have to be a good friend to them, and they will then be good to me. But without my treating them as friends, they will never feed us. We are in a partnership of species." In India, there is even a word meaning a "partnership of species"; there is also a word to refer to the "earth family" — that is, all species together.

Shiva says, "There's now data coming out of India that show that the agricultural real yields, before colonialism destroyed the practices, were at least seven or eight times higher than the Green Revolution yields. These are not anecdotes. This is documented data from the tax records. So we had a very high productivity system, which is why Alfred Howard said, 'What I see in the fields of India is something as perennial and as long-lasting as the prairies or the ocean, because they have worked out their agricultural system to perfection.' These kinds of practices are part of the culture of many peasant farmers all over the world. But [these practices] also have to come into the thinking of a twenty-first-century enlightened humanity, so we too can live in a consciousness beyond war with other species."

The Meek Shall Inherit the Earth

Africans are more in harmony with the natural environment, more directly dependent on the natural environment. They don't have the illusion at this stage that artificial fixes can solve the problems of life. The very poverty attributed to Africa makes [us] realize how closely dependent we are on natural life-support systems, and how delicately balanced those life-support systems are.

— TEWOLDE BERHAN GEBRA EGZIATHER,
MANAGER OF ETHIOPIA'S ENVIRONMENT
AND PROTECTION AUTHORITY

A lot of pressure is on the Third World to conform to a certain vision of economics and of farming. There is really only one place where northern technology is not in danger, so far, of overwhelming native methods in the key area of food production, and that is Africa. That places Africa in rather a unique position. Tewolde Berhan Gebra Egziather is trained as a plant ecologist. He is the manager of Ethiopia's Environment and Protection Authority, and he's also the Ethiopian delegate and head of the African coalition at the Biodiversity Convention of the United Nations. He is a gentle, diplomatic and very knowledgeable man. He says, "There is a view that Africa is now the most backward continent, because it is 'forgotten.' In fact, it can to some extent afford to be forgotten, because it is the most self-sufficient of the continents. It does not need the rest of the world to maintain itself as much as the interlinked continents do. The reason is very simple: the rest of the world depends on a small number of crops, but Africa has [a huge variety of] food crops that are specific to Africa. That is why it has been 'forgotten,' why the agricultural research and development that has taken place in the last few decades has bypassed Africa."

Modern varieties of food plants have been introduced to the continent, but with so many local crops and crop types to choose from, they haven't done well. And they won't do well — unless farmers are forced to buy them through complicated programs tying aid to petrochemical use and "agricultural development." Tewolde Egziather says modern methods do not appeal to the average farmer partly because "Africa[ns are] very aware that their lives depend very much on the well-being of their own environment and of their life-support systems. . . . They don't get the foolish feeling that science and technology will solve all the problems of humanity."

Many Third World countries have learned the hard way that science and technology often fail. The Green Revolution was a terrible experience for Thailand, Peru, India and many other countries. The initial high yields were not only illusory, but also left a legacy of disease and despoiled ecosystems, destabilization in land tenure and mass migration to the cities. Innovations are often well-intentioned, but they are increasingly viewed with reserve. Tewolde Egziather says, "I remember an American lecturer in agriculture in one of our colleges seeing our traditional plough, which has evolved over a long period not to disturb the soil unduly because, in fact, tropical soils are a lot more delicate than temperate soils. And he berated our technology, saying, 'What you need is a deep plough that will turn the soil over!' When that was tried, it destroyed the soils and their fertility. Such ill-advised but well-meaning efforts at . . . [so-called] development no doubt will continue to take place. But I hope that we are learning to catch up with our own mistakes and identify them as soon as we start committing them."

Often it was not just technologies but entire Third World ways of life, including diets, that were denigrated as primitive or backward. All over Asia and South America, for example, native staple varieties have been replaced by industrially developed soy, corn and wheat, while wonderful, nutritious crops have been forgotten, even lost. Tewolde Egziather recalls the situation in Ethiopia fifty years ago. "When I went to school, we had European-style schools for the first time in Ethiopia, and I was one of the earliest to go. One statement we used to hear very often was 'What is this grass you eat?' — as if grain, all grain, weren't grass. . . . So our agricultural researchers for a long time very seriously tried to eliminate our main cereal crop just because they thought it was inferior. Now it turns out that it has superior qualities. In terms of minerals, it is one of the best grains you can grow. It has a high lysine content. It is now recognized as a special food. This [kind of thing] has happened again and again in many countries."

We're seeing the growth of a monoculture in economics, in culture, in food production and in diet all over the world. What happens if new diseases turn up, if genetic technology runs amok or if climate change demands new kinds of crops? Ethiopia and a few other places still have the diversity of wild and cultivated plants from which to find strains needed to flourish in new situations. But Ethiopia is being pressured to become just like everyone else. Seed banks are being privatized all over the world as part of the economic rationalization-globalization mantra. Collections that were amassed from farmers with public money are being turned over to private corporations that may sequester, misplace, sell or even destroy them with impunity. (This last scenario is not far-fetched; companies often acquire other seed companies and seed banks to gain a monopoly on the market, not because they want to experiment with biodiversity.) Tewolde Egziather says, "It is now a fad, a fashion, to privatize everything, even seed banks. . . . A small number of seed companies control all the seed supply in many countries. And should something happen to that company — bankruptcy or whatever — the seed system in a country could be endangered. . . . So if we continue in the direction we are going, we are heading for a possible disaster."

When Tewolde Egziather talks about Africa being forgotten, he means that its countries are not as plugged into the Internet as other countries are. Africa is not a site of industrial development as South America and Asia are, nor is it a home for research and development like India and Thailand. "Although Africa is the second-largest continent," he says, "people think of it as one country. You can hear people refer to, for example, the Netherlands and Africa, as if they were comparable entities. Africa is huge, but the population is still fairly small, relatively, so the level of demand on the environment has not been great enough to stimulate the need for massive efforts to produce more on ever-decreasing land." Africa has the most mineral wealth of any continent; there is virtually no valuable mineral that is not found there. "That means that the world as a whole has a vested interest in taking what Africa can offer," asserts Tewolde Egziather. "And the way to do that is to keep the relatively small population disorganized. This means that the focus is not to treat Africans as trading partners, but as a source of raw materials."

But Africa is both too large and too rich in minerals, land and biodiversity to remain forgotten in the twenty-first century, and Tewolde Egziather knows it. In the Third World, there are many people like him who see in their countries opportunities for change, instead of disadvantages; who see multiplicity and adaptability, instead of poverty. He says, "I don't think there is only one way to development. . . . If you were to go back to the time of the dinosaurs, and you were to see a little mammal running about, you would never think that this mammal would succeed the dinosaurs. Who can tell which is a dinosaur and which is a mammal in our time, in this era of really frightening possibilities? That does not imply that I view the African way as the mammalian way. It is simply to say that what is successful now, and what will be successful in the future, . . . is not necessarily something linear that proceeds from what we know at this moment. Therefore, it is absolutely essential to keep our options open." Africa may have been forgotten or "left behind," but it has retained the possibility of trying other experiments. Other places, as Tewolde Egziather says, "have destroyed many of the bridges they would have had into other possibilities."

The Law of Social Diversity

A vibrant civic society is a precondition for having markets develop and operate in the way that they should.
— ADAM SMITH, EIGHTEENTH-CENTURY ECONOMIST

In the first chapter of this book, we discussed at length the importance of biological biodiversity to the survival of the planet — how a rich mix of species is absolutely crucial to the healthy maintenance of our atmosphere, soils, freshwater supplies and our own bodies. As we worked on the radio series, we learned that politics, culture and economics become unbalanced and inefficient without diversity as well. In his classic book *Making Democracy Work,* the sociologist Roy

Putnam describes his efforts to figure out why the citizens of northern Italy are considered by both outsiders like the UN and Italians themselves to be so much happier, more prosperous and healthy than those living in southern Italy. Putnam looked at every factor he could think of, including history, geographic position and industrialization, and he got some surprising answers.

What made the difference finally seemed to be the extent to which people belonged to civic organizations — voluntary groups like football and camera clubs, choirs and collectors' groups — which transcend religious, cultural or ethnic boundaries. Anthropologist Steve Rayner corroborates this. "It turns out there is an astonishingly strong correlation, about +92, between people's membership in these organizations within a region and the successful performance of the government in that region. Similarly, there's a negative correlation, about −75, between the performance of government and the systems of patronage [that] divided religious, cultural or ethnic groups employ.... So it seems to suggest that in fact there really is something very important about people being engaged with each other in things that don't appear to have any direct impact on government, or on the environment, or on any of the things that we're concerned about."

Jeremy Rifkin calls such voluntary organizations the Third Sector. He says that every non-communist country in the world has three sectors: the market, the government, and the Third Sector. "The Third Sector," explains Rifkin, "is every organization, every institution, every affiliation in a country that is not a corporation in the marketplace and not a government agency. It's much broader than non-government and non-profit organizations. It includes them, but it also includes cultural organizations, arts [groups], sports clubs. It includes church and secular organizations, fraternal lodges, service organizations, civic and neighbourhood organizations. In a sense, it's all the institutions that make up the culture of a country. This sector is far bigger than the marketing or government sectors, and if you were to wake up in your country tomorrow morning and this Third Sector had disappeared, how long would the country survive?"

Currently, we're completely focused on government and the market. We take the Third Sector entirely for granted. But like the environment, which supports the economy, it's the invisible layer that supports all of society. "We call this the Third Sector," says Rifkin, "but it's misnamed, because it's the primary sector in every country. We need to go back and understand the lessons of cultural anthropology. . . . We need to understand that this Third Sector is the primary sector; it is the wellspring upon which the other two sectors depend. The other two sectors, market and government, are derivative of the Third Sector."

If we look at the history of democracies, there is a remarkable partnership between the civil groups of the Third Sector and the success and happiness of the people in a society. Why? Steve Rayner, the chief scientist at the Pacific Northwest National Laboratory in Washington, D.C., is an adviser to countries around the world that are trying to create healthier political and social systems. He wondered the same thing. "The hypothesis that I'm currently investigating," he says, "is that these multiple overlapping memberships. . . . give you a much richer toolkit, or repertoire of societal strategies for dealing with problems, than if you only have a hierarchy, or if you only have a market. Or indeed, if you only have voluntary associationalism. You need all three of these elements present in a sort of creative tension if you're going to have a sustainable kind of government."

It appears that as in the natural world, our social world requires symbiotic and complex relationships to produce a healthy system. In fact, the richer the system, the healthier it gets. And the simpler, the sicker. "Now why should that be?" Rayner asks. "Well, if you've got only one way of doing things, you've got only one way of doing them. If you have only hierarchy, like in most governments and in business, and something goes wrong or you encounter a new situation that's not working, the only solution available to you is more hierarchy. If you have only a market and you encounter a new situation, all you can do is more tinkering with the prices. If you have only egalitarianism, or voluntary association, all you can do is say, 'Well, we must get more people involved and have more participation.' And yet, the definition of madness is surely doing the same thing over and over again and hoping the result will be different."

When we discussed biotechnology, we said it is impossible to predict what will happen when scientists introduce a new gene into an organism, because the interactions between all the various elements are so complex that they're transcalculational, meaning that the richness of a working system is mathematically extremely complex. This complexity also explains why we don't know how many species we can take out of an ecosystem before it collapses. Interestingly, social structures need mathematical complexity to work well too. Steve Rayner has tried to figure out why this is the case. He says that as soon as you have two elements in a social structure — say, government and market— "you have a slight increase in the number of strategies available. But still, it's either market or hierarchy, to use the conventional dichotomy in political science and economics. The fascinating thing is, if you introduce just one more element, a third element, the number of strategies [or] the number of elements that you can do and the number of ways you can combine them [rises geometrically, not arithmetically]. So that's just a very simple mathematical indicator of the fact that you have a huge increase in societal complexity and capacity for coming up with novel solutions."

If we should find ourselves suddenly invaded by Martians or overrun with genetically mutated crops or forced to cope with flash floods, global warming and ethnic wars, we'd obviously be better off having a lot of possible ways of dealing with the situation, rather than just one. "I think that's the key to civil society," says Rayner. "It keeps that whole repertoire in play all the time. And it exposes people to different ways of doing things so that when they encounter new situations, they can just switch strategies and experiment in ways that you can't if you have only one or even two options."

The Law of Requisite Variety

If we are just going to let markets all over the world commercialize and commodify everything, then what do we have left? The things we have been telling our children, the things that our ancestors have taught us in terms of how to value life — the integrity of creation, the integrity of all forms of life — all of these things will amount to nothing if we don't take a very active role in sustaining and developing our view of the world.

— VICTORIA TAULI-CORPUS, IGAROT TRIBE MEMBER

These days, it is widely thought that if the Third World is to become democratically governed, like most of the North, it needs prosperity, the global market and industrial development. But Steve Rayner demurs. "Money doesn't buy you democracy, that's for sure. I mean, one of the things that was always a great puzzle to me was . . . why, for example, did the former British colonies in Africa collapse so soon after independence? After all, for all the evils of colonialism, the British left those countries with nice, new parliament buildings, with pluralistic political parties, electoral machines, judges with all the robes and wigs and other paraphernalia of the modern state, and even half-decent economies. And yet within about ten years, most of them had become dictatorships and had a lot of environmental degradation occurring, along with poorer economic and health circumstances. And it seems to me that the one thing that the British didn't leave behind, and probably couldn't create, was a civil society; in other words, those voluntary associations across the tribal, ethnic boundaries that would have been the key ingredient in the stability of those societies."

Rayner has other examples. "Another interesting contrast is Pakistan and India. India hasn't had a single military coup in fifty years. Pakistan hasn't managed to get a single, civilian-elected government through a complete term of office. Why should that be? One reason might be because the independence movement in India was in fact a very pluralistic civil movement, involving different ethnic groupings, different religious groupings, different segments of class and caste, and so on, whereas Pakistan was specifically the creation of a monoculture, an Islamic monoculture. In other words, the creation of Pakistan actually destroyed, for the Pakistanis, a lot of that civic associationalism that has . . . served India very well."

Perhaps dams and stock exchanges are not the best gift from us to the Third World. We could try Rayner's methods. He says, "I prepared a paper for a conference in Islamabad, and when I presented it to my colleagues in Washington they laughed. What I said was that if we were serious about wanting to advance the development process in countries like Pakistan, we would do well to abandon large, capital-intensive projects and go out and buy Ping-Pong tables and sheet music." His point is that it's Ping-Pong tables and sheet music and football and sewing clubs that bring people together to learn new ways to relate across religious or ethnic lines, and to get things done, even if those things seem trivial, like throwing a parade or raising money for matching jackets. "The people in Washington laughed," says Rayner. "Interestingly, the people in Islamabad said, 'Well, of course!' They understood perfectly well that the key to sustainable development for them is to bring about an end to feudalism. And Pakistan, unfortunately, is very much a feudal society, where, although formally it's illegal, slavery persists to this day. The power of the landlords is very strong. The people who want to change that recognize that . . . the development of this sort of civic layer is the key to dismantling the feudal structure of the state."

The industrialized nations, with their one-track mindset — centred on one kind of culture, economics and politics — not only try to jump-start other countries with inappropriate massive development, they have also exported political ideologies. Up until the 1980s, the North even used many Third World countries as battlegrounds for the undeclared war between the Soviet Union and the United States. For example, Tewolde Egziather asserts that people died of starvation in Ethiopia in the 1970s and 1980s not because they were unable to grow their own food, but because they were at war. He says, "The disturbances in Africa have their roots in the Cold War. . . . In 1973, Ethiopia was supported by the United States, with Western Europe as a strong ally. In 1974, it was supported by the Soviet Union. In 1973, Somalia was supported by the Soviet Union. In 1974, Somalia was supported by the United States. The switch in a few months was most dramatic. . . . You can't imagine what kind of destabilization that has produced."

Terrible images of starving Ethiopians and Somalians in the mid-1980s elicited an outpouring of anguish, money and food from Western nations. But mass starvation had nothing to do with Africa's inherent incapacity to feed itself. "In 1984–85, we had one of the biggest food deficits in anybody's history," Tewolde Egziather says. "In 1994, we still had quite a big food deficit. In 1995, we fed ourselves very well, and the prospects looked good. And in 1997, we have exported quite a substantive amount of food. In such a small number of years, such a dramatic change is not possible. The simple reason [for the improvement] is that the instabilities were removed. People were able to mind their business, to go on with living. And life returned to normal in a very short time."

Of course, there were internal problems as well. War and mismanagement worked together to erode a wise, experienced culture's ability to manage land and food. Tewolde Egziather says, "As a reaction to the external world, we created a strongly centralized government. And when you centralize, your number-one enemy is local community, so you destroy local organization. That meant the disappearance of age-old systems of environmental management. The new centralizing state didn't have the capacity or the experience to replace what it was destroying. So it destroyed environmental management without trying to put anything in its place."

Efforts are now being made to strengthen local organization rather than sacrificing everything to central authority. "People have spontaneously organized themselves to manage their environment much better," Tewolde Egziather says. "My own village, the village I was born in, when I went [there] in 1973, I was most depressed. There was virtually not a tree left. I went back six years ago, and it looked like a virtual forest with so many trees! It's the most pleasant transformation I have ever seen, simply because people were allowed to mind their business. If we are allowed to be, we will be."

Many other peoples in the Third World are saying the same thing. Victoria Tauli-Corpus is a member of the Igarot, an indigenous mountain group in the Philippines. She also works with an indigenous coalition and is the liaison officer for the Third World Network in the Philippines. She lives in an area that is being invaded by Canadian gold-mining companies; these companies are being given carte blanche by the Philippine government, which in its quest to follow the First World lead grants corporations free access to resources in the name of globalization. The government is composed mostly of wealthy people who are as far removed from the daily life of Philippine peasants and indigenous people as are the middle class of the First World. As happened in Somalia, Yugoslavia and Mozambique, the government has bought in to the single vision of prosperity that requires slashed social programs, low wages and increasing advantages to transnational corporations in trying to be globally competitive. But the miners have not been able to get much gold out of the mountains yet, and the people who live there are resisting them, just as the Ogoni did in far-off Nigeria.

Tauli-Corpus, like Oronto Douglas, lives this struggle every day. She says her husband is involved in the resistance and has been threatened by local employees of a Canadian gold-mining company. The Igarot want to control their own lands, but not just for their economic resources. She says the whole concept of this kind of competition has always been discouraged by her people, because it clashes with their values. She says, "The reason the resources are still up in our mountains is because we have a very simple lifestyle. We haven't squandered them. We really have used them sustainably. We look at them as part of the whole community, because they're not just for us, but for future generations. I think that this whole kind of world-view is really the wealth that we have. And it's why I think the indigenous peoples. . . . are on a very high moral ground. We feel that we still have that kind of strength left to defend what we have, despite what [others] have said in the past — that we were backward, unscientific, pagan, etc. Now we feel that the values we have are actually the things that this world needs the most."

Currently, we are moving inexorably towards a system where there is only one accepted, enforced way of doing things. But living in a world that has no variety, no diversity and no adaptability in its human communities and belief systems is very dangerous, just as dangerous as using up all our natural resources. What would it mean to lose the world-views and value systems that groups like Ethiopian farmers, the Maya of Chiapas, the Igarot, the Ogoni or the Okanagan have to offer? Steve Rayner sums it up in two sentences: "Social and cultural diversity are fully as essential to the welfare of the planet as biodiversity is, and for very much the same reasons. If you violate this law of requisite variety, you have an unsustainable social system." And an unsustainable planet.

CHAPTER 9

COMPLEX PLEASURES

Thought without concrete action is demoralizing.
— RUTH STEPHENS MIDDLETON,
ELIZABETH MAY'S GRANDMOTHER

The facts are in and the conclusions undeniable. We know about the amount of the world's forests being cut down annually, the physical changes in the atmosphere, the spread of toxic pollutants, the depletion of the oceans and rising human numbers and their demands. It's clear that we're pushing the limits of this planet's ability to support us, its ability to regenerate clean air, water, productive soils and energy faster than we can use them up. It's also clear that we have very little time left to come up with new ways of living and new ways of using and sharing what we have. Denying that there is a serious problem, or giving in to a sense of impotence or hopelessness, is to render a catastrophe inevitable.

We have to fight despair. Nelson Mandela must have been sorely tempted to give up during his quarter-century of confinement, and East and West Germans must have wondered whether the Berlin Wall and the border between them would ever come down. Yet Mandela and the Germans triumphed over apartheid and division because they persisted and never abandoned hope. The ecological crisis now under way demands that we cling to hope and continue to strive to avoid eco-collapse.

Human beings are often at their best when responding to immediate crises — car accidents, house fires, hurricanes. We are less effective in the face of enormous but slow-moving crises such as the loss of biodiversity or climate change. When the crisis is environmental and global, we feel not only frightened and overwhelmed, but also insignificant and helpless.

The Sierra Club's Elizabeth May believes that no matter how overwhelming these problems have become, we can still act to mitigate them. She says, "This is not a parade on environmental problems that...we can afford to watch as observers. We are not observers. We are no more observers than when you're sitting in a doctor's office and the doctor explains where the cancer is in your body and what it's doing. You are not an observer to that process. You'd better become a participant pretty quickly, and you'd better understand that there are things you can do that will improve your chances."

With major environmental problems, as with a terrifying medical diagnosis, our first reaction may be to feel depressed or to avoid confronting the issue altogether. We may find a distraction and pretend it will all go away, or we may simply question the accuracy of the diagnosis. But anyone who has been faced with the challenge of healing knows that such responses lead only to a quicker decline. We're not dead yet, and as May says, we ought to be thinking, "Right, the prognosis may not be good, but I can change the outcome through things that I can do."

If a doctor warns us that unless we diet, stop smoking and start exercising, we are at great risk of a heart attack, our response can influence the outcome. May says, "We're being told by the global doctors, 'You'd better cut down on the smokestacks. Stop partying beyond your means. Start living within the planet's ecological means. And then you can have a long and healthy life.' We have to recognize that it's our lives, our bodies, our health, our planet [that are at risk]. We are participants. We have to be involved and engaged at a very active, deep and personal level."

May herself is extremely engaged and active. I've long admired her, and am proud to have her as a friend. Her energy and conviction brought her national attention when, as a university student, she fought pesticide spraying for spruce budworm in Cape Breton. The emulsifying agent used in the pesticide was eventually linked to Reye's syndrome, a deadly swelling of the brain that affects children. The pesticide mix has also been blamed for reduced salmon runs in the East. May's actions helped stop the spraying in Nova Scotia, and she went on to become an influential adviser to the federal environment minister in the late 1980s. When he approved a huge dam project on the Rafferty and Alameda rivers in

Saskatchewan, May resigned so she could speak out against this decision.

Elizabeth May comes by her activism honestly — she was raised that way. "It comes straight from something my grandmother Ruth Stephens used to say: 'Thought without constructive action is demoralizing.' So there is absolutely no point in learning about these issues and thinking about these issues unless you're prepared to take constructive action. I mean, my mom's paralyzing fear for the future was of mutual nuclear annihilation from the arms race. My first press conference, I was sitting on Mother's lap. I was two. She was protesting against atmospheric nuclear weapons testing, which actually was stopped with a test-ban treaty. If you'd asked my mom back then, 'If we don't change, where are we headed?' she'd have said we were headed to a world where the levels of strontium-90, the levels of childhood leukemia, would have been through the roof. As it is, childhood leukemia has increased. Yes, we poisoned the atmosphere for quite a while. But action did occur."

Now that countries rarely explode nuclear bombs above ground, we look back on the debate over atmospheric testing and fallout as something that was solved politically because our leaders gradually understood the danger. We forget what really happened. There was a massive, global movement of ordinary people, most of them women, who said no to atmospheric testing. They marched, staged sit-ins, raised money, formed blockades, marched in parades and held press conferences. "In those days, my mom was just a housewife volunteer," May remembers. "But because people like her got busy, they changed the whole damn world. And we can do it in our generation."

May knows all the ways people can become discouraged. She says, "One of the things that we mustn't do in our current moment of struggle is try to assess if we're winning or losing. By any reasonable measurement, we're losing. So let's not waste our time with that. What we have to do is continue the struggle for fundamental change. We do have our moments. We do have our opportunities. And whether we're trying to arrest biotechnology before it becomes a ubiquitous food source and we have absolutely no choice about it; or whether we're trying to reduce the amount of pesticides that we use, knowing that those increase childhood cancers; or whether we're dealing with climate change, and trying to get any level of government to act responsibly and actually create the kind of economic signals that will get business to move — it's all the same thing. I know these changes are doable, but we need the right, clear signals. These things will come from governments, but only when they feel the heat of an enraged population breathing down their necks."

One of the things that has concerned me lately is the loss of momentum in the environmental movement. In the past ten years, we've become preoccupied with economic issues and dazzled by the information superhighway. Yet every poll on the subject, every real question that addresses the future, shows that people everywhere still very much want wildlife and clean water and sustainable industries and a future for their children that includes intact and productive natural systems.

The core of activists working on these issues, as May points out, grows slightly larger all the time. "But we need everybody in the Canadian population. We need everybody to say, 'This is my personal commitment. Even if it's only an hour a week, I'm going to do something to ensure that when my kids are grown, they're not going to be looking at pictures of the African elephant and seeing it the way we look at pictures of the dodo. I don't want my kids to look at a map that shows where the low-lying island states *used* to be before they were inundated by melting ice caps. I don't want my kids growing up in a world where the levels of planetary disruption create a desert in the northern Amazon, which the Hadley Meteorological Centre in England is now predicting unless we deal with greenhouse gas emissions.'

"These are human-created problems," May reminds us. "The solutions can be created by humans too. But nothing moves without a very, very motivated, engaged, committed and dedicated public movement." If we applied the same energy to figuring out sustainable technologies and sustainable lifestyles that we do to trying to make the most money in the shortest period of time, creating a new weapon or inventing a new technology, I'm sure we could arrive at true sustainability very quickly. The idea that politicians are too corrupt or distant, and that we ourselves are powerless to do anything that makes a difference, is, as May says, "one of the most pervasive, pernicious and evil myths out there. We're not powerless. We're damn lazy. We have tremendous power in our society. We can, in fact, move the whole world in a different direction. We just have to care enough about it to make it a priority in our own lives."

And a Child Shall Lead Them

> *If the members of a local community want their community to*
> *cohere, to flourish, and to last, here are some of the things they*
> *[should] do: Always include local nature — the land, the*
> *water, the air, the native creatures — within the membership*
> *of the community; . . . ask how local needs might be supplied*
> *from local sources; . . . see that the old and young take care of*
> *one another; . . . always be aware of the economic value of*
> *neighbourly acts; . . . always care for [your] old people, and*
> *teach [your] children.*
>
> — WENDELL BERRY,
> FARMER AND PHILOSOPHER

In terms of who holds power, perhaps the lowest on the social totem pole
are the very young. We pay a lot of lip service to ensuring children's
rights, but child mortality and child poverty have increased dramatically
under our new economic order, even in the developed world. Children
don't have any legal say in our political and social decisions. They can't
vote, they're not protected by unions, and when they talk to adults we
rarely take them seriously. And yet even they can teach us a thing or two
about making a difference. Let me give you an example.

In West Vancouver, a group of about twenty children and their parents formed Orca, a nature club, one of those Third Sector groups that
cut across age, language and religious lines that Steve Rayner believes are
so central to creating a functional society. Club members did simple
things such as kayaking, hiking and designing projects to help them learn
about wild plants and animals or the stars. On a study project, while root-
ing around a stream, they discovered an unusual creature, a tailed frog.

The first thing they did was call the University of British Columbia
to find a scientist who could tell them more about the little creature.
They were informed by the astonished biologist that these frogs are very
rare and were believed not to occur south of Squamish. The youngsters
helped the biologists establish that densities were higher in the suburban
stream than up north in the wild, and they realized immediately that the
habitat was special. These tiny frogs are the size of your thumb and are
the only species in North America to live in clear, fast-running streams.

They have other unusual features as well: they breed internally and maintain a tail-like appendage even as adults. Then, the club members discovered that this very stream was due to be developed for a housing project, thereby putting the frog's habitat at serious risk. The children decided, on their own initiative, to make a submission to the West Vancouver city council, because, as they said, "there are no laws to help the frogs." They wanted to try to convince the council members to make the developer change his plans and accommodate this species.

Four of the children wrote speeches and made the presentation. Eleven-year-old David Maszaros and twelve-year-old Kathleen Folley were two of the children involved. David says of that first meeting, "I don't think they took us very seriously at all." When I asked them if they had been nervous, Kathleen replied, "Yes! Because . . . well, they're bigger!" But luckily, a television reporter got wind of the story and interviewed the children. Children and frogs make a nice news diversion, and they're visual. So when the Orca kids returned to city hall a second time, there were video cameras present to record it. David recalls, "By the fourth time, when we got there, there were, like, nine, ten TV stations all just filming us. And there were radio broadcasters."

Uncomfortable with such public scrutiny, the councillors began to take the situation more seriously. The upshot was that the Orca members, thanks to their media exposure, were able to persuade the developers to leave a generous buffer zone around the stream for the frogs, divert all waste water away from the creek and refrain from cutting any of the old-growth trees growing along its banks. David says proudly, "We had a huge effect, I think. They started to take us seriously after about the second or third time. . . . They could see we had a really big point. The frogs are a blue-listed [extremely rare] species!"

Staff members in the ministry of provincial parks told David's father, "These kids have done more to protect our creeks than anybody in the last thirty years." I asked David how that made him and his fellow Orca members feel. He replied, "Well, we feel good! We went up and had a big influence; we saved animals who can't speak for themselves." Of course, you might say the kids were lucky; they live in the affluent North, they're cute and they attracted media attention. But the fact remains that a group of informed and committed children — normally the most powerless people in our society — fought city hall, big business and big money — and won.

Five or Six Very Difficult Things You Can Do to Help Save the World a Little Bit

> *This is the one possible chink in the armour of the ... monolith represented by the television networks, Disney World, the suburb and the shopping mall, and all the kind of overwhelming material-consumption features of our lives. If those things made us as happy as they claim, then it would not make any difference what environmental arguments they raised. The fact that they don't make us all that happy is their ... Achilles' heel.*
>
> — BILL MCKIBBEN, JOURNALIST

One of the most powerful environmental books of the past ten years was *The End of Nature* by Bill McKibben, a journalist who lives in the Adirondacks. *The End of Nature* is a frightening vision of what the world has become and where it is heading. His book has been likened to a modern *Silent Spring,* the seminal work by Rachel Carson that catapulted the environment into everyone's consciousness.

McKibben's book focuses on climate change as a result of global warming. It's one of our most difficult problems, because solving it will involve basic changes in lifestyle: phasing out fossil fuels, changing trade and economic structures so that economies function locally and we don't need so much energy for transport, and much more. McKibben hasn't been afraid to tackle the really big issues that underlie our current problems, and he isn't any more paralyzed by the enormity of the task than were Elizabeth May or the Orca kids. When people ask him what they are supposed to do about such horrendous, systemic problems as overconsumption, overpopulation and global warming, he says, "In practical terms, there are many answers, all of them both simple and difficult. Someone wrote a book once called *Fifty Simple Things You Can Do to Save the World.* There were some pretty good ideas in that book, but it was a very ... American notion — that there are going to be fifty things you can do to save the world, and they are [all] going to be simple. My work has basically been writing many chapters of a long book called *Five or Six Unbelievably Difficult Things You Could Do That Would Help a Little Bit.*"

Where do we start? McKibben is the father of one child, a six-year-old girl named Sophie. He says, "We've got to address questions of our population. That means we have to address the most difficult and intimate questions of how many children we're each going to have. For those of us in the developed world, it makes real sense to think about and explore single-child families for a couple of generations." And of course, it's not just a question of numbers of people. McKibben says, "We've got to think about how much we consume." The figures are clear. If we got rid of 80 percent of the world's population tomorrow by eliminating all the poor people, we'd *still* be in the predicament we're in now. That's because those of us who live in the First World, although we make up only 20 percent of the world's population, consume more than 80 percent of the planet. We're long past using up all our biological interest and are now destroying natural capital and, with it, our children's future.

Is consumption on this level normal? Does everyone "naturally" want to consume on the scale we do? That certainly seems to be what the popular media would have us believe. Of course, people have always been interested in wealth and material security. But since the Second World War, our culture and our government policies have actually *discouraged* thrift, personal savings or debtlessness, while encouraging and rewarding ever-rising patterns of consumption and debt. We've been exhorted by ads, taxes and our global media culture to believe that having more money in order to buy more things is the real ticket to happiness; that the virtues of the past, like frugality and self-denial, were mistaken, and now being truly happy largely means indulging ourselves. But this entire pattern of thought could simply be wrong. "We've been told that the more we have, the happier we'd be," McKibben says. "But a look around us doesn't seem to bear that out."

Since the 1950s, we've almost tripled the amount of material goods in the average North American's possession. Even students without enough cash to eat properly own TVs, computers and cars. However, fifty years of surveys asking people to rate their happiness show absolutely no correlation between the attainment of material goods and personal satisfaction. Once we've got beyond having enough food and clothes and a roof over our heads, we're not made much happier by extra consumer goods. In fact, the number of people who say on these survey forms that they're very happy has actually *declined* from its peak back in the 1950s. "Material goods aren't making us happier now," says

McKibben. "We've reached some point where we have enough, and the struggle to get more makes us not more happy, but probably less happy."

A group in Seattle called the New Road Map Foundation is actively looking for ways to enable ordinary, middle-class people to be both happier and less of a burden on the Earth. One of its founders, Vicki Robin, says, "The single most important thing anybody can do now for the environment and for the economy is to save. For the environment, money not spent is resources not consumed at some level. And money saved is putting yourself on a firmer financial footing in a very, very scary and shaky world."

It's interesting how quickly the very suggestion of buying less and saving more, those two notions of sane, stable, responsible people only a generation ago, have come to sound completely radical. That's because we really have come to believe that if you don't do your share by buying a new car or a new kind of soft drink, you'll contribute to job losses and a general economic slide. Vicki Robin says that belief in constant growth and increased consumption is madness. It may have made sense fifty years ago, given our understanding of the world at the time, but now it's just helping us avoid facing ecological limits or the population issue. As Herman Daly put it, it's just helping us to avoid the issue of sharing. Robin concurs. "What constant growth actually does [not do] is . . . give us the opportunity to develop. It's like a human body. We don't grow forever; we grow until we reach a mature size. And then we develop — we develop our intelligence, our skills, our experiences in life. We become ever more beautiful human beings because of what's going on inside."

As we mentioned earlier, nothing in nature grows forever, except cancer cells (and even they die in the end). "A beautiful tree grows to a certain size and then it can produce fruit," explains Robin. "In fact, if it's pruned, if it faces restrictions and challenges, it will produce more and better fruit. This principle is the same throughout nature." She says that when ideals as sensible as thrift and conservation become radical and abnormal, it reflects an actual disease in society.

The way we live has less to do with individual choices and more to do with the general bent of our society than many of us realize. We forget that we don't *need* everything. As Robin says, if you've noticed that no matter how much stuff you get, you don't feel satisfied, it's probably because material things satisfy human beings only so much.

Stuff

We're the richest country on earth, yet half of us say we can't afford the things we really need — and that includes many people with incomes over $100,000. Something is wrong with this picture.
— EDITORIAL, *THE UTNE READER*, DECEMBER 1998

If we imagine that the fullness we yearn for can be reckoned in dollars . . . or purchased in stores, there will be no end to our craving.
— SCOTT RUSSELL SANDERS, IN *AUDUBON*, JULY/AUGUST 1998

There are only twenty-four hours in a day. We have to sleep, eat, work and have a social life. Our time on Earth is limited, and there's only so much available for the things we enjoy. Our money is hard-earned and it's nice to indulge ourselves. "We all acquire things from birth to death," Vicki Robin says. "And we enjoy material goods. They're pretty. They're soft. They allow our lives to be a little bit more comfortable, a little bit more convenient, warmer, drier. There are many reasons why acquisition of things will make our lives better. But we have to be sure that all of the things that we are acquiring really are making our lives better. That's the distinction that I'm trying to draw. There are some things you acquire that indeed improve your quality of life, but there are others that you just buy out of habit because other people have them or because you were in a hurry. Sometimes you buy something because you saw it on television; before you saw it on television you didn't want it, but now you do. And what you find is that there is a point in your whole process of consumption where that extra product actually doesn't bring you any extra fulfilment. It actually undermines your fulfilment."

Vicki Robin co-authored with her late partner, Joe Dominguez, a best-seller called *Your Money or Your Life*. The basic premise is that to make money, you hire out your life at so much an hour. If you spend that money in ways that don't make you happy, you're literally wasting your life. "You have to spend a certain number of hours of your life [earning the money] for every item that you buy in a store, every consumer product you buy, every lunch or dinner out," explains Robin. "You're paying for these things in the hours of your life. So is it making your life five hours happier to have that fifth pair of slacks? If it is, that's an okay thing to have. But if it isn't, then you'd better think twice about it." Living this way means living frugally. It means not buying so many things in order to have time off from earning money.

While doing his research, Joe Dominguez realized something. "As he looked more deeply into it, he realized what makes life fun, interesting, challenging and rewarding is what he called 'putting love out into the world,'" recalls Robin, "finding ways to make life better for other people — and for the Earth."

Robin continues, "The real epiphany [for me] came when I realized the environmental consequences of the level and pattern of consumption in North America. I became aware of how consumption is the driver behind almost every environmental problem. We will find that there's almost always a demand for a product or a service driving any particular environmental problem. If we could adjust our consumption, we could take the pedal off the floor, and then we could decelerate our stress on the environment. When I made that link, I became very passionate about teaching about consumption and becoming an activist on this issue."

Vicki Robin's epiphany runs counter to what we are usually told, which is that the economy delivers all the goods we buy: food, cars and a clean environment. In reality, every bit of the material in all products, as well as everything used to extract, process and manufacture them, comes from the Earth. One of Robin's favourite examples is to consider something as ordinary as a pen: "I took a look at the pen, and I thought, 'Where does the plastic for the body of this pen come from?' It comes from fossil fuels that have to be pumped out of the Earth, that then have to be transported to the place of manufacture, and then have to go through many processes with many chemicals to make the plastic of the body of the pen. And I thought, 'Well, the ink. Where does the ink come from, and what is the ink made out of? I'm sure it's not a vegetable, soya-based ink. So maybe it's carbon, and where does carbon come from? Well, it's coal, or a wood product.' So I began to look at the pen not as something I wanted to buy and have, but as something I had asked the Earth to give me."

Any consumer item you can think of — from your computer screen at work to the can of pop you had on your break, the wheels on your car and the crown on your tooth — comes out of the Earth. Not only does any such object come out of a finite amount of metals, wood or fossil fuels, but whatever remains when we're done with it has to go back to the Earth. Robin says, "I realized that I'm going to use this pen for a limited period of time, and then I'm going throw it away. And I started to realize that there is no place you could throw this pen where it's actually going to decompose and that particular conglomeration of chemicals and minerals can actually become an Earth that can grow things again. So I began to realize, well, wait a second, even if I have the money for this pen — even if I want it — is it something that I really need, and that I'm willing to say to the Earth, 'I want you to give me this pen?'"

People like Vicki Robin know that we need pens and shoes and telephones, and that we can't feel guilty about using them. She simply wants us to remember that "everything we interact with on a daily basis comes out of the Earth and goes back to the Earth and deserves to be treated with tremendous appreciation, gratitude and respect. This awareness, rather than sending me into guilt, sends me into gratitude. I think how lucky I am, and how lucky we all are, to have these simple, simple things that make our lives easier. The more gratitude you feel for the things that you have, the less you're going to be inclined to overconsume."

Vicki Robin and the other members of the New Road Map Foundation do not feel that they are anti-material ascetics who don't like sensual pleasures. They feel the opposite: that they want people to revel in material things by paying closer attention to them. She says, "Once you have something that you really like and enjoy, *really* like and enjoy it! And like and enjoy it for many years. And when you have to get rid of it, make sure that you put it in a place where other people can like and enjoy it. It is really an appreciation of the material world, and an honouring of the life energy that it took for you to purchase that thing, and also the life energy it took from the Earth to create that thing. . . . So when you drink your cup of coffee, take time to really appreciate that coffee. . . . We don't take the time to really reflect on our experiences, reflect on the things that we have brought into our lives, and say, 'Isn't this wonderful? Aren't I lucky?' And maybe another question is, 'How can I share this with other people?'"

Family, friends, community — these are the sources of the greatest love and joy we experience as humans. We visit family members, keep in touch with favourite teachers, share and exchange pleasantries with friends. We undertake difficult projects to help others, save frogs or protect a wilderness, and in the process discover extreme satisfaction. We find spiritual fulfillment in nature or by helping others. None of these pleasures requires us to consume things from the Earth, yet each is deeply fulfilling. These are complex pleasures, and they bring us much closer to real happiness than the simple ones, like a bottle of Coke or a new minivan.

Eating Right

> *In Japan it's referred to as "farming with a face on it."*
> *Europeans call such arrangements subscription farming.*
> *"Linking farmers with consumers" is the [phrase] used in the*
> *United Kingdom.... All these terms translate into [a]*
> *dynamic new [global] development in small-scale farming.*
> *Community-supported agriculture, or CSA, ... serves as an*
> *umbrella for farmers striving to achieve a number of goals:*
> *mutually beneficial relationships with ... consumers;*
> *environmentally sustainable farming practices; and public*
> *education on ... agricultural issues.*
>
> — DANIEL IMHOFF, JOURNALIST

There are a lot of ways we can act to conserve the Earth. Like the Orca Club children, we can take an interest in endangered nature and try to help out locally. We can follow Bill McKibben's advice and work on big issues like reducing fossil fuel consumption and curbing population growth. Or, like Vicki Robin, we can simply consume less and enjoy ourselves more.

One issue of vital concern to everyone is food. Our disconnection from the Earth is epitomized by our relationship to food. Most urban people associate food with supermarkets but fail to connect it with the land. Brewster Kneen lives in rural British Columbia and publishes a monthly newsletter called the *Ram's Horn*, which deals with agricultural issues. He informs people about how industrial farming, biotechnology and agricultural patenting intrude into their lives, and how they can resist systems that overuse fossil fuels and exhaust the soil. One of his favourite ways to fight back is through community-supported agriculture (CSA).

It's a movement that has spread over all of North America, and it's available to almost anyone living near a big city in Canada or the United States. It works by bringing an urban family together with a farmer to share the risks of producing food. The family pays in advance for its vegetables — say, a summer's supply of sweet corn and tomatoes or a winter's supply of potatoes and onions. With the prepayment, the farmer's susceptibility to unexpected pest outbreaks or exceptionally bad weather is removed, because he or she is allowed to substitute, for example, more tomatoes or zucchini if the corn crop fails; the farmer is assured of a market and doesn't have to depend on huge industrial entities, trucking, middlemen, preservatives or crop varieties bred for long shelf life instead of flavour.

As Kneen says, "People can say, 'Look, we have our family doctor. We have our dentist. And [now] we have our family farmer who looks after us. We have a responsibility to that farmer.' So if it doesn't rain, we don't say, 'Hey, farmer, you failed us.' Food production is a shared thing. He or she had nothing to do with the drought." This means the farmers don't have to go to the bank for loans to get the seed in the ground. They don't have bites taken out of their profits because they have to arrange for middlemen to transport their harvest. "You've begun to attack dependency and distancing in the food supply," explains Kneen. "You eliminate the debt factor." You can also get more variety. You can ask your farmer to grow arugula or bok choi or any vegetable you have trouble getting. And they can introduce you to their favourites. One Japanese CSA farmer presented her clients with different kinds of greens they'd never seen before, and then she taught them how to cook them. Kneen says, "I remember being with them, and those clients were all coming back and saying, 'Hey, that was fantastic! It was so good! I've been eating this iceberg lettuce all these years, and you mean there's all these other kinds of greens we could have?'"

Arrangements like CSA mean that in a bad year for potatoes, people learn to eat cabbage or turnips or whatever other vegetable produced well. They learn that nature is always changing, and that every year is different. Farmers start producing chickens when they learn that chickens can help with the weeding and insect control, and then they benefit from fresh eggs as well. They start growing heirloom vegetables and saving seed. They even start to share. In any given year, there's always a surplus of pumpkins or tomatoes or whatever, and that surplus can be sold cheaply to people who don't have the money to buy into the plan up front, or donated to food banks. "What you're really doing," says Kneen, "is reconstituting a community and a social life around food, which is quite proper." In fact, most CSAs quickly get into having feast days and harvest dances. Kneen says, "You're creating a whole new culture. And I think that's what we have to realize we're doing, and that's what we need."

Getting Control

> *Many, many years ago, culture was ours. . . . Bit by bit we lost control of our own culture, and suddenly corporations are doing all the talking. They're . . . telling all the stories. And bit by bit, the whole of our media culture has become one large advertisement for a lifestyle of consumption. . . . And now the big job ahead is to start telling our own stories again, to get dominion back over our culture.*
>
> — KALLE LASN, EDITOR OF *ADBUSTERS*

Perhaps you're not that focused on food or the country life; you're urban, young and interested in the Internet, movies and mass culture. You could check out *Adbusters,* the magazine that Kalle Lasn produces. This glossy magazine gives voice to a growing global movement called culture-jamming. Lasn is an ex-adman who was radicalized when he realized he couldn't go into a television station in North America — even if he had the money — and buy air time to put on a message he believed in. That's because there's a kind of censorship that has outlawed messages that don't conform to the current paradigm of endlessly growing economies and frenzied consumption. Lasn says, "The real problem facing us is our own culture in all its different aspects, be it our nutritional agenda or our transportation agenda or even the way that we run our society's information delivery systems. Somehow, the whole culture has now become dysfunctional. If you want to fix things, you have to deal with the culture, part by part; but you have to think of it as one huge dysfunctional culture that needs to be jammed back onto a sustainable path. We see ourselves as culture-jammers. We're trying to launch the new social-activist movement of the Information Age. We

use anything we can to get our consumer culture to bite its own tail —
and to slowly veer it off in the directions we believe it has to go to
become sustainable."

Adbusters specializes in spoof ads: perfect replicas of the style and
glossiness of Madison Avenue. One ad, for example, features Joe Camel
getting chemotherapy in a cancer ward; another shows the famous bottle
of Absolut vodka drooping like a dysfunctional penis, to remind the
viewer that drinking increases impotence.

Adbusters gets pro bono work from professionals, leaked memos
from inside the corporate world and donations from inspired amateurs.
To remind people what consumption does to the Earth and to their own
lives, the magazine sponsors a global holiday, Buy Nothing Day, on
November 26, just as most North Americans are gearing up for the pre-
Christmas shopping orgy. Articles share strategies, such as teaching
people to turn out the lights on billboards, hang up consumer-disruptive
signs in malls or alter signs and logos to expose reality (one wag glued a
cartoon balloon over the heads of two Marlboro cowboys so that one
was saying, "Bob, I miss my lung"). In short, *Adbusters* is constantly controversial, and the magazine faces lawsuits every day. Lasn writes about
the kinds of things most of us are afraid to because of libel chill, SLAPP
suits, and the sheer, overwhelming power of corporate money the world
over. The staff members of *Adbusters* live on a shoestring, and they are
prepared to go under financially and resurface tomorrow. But the magazine is one way urban people, who may not be inclined to wade in
streams looking for frogs, can use their creativity and talents and get
involved in saving the Earth.

The Media Foundation, which Lasn also runs, tried to sue the CBC,
among other broadcasters, for refusing to air its ads against cars and television, ads that criticize globalization and the neo-liberal economic
agenda. The foundation has the money to pay for the air time, and its
message isn't racist or pornographic; yet it doesn't have the freedom to
put it on the airwaves. The CBC at first signed a contract to air the spots,
then changed their minds, Lasn believes because of pressure from other
advertisers. They then broke the contract. Lasn says they have made it
clear that they believe that the CRTC allows them to manage their airwaves
any way they see fit, and they do not want to run the foundation's ads.

Lasn took the case from the B.C. Supreme Court, through the

Court of Appeal; the Supreme Court of Canada refused to hear the case. He has now gone to the World Court at the Hague, demanding redress under Article 19 of the Universal Declaration of Human Rights. He's fighting for what he calls the right to communicate. He says that since the Magna Carta and the Bill of Rights, people have been fighting to be heard and to have input into the decisions made by the elite groups that govern us. "I think that in this Information Age of ours, we need a new set of human rights," he says. "From television to cyberspace, we have to make sure that the corporations don't run away with the ball; that we, as citizens of the world, have, in our own constitutions and also in the UN charter, a little clause that gives us this new right, the right to communicate."

The right to communicate is one step beyond freedom of speech. "Freedom of speech simply means that you're allowed to stand up in a park on a box and say what you want to people who are passing by," Lasn explains. "But freedom of speech doesn't give you access. The really important battle of our Information Age is the battle for access. And if we can win this battle and win the right to communicate legally, then I think we will have a level playing field between citizens and corporations. We would be able to talk back to the corporate image factory. We would be in a position to create alternative futures and to pursue alternative visions, and eventually to create the sort of a world that we need rather than the sort of the world that the corporations are trying to railroad us into at the moment."

How Hard Do We Have to Try?

> For two and a half years, I was living in a 500-year-old oak. It wasn't just that tree; there were a lot of others — and crops — that we were trying to save.... Now they've chopped all the trees down. It's something we've just got to deal with. I went back to see it, and I sat on the stump of my oak. It was, like, two feet high. And I cried for about four hours.
>
> — ROBIN FORMAN-QUERCUS, TREE PEOPLE

People often ask me how far we should go to protect the Earth and force social change, while still remaining within ethical boundaries. In

England, a group committed to non-violence is pushing this particular envelope. They call themselves Tree People and Diggers. Tree People actually live up in trees for months at a time to prevent them from being cut down for timber or for development. High in the branches, the activists build simple wooden platforms on which they pitch tents. They also construct a system of rope bridges to move from tree to tree. Professional climbers have to get them down, and that takes time and money. The action holds up construction and adds greatly to the cost of any development. The tactic of the Diggers is to dig tunnels under-ground and chain themselves to concrete blocks many metres below. That prevents bulldozers and heavy equipment from coming in, because they'd be crushed. It can take even longer to get the Diggers out than it does to remove the Tree People.

In Manchester, in northern England, approval was granted in 1997 to build a new airport runway by filling in and paving over a forested river valley outside the city. Many of the people who would benefit financially from the expansion were also on the planning board that approved the runway. But to the local residents, the trees and river valley were far more precious than the airport expansion. Besides, air traffic was already creat-ing health problems. The citizens tried every legal means to save their valley, but they failed. So they turned to the Diggers. One Digger, Andy, told me, "About five years ago, the normal way of protesting was to lobby MPs, to write to the local government, the local councils — you know, the people who had given permission to develop. And gradually people realized that just didn't work and non-violent direct action was the only way to do it. . . . There are now thousands and thousands of people of all ages in this country who are doing direct action against development through building tree houses."

This strategy still works, but there aren't always suitable trees near a site, and there are other problems. "Now they employ professional rock climbers to come up and get us, and they're good," says Andy. "So we took to digging holes and putting a barrel of concrete at the bottom, which had a steel tube inserted in it. You put your arm down to it and you handcuff yourself to a bar. This proved to work. It was taking them longer and longer to get people out. Then suddenly somebody thought, 'Well, I've dug a hole down, why don't I just start digging off?' and the tunnels started."

It seems crazy, but it's not. Through their methods, the Tree People and the Diggers not only attract publicity and prompt public discussion, they also damage the bottom line. Andy says, "Now it's got to a point where it's taking them weeks to get us out at a cost of a lot of money, which is the way to beat these big firms. At the stage we're at now at Manchester, they set aside a budget of £4 million to evict us. It's now up to £6 million, and there [are] still three camps left. The largest of the tunnels is 70 to 80 feet down, 70 to 80 feet in, with twists and turns and steel doors they have to break through, which is again the lock-on idea, with concrete with locks on them. So even when they break through all the doors and get to you, they've then got to dig you out by hand, out of the concrete, because you're handcuffed to a block of concrete with your arm inside it on a metal rung. And the whole thing is just a way of costing them so much money that they say, 'We can't afford to do this.' "

If this was tried in countries in North or South America, there would probably be injuries or even deaths among the protesters. But in Great Britain, squatters' laws protect the diggers long enough for them to get their tunnels started. And public outcry would be enormous if violence was used against them. As it is, the Diggers still risk a lot by being forcibly dragged out of trees and living for months underground. When I first heard of them putting their bodies on the line in these incredible ways, I thought they must be wild fanatics or people with a death wish. But I changed my mind when I met them; they are some of the most gentle, clear-headed people I've ever encountered.

Andy says, "We're not really a special kind of people. It's just that this is how we want to protest. These tunnels are built as safe as we can build them or we wouldn't stay down here. We don't want to die, but we do want to stop this runway from being built. Great Britain is a very small place, and it's a beautiful place. And at the rate that it's being destroyed, it's just going to be a concrete jungle. There's going to be nothing left. We're fighting for our children now. It's not for us."

Andy is not just indulging in rhetoric. The day before he was interviewed, just after he was forcibly evicted from his tunnel, he'd learned some exciting news: "My girlfriend is down the tunnel at the moment. We've just found out she's three months pregnant. I've got no fears about her being there, because she's down there to protect our child. That child has got to have a future. It's got to be able to breathe. It's got to be able to go to parks. It's got to be able to go to woods, to know what birds are."

Andy and his fellow activists were passionately supported by the local people, including the renowned Terry Waite, the heroic Anglican minister and hostage negotiator who was held captive by terrorists in Lebanon between 1987 and 1991. A corps of housewives was smuggling food and water to the activists, bringing them warm blankets and doing their laundry. I interviewed one of them, Catherine Mitchell, who said, "We didn't want this runway because of pollution, environmental damage, the destruction of some beautiful old houses and land, and just the spread of the noise and pollution. . . . We tried for five whole years to stop this the democratic way, but power and greed have won over."

Mitchell's frustration was shared by the other supporters of the Tree People and the Diggers. "Before the Tree People came to camp," she says, "we were just wandering around wondering, 'What else can we do?' We were so angry; we never expected all our methods — petitions, letters, an inquiry — to lose. But these people came with their funny haircuts and tatty clothes, and their strong ideals and intelligence and integrity and humour. They are very loving, very peaceful. And it's done something to a lot of people. They've enabled a lot of the villagers to become close friends because we're all working together. . . . I mean, you've got a conscience, and if you start doing something you get this amazing energy. We're all sort of energized by it, because we feel we're doing something."

Mitchell is not alone in discovering that by acting, one gains energy and power. Fiona is a twenty-two-year-old college student who spent three months living in one of the trees near the Manchester airport. She didn't set out to do that. She says, "I always followed this sort of stuff on the news. . . . But until you're actually there in the middle of it, well, for me anyway, it didn't feel as real as it does now. Now it feels absolutely crucial. I understand what's going on. I understand that we're in an emergency situation and we have to take action. And we're the people to do it. . . . I mean, I'd love to be able to just get on with my life and enjoy it and do the things I want to do. . . . And it's really annoying that you can't get on with your life because the planet is being destroyed. But I, personally, can't just ignore it, because it's part of me. It's part of all of us, you know. I think a lot of people don't see the connections between things, the connections that run through everything. We have to take care of everything, because it's all part of the same thing."

It's easy to become so preoccupied with the details of living — getting up, going to work, dealing with family crises — that we fail to recognize or even care how we could make any difference and help to right the wrongs in the larger world out there. We don't usually come face to face with the opportunity to do something to make a difference for a bigger cause. Fiona has, and she knows how to get started: "You just have to try one small thing. Just do one thing, and you'll see it work and it'll encourage you. It'll give you spirit. You'll know that you're on the right track. . . . All I did was come here for the day because I felt like it. I felt an urge to do it, a pull. And now I've been here three months, and now I know what I want to do with my life. It's really just a small step. . . . The easiest way to do it is to think about your children and what they're going to say to you. And it's as simple as that. You know, 'What did *you* do, Mother?'"

The runway at the Manchester airport did get built, although the Diggers and the Tree People delayed it for months, at a cost of millions of pounds. But this setback hasn't discouraged them. They say they're lifers. It's not a game; it's a fight for their children's future. Others in different parts of the world are putting their bodies on the line for the same reasons.

Saving the Whales

> *One of my best friends the summer of 1960, when I was nine*
> *years old, was a beaver. . . . The next year, when I went back to*
> *our camp, I couldn't find him. I found out that trappers had*
> *taken all the beaver over the winter. I became pretty angry, . . .*
> *and when I was ten, eleven, twelve, I started destroying the*
> *trap lines, collecting leg-hold traps and generally being a*
> *nuisance in the neighbourhood for disrupting duck hunts and*
> *deer hunts.*
>
> — PAUL WATSON,
> HEAD OF THE SEA SHEPHERD SOCIETY

Paul Watson is a Canadian known around the world for his daring efforts to stop the killing of whales and seals by direct intervention. Although he was one of the originators of Greenpeace, he broke away from that group to form the Sea Shepherd Society, which is dedicated to protecting marine mammals. As captain of the ship *Sea Shepherd,* Watson cuts a swashbuckling figure, charging between whales and their hunters. I asked him how he ended up spending his life sinking whaling boats and getting beaten up by enraged sealers. He told me the dramatic and moving story of a day that changed his life.

"In 1975, we had encountered the Russian whaling fleet just off the coast of northern California. We'd come up with this idea to put ourselves in small inflatable boats, to put our lives on the line, reasoning that nobody is going to kill a whale if they've got to risk killing a human being. We were reading a lot of Gandhi at the time and we were quite naive. . . . Anyway, Bob Hunter and I were in a small rubber boat, and we were blocking a Soviet harpoon vessel. This 150-foot steel vessel was bearing down on us at twenty knots. And in front of us, eight magnificent sperm whales were fleeing for their lives. Every time the harpooner swivelled the harpoon, I would manoeuvre the small boat . . . to block his path; this worked for about twenty minutes. Then the captain came down the catwalk and screamed into the ear of the harpooner . . . and we knew we were in trouble. And a few minutes later, the harpooner fired the harpoon over our heads and this 150-pound exploding grenade zoomed over our heads and slammed into the backside of one of the females in this pod of sperm whales. And she screamed. Blood was squirting everywhere. The largest whale in that pod suddenly rose up and dove.

"We'd been told by all of the experts that the whale would attack us, because we were the smallest targets and it would be very angry. As we waited with a great deal of anxiety for fifty tons of very angry animal to come up underneath us, the ocean erupted behind us and we turned in time to see the whale hurl himself from the water straight at the Russian harpooner who was on the bow. But the harpooner was waiting for him, and he very nonchalantly pulled the trigger and sent a second harpoon, at point-blank range, into the head of the whale. The whale screamed and fell back in the water, blood everywhere now. And as he was rolling and thrashing about, I caught his eye. And he saw me. Then he dove.

"I saw this trail of bloody bubbles coming straight towards us, real fast. The whale came up and out of the water at an angle, so it looked like he was just going to come forward and crush us. And then it was almost as if he stopped in mid-air. He was so close I could have reached up and grabbed one of these six-inch teeth. I looked up into this eye, which was the size of my fist, and what I saw in that eye was understanding. That whale really knew what we were trying to do, because the easiest thing for the whale to [do] was to come forward and crush us or seize us in his jaws, and he did neither. He just very slowly and deliberately and with great effort slid back beneath the waves and died.

"There was something else I saw in that eye, and it was pity. Not for himself, but for us, that we could be engaged in this kind of blasphemy, where we could so wantonly destroy life. And for what? The Russians in this case were killing the whales to provide lubricating oil for ICBM missiles. We were wiping out a species in order to make a weapon meant to destroy human beings. It was absolute insanity.

"And as I sat there in that small rubber boat, . . . the water turning red around me, I began to think, 'What is this all about? Why are we doing this?' And I said to myself, 'For the rest of my life, I'm going to pledge to protect as many of his kind as I possibly can.' And personally I don't really care what people think about what I do. My satisfaction comes from living up to that obligation and protecting whales directly by destroying the illegal vessels that are out there destroying them."

Paul Watson's passion for his life commitment is unmistakable — and essential. Much as we'd like politicians to take the burden from the shoulders of individuals and care for the Earth, they haven't. The real force for environmental protection still comes from individuals and thousands of non-governmental organizations around the world. "The only thing that has ever really made a difference in any social movement has been individual initiative, individual passion," Watson argues. "Anthropologist Margaret Mead once put that very distinctly when she said, 'Never depend upon institutions or government to solve any problem. All social movements are founded by, guided by, motivated and seen through by the passion of individuals.'"

Paul Watson has been on the frontlines, protecting wildlife for thirty years, and he speaks from experience. He has many examples of what one person can do. "A few years ago I had a man call me from Glasgow, Scotland, and he said, 'They're killing grey seals up here. What are you going to do about it?' My answer to him was: 'I'm not going to do anything about it. What are *you* going to do about it?

You're Scottish, you do something about it.' And he said, 'Well, what can I do? I'm just one person.' Well, we talked to him and encouraged him, and he set up a Sea Shepherd group in Scotland. And in only three years, they shut that hunt down. He was an architect, so he wasn't a professional conservationist or anything. It just shows you what one individual can do if [he's] given the encouragement to see what kind of power [he] can have."

Complex Pleasures

The story of the twentieth century was finding out just how big and powerful we were. And it turns out that we're big and powerful as all get out. The story of the twenty-first century is going to be finding out if we can figure out ways to get smaller or not. To see if we can summon the will, and then the way, to make ourselves somewhat smaller, and try to fit back into this planet.

— BILL MCKIBBEN

As I've said repeatedly in this book, if we want to learn how to live in balance and harmony with our surroundings, we need input from many different people and cultures. Scientists and researchers can document the state of the planet, but we also need the perspective and knowledge of other cultures, especially those that have always depended on nature for physical and spiritual sustenance. Matthew Mukash, the chief of the Cree of Great Whale in northern Quebec, was born in a teepee in 1951, hundreds of kilometres from what we call civilization. Until he was nine, he and his family followed a completely nomadic way of life. Mukash spent his childhood among caribou and bear, wild geese and arctic char, on the huge rivers, muskeg and black spruce barrens of the Far North. But he yearned for a modern education, and eventually ended up studying at McGill University in Montreal.

Mukash recounts: "When I decided to go to school, my father told me, 'You have grown up in the traditional way. You have our traditional knowledge of survival and all that means. Now you have to learn the other way. I don't want you to lose what you already have. You have to keep on practising your way of life. You have to remember the teachings that you received from me and from the elders.... [Remember] what they tell us. Do what you want. Go get your education. But you always have to remember that there's a purpose for you as a Native person. There's a purpose for every nation in the world to be, to exist. That's because each nation has a particular gift. If you put those gifts together, you will find answers for the whole of humanity, for the protection of the Earth and for living a good life.... This is what the elders are saying.'"

Just as with Tewolde Egziather describing the importance of Africa in a changing world, Mukash's father was talking about the importance of a variety of beliefs and perspectives held by different peoples for our long-term survival. As circumstances change, one cultural system may be specially placed to offer an adaptive value that will add to our prospects for survival. That's why, at this critical juncture in the relationship between human beings and the Earth, we need elders of every human group who will share their knowledge and ideas.

It's worth our while to pay attention to people like the Cree, who have lived in the same place for more than 5,000 years without destroying the ecosystem around them. The Cree know they need to understand us, because our dominant culture so profoundly threatens their way of life. Mukash says, "I had to learn about the history of the world, about modern life. I got a degree in political science. I know how politics works; I know the history of law, the history of philosophy. And for me it helps, because there are certain people who are gifted to ... be messengers to other nations. And every nation has those people."

Matthew Mukash says the Cree elders think it's important to offer their own insights to other people, to talk to them and share these teachings. "People in modern society, the elders say, ... are doing things without thinking of the sacred. You know, everything is done in the absence of the sacred. But the Cree say that everything is balanced. If any element in a human being is missing, then there are problems. That's why so many people do things to ... satisfy their own needs, rather than trying to meet the needs of the whole of humanity."

The Cree elders say that our way of life, for all its comforts and pleasures, is missing a key ingredient, and that is human spiritual fulfillment. That doesn't mean that they reject all our knowledge and wisdom, or that they deny the benefits of modern medicine, transportation or information technology. The elders appreciate and accept the advantages and comforts of modern life. They just want them placed into a broader context of a useful and balanced life. Mukash says, "We're here for a reason. We're not here to make money. It's good if you make money. You can get a car; you can have a cottage in the country. But if that spiritual aspect, that spiritual element, is not part of your life, then you're breaking the law. And as an individual, you're off balance."

Mukash says that if we can pull back from our destruction of the natural world, from our fears of poverty, from our dislike of sharing, especially from our wars, we will be able to see what we need to do. "All the problems that we have with regards to the economy, to the environment, all the problems of human conflict in the world — they all have to do with the absence of that balance that should be there. This is the knowledge that our elders are passing on to us, and it's very intense. It's very difficult to understand, but all these things that happen in the world, they're happening because there needs to be a balance."

Bill McKibben also agrees there needs to be balance in life. To find the peace and happiness we seek, he says we need to look at how we're made. "We arrive here with this collection of limbs and muscles and emotions and reason and senses. Clearly, we were designed for something more than reclining on the couch, flicking the remote control. And we were probably designed for something more than obtaining money so we can purchase things with it. . . . We're built for challenge, for things that are difficult, for walking up mountains, for taking on real problems around us. And we're built, I think, for some sense of contact with the divine — however you want to define that — for some sense that there's something larger than us around."

We've come to see the creature comforts our culture provides as the sole purpose of life. When we're very young, our needs are simple — warmth, food, physical comfort, a little stimulation. But as we grow, our pleasures become far more complex. Our current culture seems to have responded by giving us more and more of what made us happy as babies. But a mature organism is not the same as an inexperienced, growing one. Mature organisms flower and fruit; they produce and share; they don't just feed and take. McKibben says, "I set up and helped run a small homeless shelter in New York City when I lived there. And given all the charms and excitements that New York has to offer — fine restaurants and going to the ballet and so on — that should have been only a kind of onerous duty. But in fact, it was the most fun, in many ways, that I had in my whole time there, because it was real and useful and took full measure of my emotions and abilities, not just my ability to think or to write, but the ability to use my muscles and my hands and my emotions."

Think about the last time you volunteered at a shelter or a bake sale, went to visit someone who was sick or helped a neighbour plant her garden. McKibben says, "We know that once you volunteer to do something or go out to help people, the pleasure is mostly yours. We're clearly built to be of service. That we are able to be convinced otherwise, convinced that our pleasures will come from focusing entirely on ourselves, is just one of several great lies that the twentieth century has tried to foist on us."

What this century should have taught us is to reflect much more deeply before implementing new projects. If we want to overcome child mortality worldwide or increase life expectancy, we will eventually have to place limits on the number of children we can have. If we want to increase agricultural crops, we'd better make sure that this will not negatively affect the natural ecosystem services on which those crops depend. We can increase our material satisfactions with computer games, more television channels and bigger cars and homes, but giving attention to such things uses up much of the time and energy we could be putting into the familial, community and spiritual needs that are so basic to our nature. Matthew Mukash says, "I was always taught that life has to be difficult, because if you're comfortable, there's no room for spiritual growth because all you focus on is your physical needs. . . . That's why our elders today [are] always on the land. They say, 'You stay in the community, you stay in a house. There's nothing to do! You watch TV. What does that bring you?' They go out on the land. They chop wood. They fish, make things. For them, life has to be difficult."

At first glance, this sounds like more asceticism. But that's too glib a dismissal. The most coddled Yuppie waxes ecstatic about her new gym or trainer and how hard he makes her work. We spend our time and money on vacations climbing mountains and shooting rapids. The extreme wealth in industrialized countries has made a cornucopia of food available year round and machines to perform our labour, and this has resulted in epidemic levels of obesity and heart disease. Down deep, we know that life might not be as easy if we started cutting back the luxuries and began sharing with others and helping to conserve parts of the planet. But we might also discover that life would be a whole lot more fulfilling, even a great deal more fun. As Mukash says, "The three parts of you have to be in balance: your physical health, your mental health and your spiritual health. They all three have to be functioning. If your spiritual side doesn't function, then you become greedy. This is a natural teaching; it's common to all nations. And that is what the problem is. We're way off balance."

As a species, humanity is in its infancy. We appeared very recently in evolutionary time and have exploded as an unprecedented force in this century. We know that we are exceeding the sustainable limits of the planet's carrying capacity. It's not deliberate; it's simply the collective impact of all we do. Our radio series and this book have examined some of our most cherished notions about science and technology, information and economics, to reveal how they too create an imbalance with our surroundings. The challenge is to restore the balance between our needs and the Earth's capacity to supply those needs and absorb our impact.

The psychiatrist and author Robert Jay Lifton once told me a story about Hiroshima after the atomic bomb was dropped on it. A rumour spread among the survivors that nothing would ever grow again in the city, that the soil had been sterilized forever. Despite the horrific death toll and the terrible suffering, the survivors were anguished even more by the thought that nature itself might have been destroyed by the great weapon. Only when plants began to grow again did the wave of horror and despair subside.

Lifton's poignant story reminds us that we emerged from nature, remain embedded in it, and need it to nourish us physically, socially and spiritually. We may not think about that very often, but as the Hiroshima story reveals, the very thought that we might be capable of destroying the source of all life is too much to bear. The path we are now on leads to the destruction of nature. It is suicidal and too horrific to contemplate. We have to listen to all the voices around us, telling us to harmonize those needs, so that we can restore the balance we so desperately need.

REFERENCES

Much of the information contained in this book comes directly from the taped interviews for the radio series on which this book is based. However, we also benefited from published and Internet information sources, which we list here for each chapter.

INTRODUCTION
Rachel Carson's *Silent Spring* (Boston: Houghton Mifflin Company, 1962) has been a continual reference and inspiration in a variety of contexts throughout this book. Her biography by Linda J. Lear, *Witness for Nature* (New York: Henry Holt and Co., 1997), has served as a fresh reminder of the enormity of her contribution to the environmental movement.

CHAPTER 1
BUGS Я US
Information on the expectations for and actual results of Biosphere II can be obtained from a large variety of newspaper and periodical sources. A few examples are: the cover story of *Current Science*, "Biosphere II: Scientists Make Home in a Dome" by H. Westrup, March 29, 1991; "Weird Science" by J.M. Laskas and P. Menzel, *Life*, August 1991; "Sealed Up," in *New Scientist*, September 21, 1991; "Lost in Space" by P. Heard, in the *New Republic*, January 21, 1991. Some descriptions of the problems that began to arise can be found in "Bubble Trouble," in *Harper's*, February 1992; "Biosphere or Biobust" by N. Zeman and L. Howard, *Newsweek*, February 24, 1992; "Lean Times for Glasshouse People," *New*

Scientist, December 5, 1992; "People in Glass Houses" by Michael Hirschorn, *Esquire*, August 1992; and "Biosflop?" *Environment*, July/August 1992.

We referred especially to Edward O. Wilson's *The Diversity of Life* (New York: Norton, 1992), and to two tomes he edited for the National Research Council and the Smithsonian Institution, entitled *Biodiversity* (Washington, D.C.: National Academy Press, 1988) and *Biodiversity II*, by Marjorie Reaka-Kudla and Don Wilson as well (Washington, D.C.: Joseph Henry Press, 1997). Another guide to the subject is Paul and Ann Ehrlich's *Extinction: The Causes and Consequences of the Disappearance of Species* (New York: Random House, 1981). Norman Myers's classic, *The Sinking Ark* (Oxford: Pergamon, 1979), is still useful.

For those interested in finding ways to increase the vital protection of biodiversity, consult the last ten years of papers from the World Resources Institute (WRI) in Washington, D.C., as well as biodiversity subjects in *State of the World*, the yearly publication of Lester Brown's Worldwatch Institute, also in Washington, D.C. (see the end of this book for addresses). Stuart Pimm's *The Balance of Nature: Ecological Issues in the Conservation of Species and Communities* (Chicago: University of Chicago Press, 1991) is a useful resource.

The classic publication on the Gaia hypothesis, now upgraded to a theory, is James Lovelock's *Gaia: A New Look at Life on Earth* (Oxford: Oxford University Press, 1979), and his update, *The Ages of Gaia: A Biography of Our Living Earth* (New York: Norton, 1995), but there are many others, including works by his collaborator, microbiologist Lynn Margulis, such as *Microcosmos*, with Dorion Sagan (New York: Summit, 1986). The understanding of the Earth as a superorganism has not diminished since *Gaia* was written, but has become increasingly supported by research and the hard sciences, like chemistry and physics, and by the mathematical model called "Daisy World." Stephen Schneider and P. Boston edited the seminal *Scientists on Gaia* (Cambridge, Mass.: MIT Press, 1991), the first "establishment" scientific conference on the Gaia hypothesis, and the one that established it as legitimate ground for further research. Fritjof Capra's latest book, *The Web of Life* (New York: Anchor Books, 1996), is a rich source of food for thought for those who wish to understand what physics is now offering biology. We also recommend *The Value of Life: Biological Diversity and Human Society* by Stephen R. Kellert (Washington, D.C.: Island Press, 1996) and *The Biophilia Hypothesis*, coedited with E.O. Wilson (Washington, D.C.: Island Press, 1993), for insights into the philosophical, ethical and emotional importance of biodiversity to human life.

Orrie Loucks's studies on forest dynamics and air pollution effects are featured in *Appalachian Tragedy*, a photo volume edited by Harvard Ayers and published by Sierra Club Books. Loucks is also the senior editor of a useful new textbook, *Sustainability Perspectives for Resources and Business* (New York: Sierra Sea Press, 1999).

The symbiosis between salmon and forests has been described by Tom Reimchen in his articles "Bears, gardeners of the forests," *The Vancouver Sun*, September 30, 1999, and "Bears: A Vital Link for Salmon, Trees," Victoria *Times Colonist*, September 14, 1999. It was also explored in an article by Francis Backhouse in the Sept./Oct. 1999 issue of *Canadian Geographic*, "Fewer salmon. Fewer bears. Fewer trees?"

For more detail on the increasing links between astrophysics, philosophy and religion, see Brian Swimme's *The Hidden Heart of the Cosmos: Humanity and the New Story* (San Francisco: Orbis Books, 1996) and, with Thomas Berry, *The Universe Story* (San Francisco: Harper, 1994). For a more detailed discussion of the Okanagan approach to life, see Jeanette Armstrong's article "Sharing One Skin — Okanagan Community" in the remarkably useful Sierra Club book, *The Case against the Global Economy* (San Francisco: 1996), edited by Jerry Mander and Edward Goldsmith.

CHAPTER 2
BIGFOOT

William Rees and Mathias Wackernagel's seminal study, *Our Ecological Footprint: Reducing Human Impact on the Earth* (Gabriola Island, B.C.: New Society Publishers, 1996), forms the basis for this entire chapter, and we drew from it extensively.

Useful articles include "The Value of the World's Ecosystem Services and Natural Capital" by Robert Costanza et al., *Nature*, Vol. 387, 1997; "Economic Growth, Carrying Capacity and the Environment" by Kenneth Arrow et al., *Science*, April 28, 1995; and

"Population Dynamics and Food Security" by Norman Myers in *Food Security: New Solutions for the 21st Century*, S.R. Johnson, ed. (Desmoines: Iowa State University Press, 1997).

Nancy Langston's *Forest Dreams, Forest Nightmares* (Seattle: University of Washington Press, 1995) is a remarkable general reference on the well-intentioned but often disastrous history of professional forestry. The World Resources Institute's groundbreaking *Report on the Frontier Forests of the World* deserves special attention from Canadians, as so much of this issue intersects with our own national interests and the behaviour of our governments. Refer to the organizations list at the end of this book for addresses.

Alan Thein Durning's *How Much Is Enough?* (New York: W.W. Norton & Co., 1992) has been useful in many chapters, beginning with this one, and we made special reference to his time-lapse image of the world's forests, which appears in "Saving the Forests: What Will It Take?" *Worldwatch Paper 117*, December 1993. We also referred to Patricia Marchak, Scott Aycock and Deborah Herbert's *Falldown: Forest Policy in British Columbia* (Vancouver, B.C.: David Suzuki Foundation/Ecotrust Canada, 1999).

Estimations of the amount of ocean floor destroyed annually by draggers are from *Conservation Biology*, Vol. 12, No. 6, December 1998. We used the *Maclean's* October 5, 1998, special issue on the oceans — especially "Our Dying Seas" by Chris Wood and "Breaking the Bonds" by Joseph MacInnis — as a source for recent facts and figures. To learn more about the state of our oceans, refer to Sylvia Earle's *Wild Oceans* (Washington, D.C.: National Geographic Society, 1999) or *Sea Change: A Message of the Oceans* (New York: G.P. Putnam & Sons, 1995).

Of the over two hundred scientific books, papers and reviews authored by Stephen Schneider, we referred especially to *Laboratory Earth: The Planetary Gamble We Can't Afford to Lose* (New York: Basic Books, 1997). He is also the founder and editor of the interdisciplinary journal *Climatic Change*. We found his *The Coevolution of Climate and Life* (San Francisco: Sierra Club, 1984) very thought-provoking. Schneider's *Global Warming: Are We Entering the Greenhouse Century?* caused a serious wave of concern when it was published in 1990, and remains an important work (San Francisco: Sierra Club Books).

See also the many publications of the Intergovernmental Panel on Climatic Change (IPCC), published by Cambridge University Press. For a concise discussion of the "controversy" of global warming and of environmental dangers in general, see Norman Myers and Julian Symon's *Scarcity or Abundance: A Debate on the Environment* (New York: Norton, 1992). An Internet search will provide literally hundreds of newspaper articles on this discussion; the more recent the articles, the more apparent it becomes that warming is irrefutable and caused by humans.

We obtained figures on the distributional change of world income over the last thirty years from UNESCO, *Sources 58*, May 1994. Along with many other writers, we are indebted to Paul and Ann Ehrlich for their classic, *The Population Bomb,* and its update, *The Population Explosion* (New York: Simon and Schuster, 1990). The journal *Population and Development Review* has many pertinent articles on population issues, and we relied as well on figures provided by the Population Institute in Washington; see the end of the book for further information. The Ehrlichs have also recently published another book that has bearing on the controversy surrounding global warming, and on other chapters of the book as well. It concerns what is termed "brownwashing" in chapter 3, and is called *The Betrayal of Science and Reason* (Washington, D.C.: Island Press, 1996).

Bill McKibbon's books, *Hundred-Dollar Holiday* (New York: Simon & Schuster, 1998) and *Maybe One: A Personal and Environmental Argument for Single-Child Families* (New York: Simon & Schuster, 1998), detail the ideas broached in the text. His classic, *The End of Nature* (New York: Anchor Books, 1990), has been a constant reference in this and several other chapters of the book.

Figures for the amount of toxic waste in Sydney, Nova Scotia, come from the Sierra Club of Canada. They have mounted a major campaign to demand appropriate government action, and will provide pertinent data to anyone who is interested. The Center for Health, Environment and Justice in Falls Church, Virginia, just outside of Washington, D.C., has a publications catalogue and also provides statistics and data on landfills, toxic waste dumps, and contaminants like dioxin in the United States, and will gladly provide them upon request. See the list at the end of the book.

CHAPTER 3
SEZ WHO?

The "World Scientists' Warning to Humanity" can be obtained in its entirety by contacting the Union of Concerned Scientists; see the list at the end of this book.

The chapter entitled "Food Fight" in Sheldon Rampton and John Stauber's book, *Mad Cow USA* (Monroe, Maine: Common Courage Press, 1997), outlines the lawsuit against Winfrey and Lyman and the bibliography gives a good rundown of top media stories on the issue. For a complex look at risk assessment and public communication, *Mad Cows and Mother's Milk: The Perils of Poor Risk Communication* by Douglas Powell and William Leiss (Montreal: Queen's University Press, 1997) is a good source, although it has a tendency to see environmental problems as communication problems.

We referred to Lawrence Grossman's *The Electronic Republic: Reshaping Democracy in the Information Age* (New York: Penguin, 1995). Several of Neil Postman's books were important to this chapter, especially *Amusing Ourselves to Death* (New York: Penguin, 1985). We also read and referred to David Shenk's influential book criticizing information glut, *Data Smog* (New York: Harper Collins Publishers, 1997). Joshua Karliner's Internet magazine, *Corporate Watch*, is an excellent source of information about who is doing what in the corporate world. We also referred to his Sierra Club book, *The Corporate Planet: Ecology and Politics in the Age of Globalization* (San Francisco: The Sierra Club, 1997).

A major source of information and inspiration was the classic *Four Arguments for the Elimination of Television* by Jerry Mander (New York: Quill, 1978). His most recent book, *In the Absence of the Sacred* (San Francisco: The Sierra Club, 1991), also provided food for thought in this and several other chapters. *A Pocket Guide to Environmental Bad Guys* by James Ridgeway and Jeffrey St. Clair (New York: Thunder's Mouth Press, 1999) was a useful reference. Publications from the *Environmental Working Group of the Clearinghouse on Environmental Advocacy and Research*, especially "Target: Democracy — The Effect of Anti-Environmental Violence on Community Discourse," April 22, 1997, back up EarthFirst! claims and give further examples of the kind of incidents of violence against peaceful environmental protest that we list in the book. Other papers list the corporate-funded "astroturf" groups that seek to undermine or weaken environmental legislation. *PR Watch*, a quarterly published by the Center for Media and Democracy in Madison, Wisconsin, gave us help and figures on many issues. We particularly referred to their July 1999 story, "Burson-Marsteller: PR for the New World Order," by Carmelo Ruiz. See the list of organizations at the end of the book for addresses.

Greenwash: The Reality Behind Corporate Environmentalism, by Jed Greer and Kenny Bruno (Penang, Malaysia: Third World Network, 1996), gives a fascinating history of how corporations use public relations and public perceptions to alter their image and convince us of noble environmental intentions, while pursuing the bottom line as usual. Joshua Karliner's *The Corporate Planet*, mentioned in chapter 2, was also helpful to us in chapter 3. But the single most quotable and eye-opening book we found on the issue of information was *Toxic Sludge Is Good for You: Lies, Damn Lies and the Public Relations Industry*, by John Stauber and Sheldon Rampton (Monroe, Maine: Common Courage Press, 1995); it uses black humour as it looks at the role of the media and private vested interests in obscuring, perverting or subverting environmental issues.

CHAPTER 4
UNNATURAL SELECTIONS
The senior author of this book was trained as a geneticist and has more than twenty-five years' experience as a practising scientist. The volume of articles and books that contributed to the position he takes in this chapter is far too great to include here. We attempted to pare it down to key articles and books that provide perspective on the debate.

Physicist Vandana Shiva is ubiquitous in the areas of both biotechnology and food security. We met with her four times, and also consulted some of her scores of articles, books and pamphlets on these subjects, notably *Monocultures of the Mind* (Penang, Malaysia: Third World Network, 1993) and *The Violence of the Green Revolution: Third World Agriculture, Ecology and Politics* (London: Zed Books, 1993). We also made extensive use of Dr. Mae Wan Ho's *Genetic Engineering: Dreams or Nightmares? The Brave New World of Bad Science and Big Business* (Penang, Malaysia: Third World Network, 1997), as well as her *Independent Report on Biosafety*, prepared by the Third World Network in 1997 for the biosafety negotiations taking place under the U.N. Convention on Biological Diversity.

We recommend Jeremy Rifkin's *The Biotechnology Century* (New York: Jeremy P. Tarcher/Putnam, 1998) for a balanced appraisal of what lies ahead for society in terms of this new technology. Brewster Kneen's *From Land to Mouth* (Toronto: NC Press Ltd., 1993) is a wonderful background explanation of the vertical integration of our food supply. See also his latest book, *Farmageddon: Food and the Culture of Biotechnology* (Gabriola Island, B.C.: New Society, 1999). We were continuously informed by Brewster and Cathleen Kneen's monthly newsletter of food systems analysis, *The Ram's Horn*, published in Sorrento, B.C.; see the organizations list at the end of the book. We also consulted *Overcoming Illusions About Biotechnology* by Nicanor Perlas (London: Zed Books, 1994), and *The Life Industry: Biodiversity, People and Profits* by Miges Baumann, Janet Bell, Florianne Koechlin and Michel Pimbert (London: Intermediate Technology Publications, 1996). For an overview of how biotech fits into politics and globalization, see *Earth for Sale* by Brian Tokar (Boston: South End Press, 1997). Probably the single most useful resource for the layman is Vol. 28, No. 5 of *The Ecologist*, Sept./Oct. 1998, an entire issue devoted to biotechnology and subtitled "The Monsanto Files." The articles and references in this issue pretty much cover the topic.

Specific facts and figures are as up to date as possible and therefore come mostly from journalistic sources. *The Times* (London), *The Guardian* and *The Independent* are excellent English-language sources for the ongoing genetic controversy in Europe. The Reuters news service, which appears in many papers, is following the issue, and the *St. Louis Post Dispatch*, located in Monsanto's hometown, is a rich source of articles on the controversies surrounding genetically engineered agricultural crops (see especially "Ham-Fisted Force-Feeding," April 15, 1999). We wish we could name a Canadian newspaper that is following the issue as diligently; Canadian coverage, although sometimes good, has been sporadic. See *The Province*, "Gene-tooled food going unchecked," May 14, 1999.

For details of the effects of genetically manipulated crops on beneficial organisms like the monarch butterfly, lacewings and ladybugs (pp. 101 and 124), see Bob Hortzler's article on the monarchs in

Science, January 1999, and Angelika Hilbeck's studies on lacewings for the Swiss Federal Research Station for Agroecology and Agriculture, Zurich, Switzerland, published in the *Journal of Environmental Entomology*, February 1997. We also quoted from reports of the International Meeting of Entomologists in Basel, Switzerland, in 1999, where Mark Whalon of Michigan State University said, "This heightened threat of Bt-resistence, coupled with the devastation of the beneficial insect populations that help keep plants in check, could lead to massive crop failures"; see also studies by Nicolas Birch of the Scottish Crop Research Institute on ladybird beeties, also 1999. Studies at both Cornell and Iowa State on monarchs reveal similar problems.

Israel's bomb engineered to affect ethnic Arabs (p. 101) was reported by Uzi Mahnaimi and Marie Colvin in the *Sunday Times* (London), November 15, 1998. The deformed cotton plants (p. 105) were reported in many farm journals and news media in the U.S. and Australia; see Allen Myerson, "Breeding Seeds of Discontent: Cotton Growers Say Strain Cuts Yield," *New York Times*, November 9, 1997; Bill Lamprecht, "Many Farmers Finding Altered Cotton Lacking," *St. Louis Post Dispatch*, April 12, 1998; and Robert Steyer, "Monsanto Refuses to Pay $1.94 Million to Farmers," *St. Louis Post Dispatch*, June 20, 1998.

Richard Strohman's charge (p. 106) that commercial concerns are twisting academic research has been noted for some years; see Brian Tokar's "The False Promise of Biotechnology" in *Z Magazine*, February 1992, which states, "Twenty-four leading research universities all have ten or more faculty members with . . . direct corporate affiliations in biotechnology; Harvard alone has 69, Stanford has 40 . . . in the most striking case, almost one third of the MIT biology department is tied to biotech companies." The overall picture has grown worse since that article was written.

Regarding ethics in the scientific profession (pp. 110–12), we were informed by Theodore Roszak's article in *Resurgence* (Sept./Oct. 1997), "The Soul of Science." The opposite approach — that the ethical issues surrounding cloning and other genetic interference can be dealt with through PR spin and habituation — is outlined in Oliver Morton's "Overcoming Yuk: It may be unnatural, but encouraging genetic choice in humans is not bad (it's also inevitable)," *Wired*, November 1998.

For already established incidences of biological pollution via wind, pollen, and insects as well as fears about microorganism contamination (p. 113), see Nick Nuttall, "Bees Spread Genes from GM Crops," *The Times*, April 15, 1999; and see also M. Brookes, "Running Wild," *New Scientist*, October 31, 1998. Monsanto's own lawsuits against farmers have raised the contention of uncontrolled pollen contamination in fields adjacent to or even some kilometres away from GM crops. They have been widely reported; we used an article by Marie Woolf that appeared in *The Independent*, March 14, 1999. See also "Perils Amidst the Promise: Ecological Risks of Transgenic Crops in a Global Market," 1993, by Jane Rissler and Margaret Mellon, available through the Union of Concerned Scientists.

Poison-free methods of dealing with weeds are legion and widely reported in the literature; a recent example is "Farmer's Friend" by Fred Pearce, in *Science*, October 24, 1998. On pp. 114 and 115, we mentioned the toxicity of Roundup, detailed in two heavily researched papers by Caroline Cox in the *Journal of Pesticide Reform*, Vol. 15, No. 3, Fall 1995, entitled "Glyphosate, Part 1: Toxicology" and "Glyphosate, Part 2: Human Exposure and Ecological Effects," No. 4, Winter 1995. Other papers we consulted included "Preventing Pesticide-Related Illness in California Agriculture: Strategies and Priorities," by William S. Pease et al., for the Center for Occupational and Environmental Health, the School of Public Health, University of California at Berkeley, 1993. It should be noted that Roundup is so generally toxic that researchers are even investigating its potential as an antimicrobial. See F. Roberts et al. in *Nature* 393, 1999, pp. 801–5. Many related articles are available through PAN, the Pesticide Action Network; see organizations list for details.

For an example of a possible allergenic reaction to genetically engineered materials, see J.A. Nordlee et al., "Identification of a Brazil-Nut Allergen in Transgenic Soybeans," *The New England Journal of Medicine*, March 14, 1996. Problems with synthetic insulin were detailed in a series of articles in *The Guardian*, beginning with the March 9, 1999, article "Diabetics Not Told of Insulin Risk." Another human health issue is detailed in "Meningitis Fears from GE

Crops," a story reported both on the BBC News and in The *Sunday Times* (London), April 19, 1999. The *Times* article states, "The UK's Advisory Committee on Novel Foods and Processes fears antibiotic-resistant genes will be picked up by commonly-carried bacteria, such as those for meningitis . . ."

Some of the biotech industry's increasing regulatory problems affecting profit margins are listed in Andrea Ahles's article "Biotech Companies Seek Funds from Non-Wall Street," *The Philadelphia Inquirer,* June 7, 1999; recently the Deutsche Bank has advised its investors to be aware of serious problems with biotech stocks and biotech companies (Internet Deutsche bank analysis report, September 1999). Regarding the failings of regulatory bodies in this matter, see Mae Wan Ho and Ricarda Steinbrecher, "Fatal Flaws in Food Safety Assessment: Critique of the Joint FAO/WHO Biotechnology and Food Safety Report," *Environmental and Nutritional Interactions* 2, 1998. Finally, we are particularly indebted to Richard Strohman's excellent article in *Nature Biotechnology*, "The Coming Kuhnian Revolution in Biology" (March 1997).

CHAPTER 5
YOUR MONEY OR YOUR LIFE FORMS
Vandana Shiva's published works are even more extensive in the area of biopiracy and farmers' rights than they are in food systems and biotechnology. We specifically recommend *Biopiracy: The Plunder of Nature and Knowledge* (Boston: South End Press, 1997) and *Staying Alive: Women, Ecology and Development* (London: Zed Books, 1988). A very useful overview is Ruth Hubbard and Elijah Wald's *Exploding the Gene Myth: How Genetic Information Is Produced and Manipulated by Scientists, Physicians, Employers, Insurance Companies, Educators and Law Enforcers* (Boston: Beacon Press, 1993). See also Andy Kimbrell's *The Human Body Shop: The Engineering and Marketing of Life* (San Francisco: Harper Collins, 1993).

Specific references used include articles from a special section in *The Boston Sunday Globe*, April 5, 1998, "Cashing In at Public Expense," which states, "Taxpayers subsidize an industry awash in profits, then pay onerous prices for drugs their tax dollars helped create" (see p. 131). The *Staphylococcus* controversy (p. 133) was reported in

"Biotech Battlefield: Profits vs. Public" by Marlene Cimons and Paul Jacobs, in the *L.A. Times*, February 21, 1999. For details of the organized rural resistance to GM crops in India (p. 134), known journalistically as the "Cremate Monsanto" movement, see "Farmers Group Storms Mahyco Office in Hyderabad," *The Indian Express*, Bangalore Edition, December 2, 1998, or "KRRS 'Cremates' Cotton in Bellary," *The Times of India*, December 4, 1998.

On the patent scramble for neem, mustard, ginger, castor, basmati and more, see especially "Biopiracy: The Need to Change Western IPR Systems" by Vandana Shiva in *The Hindu*, July 28, 1999. This article also explains the remarkable fact that transport of a living thing from one country to another is the only current requirement for ownership. Shiva points out that section 102 of the 1952 U.S. Patent Act does not consider use of any item, even an invention, in another country to be "prior art" that would disallow patenting. In other words, until it's patented in the United States, it's free game.

The controversy surrounding the experiments by Dr. Arpad Pusztai (described on p. 137) occupied the British media for weeks. The huge spread in *The Guardian* published February 12, 1998, lays out all the players, the chronology and the controversy. In "Food Scandal Exposed," Michael Sean Gillard, Laurie Flynn and Andy Rowell write, "[Dr. Pusztai's] team found that the liver and heart sizes of the rats were decreasing — worse still, the brains were getting smaller . . . 'It is very unfair to use our fellow citizens as guinea pigs,' said Dr. Pusztai. Two days later he was summarily suspended." We of course consulted the primary data, including the Rowett Research Institute audit report by Philip James, which disagreed with Pusztai's findings, and the October 1998 experiments by pathologist Stanley Ewen of Aberdeen University Medical School, which supported Pusztai's position. When this book went to press, the findings were still in dispute, but had not been refuted and remained worrying. The main point, supported by twenty prominent international scientists in a public statement in February, was that such preliminary findings in a government-funded agency should have triggered serious health effects research, not a forced resignation and a cover-up.

Evidence of a link between glyphosate and a dangerous cancer, non-Hodgkin's lymphoma (see p. 137), are detailed in a recent paper by oncologists Lennart Hardell and Mikael Eriksson in the *Journal of the American Cancer Society*, March 15, 1999.

Regarding liability, see for example "The Price of Disaster Will Not be Paid by Those Responsible" by Justine Thornton in *The Independent*, February 28, 1999. The "revolving door" list on p. 139 is only a small part of the picture. In the biotech special edition of *The Ecologist* (Vol. 28, No. 5, Sept./Oct. 1998) Jennifer Ferrara and others provide many more examples in their section entitled "Revolving Doors: Monsanto and the Regulators." For allegations of bribery in Canada and Britain, see "All Monsanto's Men?" by Nick Cohen, *The Observer*, February 21, 1999, which says, "Dr. Margaret Haydon told the Canadian Senate that she and her superior in the Human Safety Division, one Dr. Drennan, [in October of last year] had met representatives of Monsanto, the hormone's (rBGH) manufacturers. 'An offer of one to two million dollars was made,' she said."

The description of Monsanto's behaviour as a corporate citizen (pp. 139–40) is well documented. The best popular source is Brian Tokar's "Monsanto: A Checkered History," in the Sept./Oct. 1998 biotechnology edition of *The Ecologist*; but more detailed sources would include: "Criminal Investigation of Monsanto Corporation — Cover-up of Dioxin Contamination in Products — Falsification of Dioxin Health Studies," Cate Jenkins, *USEPA Regulatory Development Branch*, November 1990; Peter Schuck, *Agent Orange on Trial: Mass Toxic Disasters in the Courts* (Cambridge, MA: Harvard University Press, 1987); "Case of Mislabeled Herbicide Results in $225,000 Penalty," *Wall Street Journal*, March 25, 1998; Erik Millstone, "Increasing Brain Tumour Rates: Is There a Link to [the Monsanto product] Aspartame?" *University of Sussex Science Policy Research Unit*, October 1996; see references for "PCBs — Can the World's Sea Mammals Survive Them?" by Joseph Cummins in the aforementioned issue of *The Ecologist*; and see especially Dr. Samuel S. Epstein, "Unlabelled Milk from Cows Treated with Biosynthetic Growth Hormones: A Case of Regulatory Abdication," *International Journal of Health Services*, Vol. 26, No. 1, 1996. For excellent overviews of the regulatory history of Monsanto and other polluting chemical companies like Dow and Dupont, see *Greenwash*, the Jed Greer and Kenny Bruno book cited in chapter 3.

"Terminator Technology: The Threat to World Food Security," by Ricarda Steinbrecher and Pat Mooney in *The Ecologist* issue cited above, explains the issues raised in the text (p. 141). For a critique of hybrid seed, see Richard Lewontin and Jean-Pierre Berlan, "The Political Economy of Agricultural Research: The Case of Hybrid Corn, in Ronald Carroll et al., eds., *Agroecology* (New York: McGraw Hill, 1989); we consulted a special article in *The Guardian*, February 22, 1999, "Genetically Modified Food: It's Business as Usual," also by Lewontin and Berlan. The Terminator seed actually contains a poison that is set off in the late stages of production by exposure to the antibiotic Tetracycline. Technically speaking, temporary "gene silencing" of the poison gene or failed activation of the Terminator countdown could cause infection of wild relatives with sterility. The Tetracycline itself could cause problems if released in such amounts into the environment. The Terminator's potential as a weapon is known to the military, and in theory, crop diseases could be triggered by seed exports that would not kick in until activated by specific chemicals or conditions.

The story of Percy Schmeiser and Edward Zielinski, two Saskatchewan farmers being sued by Monsanto, has been picked up by most Canadian news sources. We used "Two Farmers Being Pursued by Monsanto for Growing their Seed Without a License in Landmark Cases" from *The Independent* by Marie Woolf (p. 145). On April 28, 1999, CBC Radio news reported on Agriculture Canada's refusal to provide any details about Monsanto research being conducted at the department's facilities throughout Canada (p. 139). Agriculture Canada also refused to disclose how much money they've received from the chemical and biotech company over the last fifteen years. The story was also reported in "Giant Food Companies Control Standards: Critics," the *Toronto Star*, April 28, 1999, which provided the quote from Stewart Wells.

Ray Mowling's speech (p. 146) was quoted in *Resource News International*, Winnipeg, April 4, 1999, "The Industry Isn't Taking Europe's Fight Against Agro-Biotech Lying Down." In this speech, Mowling referred to Canadian regulations to label products that have "changed in composition or ingredients relative to traditional commodities," saying that while there is a "hold" on these regulations, "there is growing pressure to implement such rules." According to the article, the American Soybean Association "recommended that the USDA work with or lean on the EU to harmonize its approval process, and include biotech in the next round of WTO negotiations." CBC News Online reported on May 3, 1999, that Canadian canola growers lost $30 million in export sales last year alone (p. 149), because of the shrinking market for genetically engineered canola, which now makes up the majority of their crop.

In the bioweapons section (pp. 150–51), documentation acquired by RAFI via a Freedom of Information application, "Biotechnology Workshop 20/20," May 29–30, 1996, held at the U.S. Army War College, outlines a wide range of military uses for biotechnology which the authors believe to be feasible by the year 2020. For action strategies, see "How Women Took On the Supermarkets — And Won" by Melanie McDonagh in the London *Evening Standard*, March 24, 1999; also "GM Food Ban Boosts Iceland Supermarket Chain," in *Business: The Company File*, March 23, 1999. Also see chapter 9 of this book and the organizations list at the end.

CHAPTER 6
FOLLOW THE MONEY
Building a Win-Win World: Life Beyond Global Economic Warfare (San Francisco: Perrett-Koehler, 1996), *Creating Alternative Futures: The End of Economics* (New York: G. P. Putnam's Sons, 1978), and *Paradigms in Progress: Life Beyond Economics* (San Francisco: Berrett-Koehler, 1995) are just a few of Hazel Henderson's books on economics. The key reference for estimating the worth of the world's natural services is Robert Costanza et al.'s "The Value of the World's Ecosystem Services and Natural Capital," *Nature*, May 15, 1997.

Herman Daly's work in this field is unsurpassed; a few of the books we recommend are: *Steady-State Economics* (Boston: Beacon Press, 1997), *For the Common Good*, with John Cobb (Boston: Beacon Press, 1989), *Valuing the Earth, Economics, Ecology and Ethics*, with Kenneth Townsend (Boston: MIT Press, 1993), and *Beyond Growth: The Economics of Sustainable Development* (Boston: Beacon Press, 1996).

The fascinating statistics on p. 160 and the Barber Conable quote on p. 161 came from Clifford Cobb and Ted Halsted's *The Genuine Progress Indicator: Summary of Data and Methodology* (San Francisco: Redefining Progress Institute, 1994). See the organizations list. For the "Eaten Alive" section, see the recent article on *Pfiesteria* by Joanne Burkholder in *Scientific American* (August 1999). The Cindy Watson story told on pp. 166–67 was reported in Bill Moyers's television special "Free Speech for Sale" broadcast on PBS, July 1999. Specific articles such as "The Failures of Bretton Woods" in *The Case against the Global Economy* and "Toxic Empire: The World Bank, Free Trade and the Migration of Hazardous Industry" in *The Corporate Planet* back up Morris and Glaesbeck's charges in our section entitled "Corporate Morality"; the latter article also details Union Carbide's behaviour in Bhopal.

David Korten's books, *When Corporations Rule the World* (New York: Kumarian Press, 1995) and his latest, *The Post-Corporate World: Life After Capitalism* (New York: Berett-Koehler and Kumarian Press, 1999), provide more background to his positions. He is also involved with *YES! Magazine*, an organization looking for positive futures for the world; see organizations list. The statistics on p. 173 are taken from *World Bank, World Development Report 1990, Poverty*, Washington, D.C., 1990, and *The Globalisation of Poverty* by Michel Chossudovsky (Penang, Malaysia: Third World Network, 1997).

We obtained figures on the distributional change of world income over the last thirty years from UNESCO, *Sources 58*, May 1994.

John Cassidy's figures on middle income decline were published in "Who Killed the Middle Class?" in the *The New Yorker*, October 16, 1995. Regarding perverse subsidies, see Alan Durning's *How Much Is Enough?* and his booklet, *The Car and the City*, referenced in chapter 2. An indispensible book for anyone interested in the historical evaluation of modern culture is John Ralston Saul's *Voltaire's Bastards* (Toronto: Penguin Books, 1992) as well as the book version of his Massey Lectures, *The Unconscious Civilization* (Toronto: House of Anansi Press, 1995). For more details about "Natural Capitalism," see Paul Hawken, *The Ecology of Commerce: A Declaration of Sustainability* (New York: HarperBusiness, 1993).

CHAPTER 7
GLOBALIZATION BLUES
The most indispensible book to this chapter and a layperson's excellent overview of the entire globalization controversy is the five-hundred-page tome *The Case against the Global Economy*, edited by Jerry Mander and Edward Goldsmith (San Francisco: Sierra Club Books, 1996), which includes satisfying articles by a great many of the people quoted in other chapters of this book (Ralph Nader, Vandana Shiva, David Korten, Andy Kimbrell, William Greider, etc.). It's a good idea for anyone to read or reread the touted father of modern, classical economics, who actually put things differently than we are led to believe — see Adam Smith (1776), *The Wealth of Nations: Books I–III* (Harmondsworth, Middlesex: Penguin, 1978). Joshua Karliner's *The Corporate Planet* (San Francisco: Sierra Club Books, 1997) was extremely useful here and in chapter 3. We also made good use of John Cavanaugh's book co-authored with Richard J. Barnet, *Global Dreams: Imperial Corporations and the New World Order* (New York: Simon & Schuster, 1994). Cavanaugh has co-authored eight other books on free trade and transnational corporations.

For a detailed analysis of the on-the-ground effects of NAFTA in Canada, the United States and Mexico, see *Pulling Apart, The Deterioration of Employment and Income in North America Under Free Trade* by Bruce Campbell et al. (Ottawa: The Canadian Centre for Policy Alternatives, 1999). *MAI: The Multilateral Agreement on Investment and the Threat to Canadian Sovereignty* by Tony Clarke and Maude Barlow is a must-read for every Canadian (Toronto: Stoddart, 1997). There are many additional publications about NAFTA and free trade available from the Council of Canadians; see organizations list.

To learn more about the global economy's input into recent famine, genocide and war, see Michel Chossudovsky's *The Globalization of Poverty: Impacts of IMF and World Bank Reforms*, mentioned in chapter 6, or his recent article for the *Journal of International Affairs*, "Global Poverty in the Late 20th Century" (Columbia University, Fall 1998). See also "Control of the World's Food Supply" in *The Case against the Global Economy* and Vandana Shiva's *Ecological Cost of Economic Globalisation*, referred to in more detail in the notes to chapter 8.

The MMT controversy was widely covered in the Canadian press and on CBC. See for example "Fuel Additive Debate Recharged" or "Ottawa Reintroduces MMT Bill: Proposed Ban on U.S.-Made Substance Could Start Trade War" in the *Globe and Mail*, March 25, 1996; "Banning MMT Prudent and Responsible" in the *Financial Post*, April 3, 1997; and "Lawsuit Looms Over MMT" in the January 29, 1997, issue of the *Sarnia Observer*. A visual map showing the human and environmental cost of gold and other metal mining in the Third World is outlined on the back page of the October 1999 issue of *Harper's* magazine. Regarding the SLAPP suit controversy on pp. 209–10, a typical local article on this subject would be the spread in the Montreal *Gazette*, December 7, 1996, "Silencing Citizens," by Debbie Parkes, dealing with local corporate suits against mostly environmental activists. On p. 214, perverse subsidies estimates come from Ralph Estes, *The Tyranny of the Bottom Line* (San Francisco: Berrett-Koehler, 1996).

For a fascinating overview of how one corporation works to corner the global market, see Brewster Kneen's *Invisible Giant: Cargill and Its Transnational Strategies* (Halifax, N.S.: Fernwood Publishing, 1995). Jeremy Rifkin's *The End of Work: The Decline of the Global Labor Force and the Dawn of the Post-Market Era* (New York: G.P. Putnam's Sons, 1995) is an instructive and even hopeful look at the future.

CHAPTER 8

THE OTHER WORLD

The accusations against Shell by the two people interviewed, Oronto Douglas of Environmental Rights Action, Nigeria, and Danny Kennedy of Project Underground, are backed up by the following published sources. On general background information: *Drilling to the Ends of the Earth: The Ecological, Social, and Climate Imperative for Ending Petroleum Exploration*, by Stephen Kretzmann and Shannon Wright, published by Project Underground and Rainforest Action Network, 1998; *Independent Annual Report: Human Rights and Environmental Operations Information on the Royal Dutch/Shell Group of Companies 1996–1997*, also by Kretzmann and Wright, published by Project Underground, Rainforest Action Network and

Oilwatch, 1997; *People and the Environment, Shell Petroleum Development Company of Nigeria Ltd. Annual Report,* 1997, put out by Shell International. Specific information provided in interviews is backed up by World Bank figures, which point out that millions of people have flocked to the Niger Delta in hopes of development employment, but Shell still only accounts for 1.3 percent of modern sector employment in the entire country; see World Bank, "Defining an Environmental Development Strategy for the Niger Delta," Vol. 1, 1995. See also the World Council of Churches, "Ogoni: the Struggle Continues," (Geneva, 1996). Project Underground undertook the research detailed on pp. 226–27 in April 1997; the samples were analyzed by Citizens Environmental Laboratory (CEL) Cambridge, MA. For the dangers of flaring and hydrocarbons, see *EC Directive 75/440/EEC* and *Greenpeace Oil Briefing #7,* "Human Health Impacts of Oil," Greenpeace UK, January 1993. The *New York Times* covered the Smithsonian Tropical Research Institute's work in Panama, where the levels of spilled oil reached similar levels as in the Niger Delta. These levels were termed, in a comparable tropical mangrove system, "catastrophic," and amounted to a "chronic oil spill" every time the rainy season arrived (December 21, 1993).

Shell's admissions of payments to the military are based in part on a letter to Paul Brown and Andy Rowell from Eric Nickson, Head of Media Relations for Shell International (6/11/96). This letter also admits to providing transport for security forces on two occasions that involved loss of Ogoni life. However, as Kretzmann and Wright note, "The company maintains that they were merely protecting their interests and unconnected to the military activity." A number of memos that seem to point to "the existence of a coordinated effort between Shell and the military to suppress dissent" are also detailed in Project Underground's *Independent Annual Report* cited above. Please note that there are at least eleven statements on record from Shell denying military connections, and there are as well many other charges of wrong-doing and intimidation from the Ogoni. Owens Wiwa, Ken's brother, says that Brian Anderson of Shell Nigeria said he could free Ken, then imprisoned by the Nigerian military, but only if the international protest against Shell were called off and the environmental damage disallowed. As the *IAR* states, "Shell disputes Dr. Wiwa's account of the meetings, but gives no plausible alternate explanation for the reason for the meetings."

Redefining Progress can provide figures, brochures and ideas on how to reevaluate, remeasure and remake daily life; see the organizations list at the end of the book. We again consulted Jerry Mander's books mentioned above and John Cavanaugh's *The Corporate Planet*. References to the Green Revolution appeared in chapter 4; see also Lappe, Collins, Rosset and Esparza, *World Hunger: 12 Myths* (Grove/Atlantic and Food First Books, 1998) and Andy Kimbrell, "Why Biotechnology and High-Tech Agriculture Cannot Feed the World," in *The Ecologist*, Sept./Oct. 1998.

Vandana Shiva, Afsar Jafri and Gitanjali Bedi's *Ecological Cost of Economic Globalisation: The Indian Experience* (New Delhi: Research Foundation for Science, Technology & Ecology (RFSTE), 1995) details the studies brought up on pp. 238–40.

For famine, food shortage and population figures, see any number of the Food and Agricultural Organization of the United Nations (FAO) reports, notably *Food Supply Situation and Crop Prospects in Sub-Saharan Africa*, Special Report No. 1, April 1993.

The analysis of lack of satisfaction with government in northern and southern Italy discussed on p. 245 comes from Robert D. Putnam et al.'s *Making Democracy Work: Civic Traditions in Modern Italy* (Princeton University Press, 1994).

CHAPTER 9
COMPLEX PLEASURES

This chapter was not about research, academic opinion or journalism. It was about activists, people who have decided to stop reading, talking or worrying and start doing something. The only printed references it mentions are Vicki Robin and Joe Dominguez's *Your Money or Your Life* (New York: Viking Penguin, 1992), Brewster Kneen's activist food system newsletter *The Ram's Horn* (where you can get information on, for example, CSAs in your area), and Kalle Lasn's activist anti-magazine, *Adbusters*. We also referred to Bill McKibben's books, listed in chapters above. Otherwise, there are no printed sources — the discussion was taken from taped interviews. We do, however, refer the reader, hopefully, to the list of activist and informational organizations at the end of this book.

ORGANIZATIONS TO CONTACT

If the issues raised in this book have concerned you, you should
know that many of our elected officials in Canada are actively
supporting policies that will make matters even worse in terms of
genetic engineering, global warming, species protection, food
safety and phasing out of toxins. Elected officials respond to
pressure, and they get a lot of it from vested interests. If you want
to exert some pressure of your own, send letters to your MP or to
the relevant ministry at the following address (the main address,
after the ministry, is always the same, and the postage is free):

  House of Commons
  Ottawa, Ontario K1A 0A6
You can also visit the web site www.net-efx.com/faxfeds
and Fax the Feds!

*For biotech, food safety, human health as related to toxins and global
warming, write:*
  Allan Rock
  Ministry of Health
  or Canadian Food Inspection Agency
  Ottawa: (613) 225-2342 Hull: (819) 997-2919
*For global warming issues, globalization issues, biotech and industrial
toxins, write:*
  John Manley
  Ministry of Industry

For climate change, forests, toxins and biotech, write:
  Ralph Goodale
  Ministry of Natural Resources
For globalization issues, the Tobin Tax, structural adjustment inequalities, or to demand forgiveness of Third World Debt and democratization of the global economy, write:
  Paul Martin
  Ministry of Finance
For globalization issues, water export and more, write:
  Sergio Marchi
  Ministry of Trade
To push for tougher legislation on endangered species, to speak out against exporting our water and to protect biodiversity, write:
  David Anderson
  Ministry of the Environment (david.anderson@ec.gc.ca)
  or contact the Convention on Biological Diversity
  Montreal, Quebec
  (514) 288-2220 *or* the United Nations Environment Program
  UNEP (514) 282-1122

If you're concerned about consumption issues, write especially to the Ministry of Trade and the Ministry of Finance. If you have questions about a specific issue, contact the Sierra Club (see address below) or Fax the Feds at the web site above.

The following is a list of effective organizations that are concerned with concrete action about the issues raised by this book. It begins with some organizations that deal with overall environmental issues, and then groups others by their topics of focus. We hope you'll be inspired to go further and learn more about what we've discussed here and in the radio series.

GENERAL ENVIRONMENTAL ISSUES

  The Corner House
  PO Box 3137
  Station Road
  Sturminster Newton

Dorset, UK DT10 1YJ
Phone: 44 1258-473795 Fax: 44 1258-473748
email: cornerhouse@gn.apc.org
Publishes monthly briefings on subjects such as climate, nuclear
contamination, biotechnology, globalization and other issues.

The Ecologist
Unit 18, Chelsea Wharf
15 Lots Road
London, UK SW10 0QJ
Phone: 44 171 351-3578
Fax: 44 171 351-3617
email: ecologist@gn.apc.org
web site: www.gn.apc.org/ecologist/
The Ecologist is a long-established bimonthly of the highest status
and credibility, published by Edward Goldsmith. It features some of
the finest experts in the world contributing articles investigating
every aspect of environmental issues — scientific, cultural and
economic.

Friends of the Earth U.S.
1025 Vermont Avenue NW
Washington, D.C. 20005
Phone: (202) 738-7400
Fax: (202) 783-0444
email: foe@foe.org   web site: www.foe.org

FOE International
PO Box 19199
100 GD Amsterdam
the Netherlands
Phone: 31 20 622 1369 email: foeint@antenna.nl

FOE UK
26-28 Underwood Street
London, UK N17JQ
email:susdev@foe.co.uk   web site:www.foe.co.uk.org
Friends of the Earth is an international environmental advocacy

organization with member groups in sixty countries that often involve themselves in direct action. FOE is democratically based, with individual groups varying widely in their campaigns. For example, the Manchester group aids the Tree People and Diggers; the Nigerian group helps those fighting corporate armies. Many U.S. groups concentrate on global warming issues, and many other British and European groups are fighting against biotech and for food purity. FOE attempts to mobilize grass-roots citizen efforts in order to rescue the planet from environmental disasters.

Greenpeace Canada
250 Dundas Street West, Suite 605
Toronto, ON M5T 2Z5
Phone: (416) 597-8408 ext. 3030
web site: www.greenpeacecanada.org

Greenpeace International
Keizersgracht 176
1016 DW Amsterdam, the Netherlands
Phone: 31 20 523 6222
Fax: 31 20 523 6200
Active in food-related issues, especially biotech.

Population Institute
107 Second Street NE
Washington, D.C. 20002
Phone: (202) 544-3300
email: web@populationinstitute.org
web site: www.populationinstitute.org
The Population Institute studies and provides figures on population, fertility, food security and other related issues.

The Sierra Club of Canada
1 Nicholas Street, Suite 412
Ottawa, ON K1N 7B7
Phone: (613) 241-4611 Toll-free: 1 (888) 810-4204
email: sierra@web.net web site: www.sierraclub.ca/national

Arguably the most active and effective general-issue environmental organization in the country, the Sierra Club of Canada spearheads campaigns on issues like biotechnology, toxic waste, pesticide reduction, forest and endangered species conservation, global corporate rule, the gas additive MMT and initiatives against human rights violations. The Sierra Club works on many levels, from public education and research to litigation and direct action, and is very different from its U.S. counterpart, operating on a shoestring and tackling issues in a more direct manner.

Third World Network
228 Macalister Road, 10400
Penang, Malaysia
Phone: 60 4 2266728 / 2266159   Fax: 60 4 2264505
email: twn@igc.apc.org   web sites: twnet@po.jaring.my *and*
www.twnside.org.sg
The Third World Network is an independent network of organizations and individuals working on issues related to development and the North – South dichotomy. It researches and publishes extremely helpful books and articles on issues pertaining to struggles in the Third World: a daily out of Switzerland, the *SUNS Bulletin*; a twice-monthly magazine focusing on GATT, the WTO and the IMF, *Third World Economics*, and the famous monthly illustrated magazine, *Third World Resurgence*. Many of the books and much of the research forming the core of this book came from TWN. The secretariat is in Penang, but it has offices in Delhi, Montevideo, Geneva, London and Accra.

The Union of Concerned Scientists
Two Brattle Square
Cambridge, MA 02238-9105
Phone: (617) 547-5552
This is a conservative group of hundreds of scientists who have banded together to investigate and publicize unimpeachable statements regarding global warming, deforestation and other issues.

CONSUMER ISSUES

Adbusters and Media Foundation
Kalle Lasn
1243 West 7th Avenue
Vancouver, BC V6H 1B7
Phone: (604) 736-9401
Fax: (604) 737-6021
email: adbusters@adbusters.org   web site: www.adbusters.org
The Media Foundation works to help people step back and analyze
the role of public relations and advertising in the world. They expose
abuses and brainwashing and especially try to fight the unregulated
spread of a corporate consumerism that is wasting the life-support
systems of the planet. There are groups practising frugality,
downsizing and culture-jamming in all major cities. Contact the Media
Foundation and they'll help you find them.
Adbusters is the glossy, radical and often funny monthly magazine
of the culture-jammer movement, people trying to get out from
under the propaganda of the profit-over-all mentality of corporate
America. Subscriptions don't help fund any corporations.

New Road Map Foundation
PO Box 15981
Seattle, WA 98115
Phone: (206) 527-0437
Fax: (206) 528-1120
The New Road Map Foundation is an all-volunteer, educational and
charitable organization concerned with the role of personal
responsibility and personal initiative in effecting positive global
changes. They see a responsible and engaged individual working
voluntarily for the common good as the key to the creation of a
humane, sustainable culture. They are deeply involved with the
growing frugality movement, which expanded greatly with the nine-
step plan of *Your Money or Your Life*, by Vicki Robin and Joe
Dominguez. They offer audiocassette courses and workbooks to
people wishing to gain control of their financial lives, with all
proceeds donated to non-profit organizations. They also help fund

other organizations and projects working towards a humane, sustainable future.

Northwest Environment Watch (NEW)
Alan Durning, Director
1402 3rd Avenue, Suite 1127
Seattle, WA 98101-2118
Phone: (206) 447-1880
Fax: (206) 447-2270
email: nwwatch@igc.apc.org

Northwest Environment Watch is a non-profit research centre looking to find sustainable, long-term ways to live in harmony with the ecological area extending between northern California and southern British Columbia and bounded by the Rockies. They create indicators to track sustainability, and publish health checkups for the region, as well as long reports like *The Car and the City,* and *What Can the Earth Afford? Beyond the Consumer Society in the Pacific Northwest.* They accept no corporate funding.

Redefining Progress
1 Kearny Street, 4th Floor
San Francisco, CA 94108
Phone: (415) 781-1191
Fax: (415) 781-1198
web site: http://www.rprogress.org

The people at Redefining Progress are pioneers in the effort to develop a new measure for national well-being to counteract the inadequate Gross National Product. Their indicator, the General Progress Index, is an attempt to measure more than just the exchange of money in judging a society's well-being. They believe that a world of true abundance lies not in more financial transactions, but in a high quality of life for all, sustained by the networks of nature and community and passed on from generation to generation.

FOOD ISSUES AND BIOTECHNOLOGY (ABROAD)

Australian Gene Ethics Network
340 Gore Street
Fitzroy 3065
Victoria, Australia
Phone: 613 03 9416 2222
Fax: 613 03 9416 0767
email: acfgenet@peg.apc.org
web site: http://www.zero.com.au/agen
This grass-roots, non-profit, public interest group monitors and tries
to protect consumer rights and to demand labelling of genetically
engineered products. They publish *The Helix*, a textbook designed
for teachers and students in Grade 12 and university, and a
newsletter, *The Gene File*.

Ecoropa
President, Christine von Weizsacker
Postfach 130 165
53061 Bonn, Germany
Phone: 49 228 9181 033
Fax: 49 228 9181 034
email: cvw@isd.de
Ecoropa is a fifteen-year-old European environmental group
specializing in biotech, agricultural issues, toxics and food safety issues.

NAVDANYA
(National Program for Conservation of Native Seed Varieties)
Director, Vandana Shiva
A-60, Hauz Khas, New Delhi 110 016
Phone: 91 11 696 8077 or 651 5003
Fax: 91 11 685 6795; 696 2589
NAVDANYA is involved with actively saving the seeds of rural India
from patenting and industrial development.

Women's Environmental Network Test Tube Harvest Campaign
87 Worship Street
London, UK EC2A 2BE

Phone: 171 247-3327
Fax: 171 247-4740
web site: www.gn.apc.org/wen
See also: www.gn.apc.org/pnhp/gs
Involved in both direct action and education against biotech in
England and Europe, WEN also has a unique research and campaign
team, four members of which are biologists or geneticists. Their
publications are used all across the United Kingdom, Europe,
Canada and South America.

For a constant stream of up-to-date biotech information that
has been rigorously screened by a microbiologist, write to
Genet@agoranet.be.

FOOD ISSUES AND BIOTECHNOLOGY (CANADA)

Biotech Action Montreal (BAM)
c/o QPIRG-McGill
3647 University, 3rd Floor
Montreal, PQ H3A 2B3
Phone: (514) 398-7432
Fax: (514) 398-8976
email: qpirg@ssmu.mcgill.ca (attn: BAM) *or*
lorrainelapp@sprint.ca *or* mercier@magellan.umontreal.ca
web site: www.ssmu.mcgill.ca/qpirg
This is a grass-roots citizens' group that arose in the wake of the
news that Canadians are eating unlabelled genetically engineered
organisms.

Rural Advancement Foundation International (RAFI) Canada
71 Bank Street, Suite 50421
Ottawa, ON K1P 5N2
Phone: (613) 567-6880
Fax: (613) 567-6884
website: www.rafi.ca

RAFI International
International office: 110 Osborne Street, Suite 202

Winnipeg, MB R3L 1Y5
Phone: (204) 453-5259
Fax: (204) 925-8034
email: rafi@rafi.org
The Rural Advancement Foundation International is headquartered
in Winnipeg, Manitoba, Canada, with affiliate offices in Ottawa and
in North Carolina. RAFI is dedicated to the conservation and
sustainable improvement of agricultural biodiversity, and to the
socially responsible development of technologies useful to rural
societies. They are currently very active in the controversies
surrounding genetically engineered crops.

The Ram's Horn
Brewster Kneen, Editor
S-12 C-11 RRRI Sorrento, BC
Phone/Fax: (250) 675-4866 email: ramshorn@jetstream.net
Brewster and Cathleen Kneen's monthly newsletter will keep you
abreast of crucial food issues in Canada and abroad for only twenty
dollars a year. They can also put you in touch with activist groups on
biotech and other agricultural issues in a Canadian city near you.

FOOD ISSUES AND BIOTECHNOLOGY (USA)

The Campaign for Food Safety
Ronnie Cummings
860 Highway 61
Little Marais, MN 55614
Phone: (218) 226-4164
Fax: (218) 226-4164
email: purefood@aol.com   web site: www.purefood.org
A public interest organization that deals with issues of food safety
and genetic engineering, the Campaign for Food Safety is allied with
the Center for Food Safety in Washington. Their campaign tactics
include public education, litigation, boycotts, media work and direct
action. CFS also publishes a free monthly electronic newsletter,
Foodbytes. You can subscribe by emailing to: majordomo@mr.nat and
then writing "subscribe pure-food-action."

The Edmonds Institute
Beth Burrows, Director
20319 92nd Avenue West
Edmonds, WA 98020
Phone: (425) 775-5383
Fax: (425) 670-8410
email: beb@igc.apc.org
web site (under construction): www.edmonds-institute.org
The Edmonds Institute is a public interest, non-profit environmental
thinktank; its current emphasis is on biosafety, intellectual property
rights and just policies for the protection of biodiversity. The
institute encourages pro bono research and policy analysis by
scientists and scholars, and its special talent is creating alliances and
coalitions with like-minded organizations and individuals. The
institute just won its litigation with the U.S. Department of the
Interior and the National Parks Service over the commercialization
of biodiversity in Yellowstone National Park.

The Foundation on Economic Trends
1660 L Street NW, Suite 216
Washington, D.C. 20036
Phone: (202) 466-2823
Fax: (202) 429-9602
email: campaign@uol.com *or* jrifkin@foet.org
web site: http://www.biotechnology.org
The Foundation on Economic Trends (FET) is a non-profit
organization whose mission is to examine emerging trends in science
and technology and their effects on the environment, economy,
culture and society. Jeremy Rifkin is its president and founder.

The Humane Society of the United States
Eating with Conscience Campaign
700 Professional Drive
Gaithersburg, MD 20879
Phone: (301) 258-3054 Toll-free: 1 (800) 444-8359
Fax: (301) 258-3081
email: hlyman@aol.com

The Humane Society of the United States is fighting for safer and more humane conditions for food animals, in an effort to also help prevent the spread of E.coli, salmonella and BSE (Mad Cow) outbreaks in humans, which they contend are a natural concomitant of present industrial agriculture. The director of their Eating with Conscience campaign, Howard Lyman, was sued by the Cattlemen's Association, along with Oprah Winfrey, for discussing on her show the dangers of Mad Cow Disease and other infections in food.

Institute for Agriculture and Trade Policy (IATP)
Kristin Dawkins, Director
Trade and Agriculture Program
2105 First Avenue South
Minneapolis, MN 55404
Phone: (612) 870-3410
Fax: (612) 870-4846
email: kdawkins@iatp.org   web site: http://www.iatp.org/iatp
IATP is working to create environmentally and economically sustainable communities and regions through sound agriculture and trade policy. The data they gather are distributed as educational materials to policy makers and the public at large. This includes a mail-order service, video productions, PSA campaigns, and conferences and computer networks.

The International Center for Technology Assessment
The Center for Food Safety
310 D Street NE
Washington, D.C. 20002
Phone: (202) 547-9359
web site: http://www.icta.org
The International Center for Technology Assessment examines the economic, ethical, social, environmental and political effects of the applications of technology, and it carries on lawsuits against government entities and corporations where necessary. The Center for Food Safety addresses the impact of our food production system on human health, animal welfare and the environment. They are fighting for testing, labelling and regulation of genetically engineered foods, preserving strict national organic food standards,

and preventing potential health crises caused by food-borne illness, including Mad Cow disease. Both are energetic sources of information and of legal action.

RAFI USA
PO Box 640
Pittsboro, NC 27312
Phone: (919) 542-1396
Fax: (919) 542-0069
email: rafi@rafi.org
See description of the Rural Advancement Foundation above, under Food Issues and Biotechnology (Canada).

Seed Savers Exchange
Kent Whealy
RR 3, Box 239
Decorah, IA 53101
Phone: (319) 382-5990
Fax: (319) 382-5872
This group grows, saves, distributes and sells organic and heritage seed. They also fund workshops for Third World participants to increase their knowledge of sustainable food cropping.

SoilFoodWeb Inc.
Elaine Ingham
President, SoilFoodWeb Inc.
980 NW Circle Boulevard
Corvallis, OR 97330
Phone: (541) 752-5066
Fax: (541) 752-5142
email: inghame@bcc.orst.edu
This organization advises, educates and provides the means for farmers to wean their soils from agricultural chemicals and learn how to build soil for sustainable agriculture.

Food safety issues information can also be obtained, in the U.S., by calling: Food First: (510) 654-4400 *or* Consumer's Union: (914) 378-2000

GLOBALIZATION ISSUES

The Council of Canadians
502 – 151 Slater Street
Ottawa, ON K1P 5H3
Phone: (613) 233-2773
Fax: (613) 233-6776
web site: www.canadians.org
email: inquiries@canadians.org
The Council of Canadians is a non-profit, non-partisan public
interest organization supported by more than 100,000 members. It
serves as a government watchdog, critic of corporate crime and
catalyst for grass-roots organizing. The Council works to protect
Canadian sovereignty and promote democratic rights. They have
proved tireless in fighting undemocratic globalized trade, tackling
such issues as unregulated, unlabelled genetically engineered food,
corporate control of the media, and the forced introduction of trade-
protected toxins like MMT.

The International Forum on Globalization
1555 Pacific Avenue
San Francisco, CA 94109
Phone: (415) 771-3394 Fax: (415) 771-1121
email: ifg@ifg.org   web site: www.ifg.org
The IFG is an alliance of leading activists, scholars, economists,
researchers and writers from twenty-five countries, formed to stimulate
joint activity and public education in response to the global economy.

Institute for Policy Studies
733 15th Street, NW, Suite 1020
Washington, D.C. 10005-2112
Phone: (202) 234-9382
Fax: (202) 387-7915
The IPS is a Washington thinktank established more than thirty
years ago, under President John F. Kennedy. These days, it is
concerned primarily with democracy and justice issues as they relate
to trade. It works closely with the fifty-eight-member Progressive

Caucus on Capitol Hill, to link its staff with national networks of scholars, activists and citizens to articulate a new progressive agenda for America at the local, state and national levels. See their web site at www.netprogress.org.

PR Watch
Center for Media and Democracy
3318 Gregory Street
Madison, WI 53711
Phone: (608) 233-3346
Fax: (608) 238-2236
email: 74250.735@compuserve.com
web site: http://www.prwatch.org/
The Center for Media and Democracy, founded by Sheldon Rampton and John Stauber, the two crusaders against green- and brownwashing described in chapter 3, keeps an eye on transnationals and their media manipulations. They publicize issues like SLAPP suits, corporate censorship and marketing to children. Their newsletter, *PR Watch*, is published quarterly.

The Transnational Resource and Action Center (TRAC)
Corporate Watch, Internet magazine
PO Box 29344, Presidio Station
San Francisco, CA 94129
Phone: (415) 561-6567
email: trac@igc.org web site: www.corpwatch.org
This organization keeps track of corporate power and analyzes the dangers to democracy and to human rights. Their Internet magazine is a rich source of information about who is doing what and how to combat it.

GLOBAL WARMING AND FOREST ISSUES

Appalacian Voices
197 New Market Center
Boon, NC 28607
Phone: (828) 963-2651

This small organization is sponsoring research and helping find solutions to air pollution effects. It also fights strip mining of forests, including mountain-top removal that supplies today's huge industrial chip mills.

The David Suzuki Foundation
Suite 219
2221 W. Fourth Avenue
Vancouver, BC V6K 4S2
Phone: (604) 732-4228
Fax: (604) 732-0752
email: solutions@davidsuzuki.org   web site: www.davidsuzuki.org
The David Suzuki Foundation is a non-profit research group that tries to study the underlying structures and systems that cause environmental crises, in order to bring about fundamental change. The Foundation commissions research, supports the implementation of ecologically sustainable models, works to educate the widest possible audience to support change, and urges decision makers to adopt policies that encourage individuals and businesses to act within nature's constraints. The David Suzuki Foundation has mounted Canada's largest and most sustained campaign to understand and find solutions to global climate change. They are involved in a watershed restoration project with the Musqueam Indian Band, and have organized the Pacific Salmon Forests Project, to help people understand how the interaction between fish and forests is crucial to the survival of both. Among other projects, the David Suzuki Foundation fights unsustainable logging and has researched ten stories of fisheries that work.

[Note: if your request or question involves David's CBC Television series *The Nature of Things*, contact them directly by email at tnot@toronto.cbc.ca, or at PO Box 500, Station A Toronto, ON M5W 1E6; Phone: (416) 205-6888 Fax: (416) 205-3579.]

Greenpeace U.S.A.
1436 U Street NW

Washington, D.C. 20009
Toll-free: 1 (800) 326-0959
Phone: (202) 462-1177
Fax: (202) 462-4507
web site: www.greenpeaceusa.org
Greenpeace is the leading independent, international organization
that uses peaceful and creative activism to protect the global
environment. Their major U.S. campaign at the moment is against
global warming.

Rainforest Action Network
221 Pine Street, No. 500
San Francisco, CA 94702
Phone: (415) 398-4404
Fax: (415) 398-2732
email: rainforest@ran.org   web site: www.ran.org
Rainforest Action Network works to protect the Earth's rainforests
and support the rights of their inhabitants through education, grass-
roots organizing, and non-violent direct action.

World Resources Institute
10 G Street NE, Suite 800
Washington, D.C. 20002
Phone: (202) 729-7600
Fax: (202) 729-7610
email: lauralee@wri.org
web site: http://www.wri.org
The World Resources Institute is a public and grant-supported
educational organization that believes a healthy environment and a
healthy economy can coexist. Current areas of research include
economics, forests, biodiversity, climate change, energy, sustainable
agriculture, resource and environmental information, trade,
technology and health. Their ground-breaking report on *The Last
Frontier Forests: Ecosystems and Economies on the Edge* is a must-read
for all Canadians.

NON-VIOLENT DIRECT ACTION GROUPS

EarthFirst! California
PO Box 83
Canyon, CA 94516
Phone: (510) 848-8724

*EarthFirst!*Journal
PO Box 1415
Eugene, OR 97440
Phone: (541) 344-8004
Fax: (541) 344-7688

EarthFirst!'s activities are detailed in chapter 3. Earthfirst works mostly on the West Coast of the United States, but does have offices in Boston. Although its members are most famous for non-violent direct action (blockades, demos, sit-ins and the like), they also help organize communities, petition governments, and educate the public, like most democratic groups.

Sea Shepherd Conservation Society
PO Box 628
Venice, CA 90294
Phone: (310) 301-7325
Fax: (310) 574-3161
To contribute money, call: 1 (888) whale-22
web site: http://www.seashepherd.org

Paul Watson is captain of the Sea Shepherd vessel and a direct-action environmental activist. For the last two decades, he and members of his Sea Shepherd Conservation Society have tried to protect sea mammals by putting themselves between harpooners and whales, and by sinking whaling ships. He has been beaten by sealers in Newfoundland, jailed in Iceland for sinking ships, and lionized by many as one of the only lines of defence left between the survival and the extinction of a constantly shrinking marine mammal population.

Other non-violent action groups include Friends of the Earth, and Greenpeace, whose addresses are listed under "General Environmental Issues."

POLLUTION AND TOXICS

Center for Environment, Health and Justice, CCHW
Lois Gibbs, Executive Director
PO Box 6806
Falls Church, VA 22040-6806
Phone: (703) 237-2249
Fax: (703) 237-8389
email: cchw@essential.org and noharm@iatp.org
web sites: http://www.essential.org/cchw *or*
http://www.noharm.org

The Center for Health, Environment and Justice helps families
protect their children from chemical poisons and their communities
from toxic waste dumps. It was founded, as the Citizen's Clearing
House on Hazardous Waste, by Lois Gibbs, the leader of the first
successful community campaign against toxics, Love Canal. CHEJ
works for, and is supported primarily by, blue-collar workers,
farmers, low-income families and people of colour. Frightened
victims of suspected toxics can turn to their Science and Technical
Assistance Program, led by Harvard-trained toxicologist Stephen
Lester. CHEJ publishes over 130 guides and fact-pacts and three
periodicals, *Everyone's Backyard, Environmental Health Monthly* and
Dioxin Digest. The tiny staff spends only 14 percent of their budget
on fund-raising and administration. This is a true grass-roots
organization, one of the most effective in the world.

Environmental Rights Action (ERA)
Friends of the Earth
PO Box 10577
Ugbowo, Benin City
Nigeria
Phone and Fax: 234 52 600 165
email: eraction@infoweb.abs.net *or* obebi@infoweb.abs.net *or*
oilwatch@infoweb.abs.net

Oronto Douglas, lawyer and friend of Ken Saro-Wiwa, the Nobel
Prize–winning poet executed by Nigerian dictators five years ago, is
deputy director of ERA. This organization attempts to disseminate

news of the human and environmental abuses by multinational oil companies, like Shell Oil and Chevron, in alliance with paramilitary and government groups in the Niger Delta. They also help coordinate the worldwide Shell boycott, and can provide information on the activities of these corporations in the Third World.

> Pesticide Action Network
> 116 New Montgomery, Suite 810
> San Francisco, CA 94105
> Phone: (415) 541-9140
> Fax: (415) 541-9253
> email: panna@panna.org

The Pesticide Action Network is a fast and scientifically reliable source of information. They know what compounds your food contains, and can tell you exactly how dangerous and common they are. PAN can also show you how to organize to limit or eliminate pesticide use in your area.

> Project Underground
> Danny Kennedy, Project Coordinator
> 1916a Martin Luther King Jr. Way
> Berkeley, CA 94703
> Phone: (510) 705-8981
> Fax: (510) 705-8983
> email: project_underground@moles.org
> web site: http://www.moles.org

Project Underground fights the toxic pollution and human rights violations of the current worldwide goldrush on metals, led in large part by Canadian corporations. They provide information, legal help and outside research to people suffering the effects of the world land-grab for minerals.

INDEX

quality of life: in cities, 186;
indicators, 185; Italy, 245;
measuring, 159; and Third
Sector, 245–47
quantum mechanics, 15
quantum physics, 14
Quebec, lawsuit against Cambior
in, 210
quinoa, patents pending on, 132

rabbits, immunosterilization of,
141–42
radicals, 83, 88–90, 91–92
Rae, Bob, 211
Rafferty and Alameda dam,
253–54
Rainbow Warrior, 91
rain forests. *See* tropical rain
forests
Rampton, Sheldon, 87
Ram's Horn newsletter, 264
Rayner, Steve, 245–46, 248, 256;
law of requisite variety, 251
realists, 89–90
recolonization, 230–33;
bankruptcy program as, 201;
multinational corporate, 226
recycling, industrial, 49
Redefining Progress Institute,
159–60
reductionism. *See* scientific
reductionism
Rees, Bill, 38–42, 44
regulation, 23, 214–15
Reimchen, Tom, 21
research: dependence on private
industry, 106; in ecology, 22
resource base, 32, 38, 174
resource exploitation, Canada,
54
responsibility, concept of, 182
Reye's syndrome, 85, 253
Rifkin, Jeremy, 113, 120,
127–28, 133, 144–45, 153,
245
riparian habitat, 30–31
risk assessment: procedures for
biotech companies, 144; tax
money for, 145
risks, in biotechnology, 110,
119–21
riverbanks, diversity of life on, 31
rivers, humans' effect on, 30–31

Robin, Vicki, 260–64
Roots, and Daishowa products,
209
Roundup, 114–15
Roundup-Ready products:
phytoestrogens in, 119;
poisonous agrochemical, 115;
transgenic crops, 148
Royal Dutch Shell, 225
royalties, on GM organisms, 127
Russia: bankruptcy program,
201; deteriorating conditions
in, 174; mapping global
forests, 54; natural forests, 53;
whaling fleet, 273–74. *See also*
Soviet Union

sacred, as human element, 276
Salk, Jonas, 131
Salk vaccine, 131
salmon, 177; -breeding
programs, 19; controversy,
18–21
Sanders, Scott Russell, 261
Saro-Wiwa, Ken, 224, 226, 228
Saul, John Ralston, 181–82
scallop fishing, 51
scepticism, need for, 82
Schmeiser, Percy, versus
Monsanto, 140
Schneewind, Olaf, 133
Schneider, Russ, 147–48
Schneider, Stephen, 56–57, 59
Schumacher College, England,
104, 144
science and technology: and
Africa, 242; unwarranted faith
in, 37–38
Scientific American, 238
scientific reductionism, 11–12,
15–16, 35; and
biotechnology, 105, 110; and
salmon species, 20
sea otters, results of
extermination of, 23
Sea Shepherd group, Scotland,
275
Sea Shepherd (ship), 273
Sea Shepherd Society, 83, 90,
273
sea urchins, and sea otters, 23
Second World War, 189, 190
secrets. *See* commercial privacy

seed banks: India, 234;
privatization of, 243
seeds, farmers and, 140–41
self-interest, and economic
system, 182
sharing: as Canadian narrative,
219–20; in the economy,
183–84; moral problem of,
184
Shell Oil, 225–27; boycott of,
227, 229; and Nigerian
dictatorships, 225; Nigerian
military weapons, 228
Shenk, David, 81–82
Shiva, Vandana, 114–16, 138,
140, 152, 154; on attitude of
farmers, 240; on biopiracy,
135; on farming, 237–39; on
World Bank and India's
wheat, 202–3
shrimp farms, destructive effects
of, 31
Sierra Club, 33, 63, 85, 93, 253;
Legal Defence fund, 209–10;
Tobin Tax, 216
Silent Spring (Carson), 67, 139,
258
Symon, Julian, 40
Sizer, Nigel, 53, 55
slavery, in Pakistan, 249
Smith, Adam, 213, 244
Snake river, dams on, 18
social activists, dossiers on,
88–89
social deterioration, UN
response to, 174
social diversity, law of, 244–47
social services, slashing of,
176–77
Society for the Prevention of
Cruelty to Animals, 70
soil: and Biosphere II, 15;
building blocks, 23; fungi, 14;
organisms, 22, 23–24
solar system model, 15
solvents, and health problems,
61
Somalia: destabilization in, 249;
failed IMF policies in, 203
Sony Corporation, 195
South Asia, famines in, 174
sovereignty, of national
governments, 195, 205

THE DAVID SUZUKI FOUNDATION:
WORKING TOGETHER FOR A SUSTAINABLE FUTURE

The David Suzuki Foundation was established to work for a world of hope in which our species thrives in balance with the productive capacity of the Earth.

Our mission is to find solutions to the root causes of our most threatening environmental problems. Then, we work with our supporters and their communities to implement those solutions for a sustainable future.

Our mandate is broad, ranging from projects on climate change, air, soil, water, fisheries, forestry, energy, and liveable cities, to defining the foundations of sustainability, how social change occurs, and the potential of new economic models.

We can only accomplish this with the support of concerned citizens who care about the environment. We invite your help.

JOIN OUR PARTNERSHIP . . . JOIN THE FOUNDATION!

NAME   ADDRESS
_____

CITY/PROVINCE   POSTAL CODE   TELEPHONE

Here is my donation of: ❏ $30   ❏ $50   ❏ $100   ❏ $500
                         ❏ $1000 National Sponsor   ❏ $5000 Founder

❏ Cheque   ❏ Money Order   ❏ Visa   ❏ MasterCard

_____

CARD NUMBER   EXPIRY DATE

SIGNATURE

Yes, I'll become a Friend of the Foundation. I authorize the Foundation to receive the following amount from my chequing account on a monthly basis. I understand I'll receive a tax credit and the benefits of becoming a Foundation Supporter.

❏ $10 a month   ❏ $15 a month   ❏ $25 a month   ❏ $_____ a month

I understand I can change or cancel my pledge at any time.
I enclose a sample cheque marked VOID for bank coding.

_____

SIGNATURE

Please return this reply memo with your tax-creditable donation. Cheques can be made payable to The David Suzuki Foundation. Thank you very much for your support.

 THE DAVID SUZUKI FOUNDATION
219–2211 WEST FOURTH AVENUE
VANCOUVER, B.C., CANADA V6K 4S2
Phone (604) 732-4228; Fax (604) 732-0752

Charitable Registration Number: BN 12775 6716 RR0001